Racial Inequality in Education

Edited by Barry Troyna

Routledge

First published in 1987 by
Tavistock Publications

Reprinted 1989
by Routledge
11 New Fetter Lane
London EC4P 4EE

Typeset by Scarborough Typesetting Services
and printed in Great Britain by
Richard Clay (The Chaucer Press) Ltd
Bungay, Suffolk

British Library Cataloguing in Publication Data
Racial inequality in education.
1. Discrimination in education – Great Britain
I. Troyna, Barry
370.19'942'0941   LC212.53.G7

ISBN 0–415–04023–X

Contents

List of contributors

Bob Carter	Lecturer at Newman College, Birmingham.
Mel Chevannes	Lecturer at the City of Birmingham Polytechnic, founder member of the Afro-Caribbean Education Trust and Chair of Wolverhampton Social Services Committee.
Andrew Dorn	Education Officer at the Commission for Racial Equality.
Olivia Foster-Carter	Lecturer in the School of Social Analysis at Bradford University.
David Gibson	Principal, Central Area of Community Education in Manchester.
Ahmed Gurnah	An active member of the black community in Sheffield, currently working for the Education Department.
Richard Hatcher	Research Fellow in the Department of Education, University of Warwick. He is active in the NUT and the Labour Party.
Paul Hibbert	Formerly Community Relations Officer in charge of Southampton Commission for Racial Equality, he now lives in New Zealand.
David Oldman	Lecturer in sociology at Aberdeen University.
Frank Reeves	Vice-Principal of Bilston Community College, Wolverhampton and Honorary Visiting Research Fellow at the ESRC Centre for Research in Ethnic Relations at Warwick University.

Sally Tomlinson   Professor and Head of the Department of Educational Research, Lancaster University.

Barry Troyna   Lecturer in the Social Aspects of Education, University of Warwick.

Jenny Williams   Principal Lecturer and Head of the Equal Opportunities Unit at Wolverhampton Polytechnic.

John Wrench   A Senior Research Fellow at the ESRC Centre for Research in Ethnic Relations, Warwick University.

Cecile Wright   Lecturer in the School of Education at the University of Leicester.

Acknowledgements

The contributors to this book have been exceptional in their co-operation and support. This ensured that the book was delivered (almost) on time — much to the pleasure (and surprise?) of Caroline Lane at Tavistock Publications. Thanks are due to Susan Pickering and Val Stephenson of the Faculty of Education at Sunderland Polytechnic for their administrative support.

At a more personal level, I'd like to thank Wendy Ball, Bruce Carrington, Andy Dorn, Bill Gulam, Chris Skelton, Jenny Williams, and, above all, Jayne Mills, for their advice and support in recent years. Finally, I would like to acknowledge how much I learned from my mum, Sylvia Troyna, who died in January 1987. Amongst many other things she had that indefinable quality: *chutzpah*. This book is for her, out of love and respect.

Barry Troyna
Department of Education,
University of Warwick

1 A conceptual overview of strategies to combat racial inequality in education: introductory essay

Barry Troyna

Some forty years on, the 1944 Education Act remains the cornerstone of the organization and thrust of the current educational system in Britain. It gave expression and legitimacy to two closely linked principles. First, that social advancement should be available to all; second, that the meritocratic structure of the education system would guarantee that personal achievement and talent would be rewarded within a competitive setting, irrespective of the age, sex, and ethnic or class origin of individual students.

Evidence was soon adduced, however, to challenge the assumptions on which the Act was designed. The research of A. H. Halsey and his colleagues was especially important in this context. These studies explored correlations between social status and the extent of social mobility in the UK, and the role of education as a mediating force in this process (Halsey 1972, 1978; Halsey, Heath, and Ridge 1980). Halsey's conclusions showed that despite the aims of the 1944 Act and a range of subsequent reformist measures and interventionist programmes, there remained a tenacious pattern of class inequality in educational achievement and attainment.[1] As he noted in 1978, the introduction of comprehensive secondary education, the raising of the statutory leaving age and the expansion of pre- and post-school provision had not generated 'the anticipated equality of access to the national heritage'. Indeed, the State's attempts to expand educational opportunities beyond the statutory leaving age had the opposite effect, in that they had 'been seized disproportionately by those born into advantageous class circumstances' (Halsey 1978: 130).

The ending of the broad educational consensus of the 1960s, which had provided the context for the promotion of programmes and initiatives to enhance 'equality of opportunity' for working class students, presaged the rise in the 1970s and 1980s of what Stuart Hall has called a period of 'regressive educational offensives' (Hall 1983: 2). Within this contemporary setting, the status of 'equality of opportunity' as an organizing principle of central government's educational strategy has been demoted, if not entirely dislodged. As Hall has put it: 'Inequality in education has become, once again, a *positive* social programme' (Hall 1983: 3).

Now, perhaps a more sanguine view of national developments could be drawn from sources such as *The Curriculum from 5–16*, a discussion document published by HM Inspectorate in 1985. There, 'equal opportunities for girls and boys' and the development of multi-cultural education are noted as 'essential issues'. HMI recommends that the place of these issues 'within the general framework' of schools should be assured (Department of Education and Science 1985: 13–15). Nonetheless, 'discussion documents' are structurally peripheral to the core of educational decision-making and there is no evidence that central government has taken this advice on board in the specification of funding or priorities. Nor does their identification as 'essential issues' in a discussion document disturb Bernard Davies' claim that the watchwords of the 1980s are: 'Elitism (rather than equality of opportunity); meeting the needs of the employer (rather than realising individual potential); responsibility and reliability (rather than self-expression and creativity)' (Davies 1986: 40).

This cynical disregard for 'equality of opportunity' in the framing of national education policy and strategy has not been replicated entirely at other levels of the state, however. Despite the constraints imposed on local state autonomy and policy options by the dominance of the central state's priorities, this same period has seen the extension of the concept to highlight the systematically negative experiences not only of working class students but also of those from other identifiable groups.

This shift from an exclusive concern with class inequalities in patterns of educational experience and achievement has been pre-cipitated by a recognition that racist and sexist impulses, above all, are pervasive within the educational system and that if left unchallenged these have the potential to undermine the maintenance and credibility of its meritocratic structure. At the very least, it has been acknowledged that these continually inhibit the qualifications obtained, courses followed, and opportunities available to female and black students (i.e. those of South Asian and Afro-Caribbean origin). Put differently, the operation of racism and sexism in the formal educational process has determined that girls and black students are discriminated against in their access to, treatment within, and subse-quent outcome from schools. More fundamentally, however, these impulses have been interpreted as signifying the educational system as an important site where the reproduction of sex and 'race' inequalities is achieved and confirmed. To a greater or lesser extent, these insights have led to a reappraisal of the way services are delivered in a growing number of local education authorities (LEAs) and individual educational institutions. Subsequently, these changes have been noted in the publication of formal policy statements which are informed by some version of antisexist, antiracist, multicultural, or equal opportunities principles. Not surprisingly, the complexion, orientation, and conviction of these policy initiatives varies between LEAs and individual institutions for reasons which have been touched on elsewhere (Arnot 1985; Troyna and Williams 1986). What is important to emphasise here is their common commitment to the mitigation of inequalities (variously defined) suffered by female and black students. The policies, therefore, provide the framework and rationale for a *manipulation* of the way education is organized for and experienced by these students in the local context.

It is the nature and efficacy of 'manipulation' as a strategic tool which is of interest here. If there is now a growing concern to combat sexism and racism and the inequalities they accentuate in formal educational settings, there remain deep divisions over the proposed rate, extent, and means of intervention. In short, the debate centres not only on the degree to which the educational system should be manipulated to promote equality of opportunity for female and black students, but also on whether this approach should be eschewed in favour of more radical challenges to the fundamental structure, ethos, and orientation of the system. This is a political and policy choice influenced, to a significant extent, by the way in which the core concept 'equality' is understood in the educational context.

As Lyn Yates has pointed out, for some theorists and researchers the basis for intervention stems from an understanding of inequality primarily in terms of 'disadvantage'; that is 'having more or less of, or possessing or not possessing the attributes and resources needed in schools.' Yates has suggested that from this perspective: 'Inequality was measured by success in school, post-school status and earnings etc. This was a liberal rather than radical definition of the problem in that the question was how to distribute achievement . . . more evenly *within* the existing system' (Yates 1986: 120–121).

Although, as I have already implied, no single or coherent meaning of equality (or inequality) in education prevails, it seems to me that Yates is wrong to consign this particular conceptual framework to the annals of history. The conception of inequality in these terms continues to give rise to incrementalist approaches to change which characterize, if not dominate, a number of current antisexist and antiracist policies and initiatives. In Jennifer Hochschild's words, incrementalism implies 'focusing on those few problems that present themselves as urgent needs rather than on the many features of a system that could probably be improved but seem to function adequately at the moment'. (Hochschild 1984: 79). If we accept this definition, then it is possible to identify a range of contemporary initiatives which conform to the model 'Inequality as disadvantage', but which operate under both liberal and radical guises. These initiatives tend to crystallize around a concern for 'achievement' in the terms designated by the system. For instance, the Girls into Science and Technology (GIST) project presumed a clear and single incrementalist objective: namely, to redress the under-representation of girls in physical science and technical craft subjects when these become optional in the latter stages of secondary education (Whyte 1986). Similar concerns are to be found in the field of both multicultural and antiracist education. It is not possible, for example, to appreciate fully the demands for curriculum reform along multicultural lines without recognizing the presumed relationship between these initiatives and the enduring concern with the 'underachievement' of black students, especially those of Afro-Caribbean origin. As those who framed Birley High School's policy in 1980 emphasized, 'Multicultural education is a whole curriculum which also involves an attitude to life. It aims to promote a positive self-image and respect for the attitudes and values of others. Such an education will improve academic attainment' (1980: 2). Similarly, the apparently radical, antiracist stance adopted by Berkshire and Inner London education authorities in the formulation of policies, reflects, on closer examination, a more traditional and liberal concern with the issues associated with the 'inequality as disadvantage' paradigm; that is, a redistribution of academic success.

For example, in the Berkshire policy statement, we are told that

'There will be racial equality in education, it follows, if and when Asian and Afro-Caribbean people are proportionately involved in teaching and administration at all levels, in higher and further education, and in streams, sets, classes, and schools leading to higher and further education.' (Berkshire LEA 1983: 5)

Following the same line, the then leader of ILEA, Frances Morrell, specified the Authority's goals as the identification of 'policies that are likely to *change* the current patterns of achievement within inner city schools' (Morrell 1984: 200).[2]

These, then, are classic exemplars of the 'inequality as disadvantage' paradigm within current antisexist, antiracist frameworks for action. Essentially, they represent liberal, or what Crosland defines as 'weak' versions of 'equality of opportunity' which are incrementalist in nature. They demand a greater or lesser extent of manipulation of resources, provision, organization, and priorities *within* the existing meritocratic and highly competitive structure of the educational system. Naturally, the techniques of manipulation may and do differ. As Nick Jewson and David Mason (1986) have indicated in their discussion of equal opportunities policies there are, on the one hand, those subscribing to 'liberal' traditions who favour the establishment of 'fair procedures'. In an educational context this approach adheres closely and gives credence to the meritocratic ideal as legitimate. On the other hand, there are those who adopt a more 'radical' stance and assign priority to the introduction of special programmes and provision, such as affirmative action, access, and conversion courses, and so on. These are rationalized on the grounds that it is imperative to overturn the effects of formerly entrenched processes of sexual and racial discrimination. But whatever the means, the goals remain the same: a redistribution of the scarce educational rewards which are on offer within a setting in which there must remain (few) winners and (many) losers. From this ideological and policy standpoint the attainment of 'equality' is inferred from patterns of educational outcome. What is especially important, however, is that *a priori* assumptions about the allocative and selective function of the educational system are accepted.

Another scenario is depicted by those who maintain that dependency on 'manipulation' as an antisexist, antiracist strategy reveals an impoverished understanding of the complex nature of sexism and racism and their relationship to education as an agent of cultural reproduction. This argument is sustained by the suggestion that such strategies promote, or at least defer to, what might be called a 'technicist' interpretation of these practices. That is, sexism and racism in education, and the patterns of inequality in outcomes which they produce, derive mainly from the inadequate functioning of educational institutions; a failure, that is, to respond competently and adequately to the needs of the various groups of students. This group of theorists does not conceive of the educational system as a neutral institution prepared to accept automatically the value and efficacy of antisexist, antiracist orthodoxies, on the basis of a well-reasoned argument. Instead, it is conceived as protective of, and an agent for the reproduction and legitimation of the culture, interests, and power of dominant groups, within which sexism and racism are constitutive features. Those who accept this perspective, therefore,

5

construe as anathema to 'equality' a system which is committed to selection, divisiveness, and discrimination and which, through the unequal distribution of cultural resources, skills, and knowledge, helps maintain and reproduce an unequal social structure. The concern of these theorists is less with the realization of a 'colour-blind', 'gender-blind', 'class-blind' hierarchy which, in principle, might be accomplished through manipulative strategies, and more with dismantling the institutional structure and prevailing ethos in education which ensures and legitimates the *existence* of the hierarchy.

The enactment of this theoretical and political stance has implications for the nature of the curriculum and pedagogy, student relationships, community involvement in decision-making processes, and modes of learning (Troyna 1987). Its advocates are heavily critical, for instance, of didactic approaches and of competitive individualism within an achievement-orientated learning environment. What they propose is greater emphasis on student participation and responsibility for learning, genuine collaboration, and group-centred approaches. They argue, quite rightly, that in a setting which encourages individual achievement and where rivalry for the scarce credentials available is inevitably nurtured, such ideals cannot be attained. Now, these are not novel proposals; as Gordon Allport observed over thirty years ago, logically they cannot be omitted from the agenda of reforms informed by antisexist, antiracist concerns:

'If segregation of the sexes or races [*sic*] prevails, if authoritarianism and hierarchy dominate the system, the child cannot help but learn that power and status are the dominant factors in human relationships. If, on the other hand, the school system is democratic, if the teacher and child are respected units, the lesson of respect for the person will easily register. As in society at large, the *structure* of the pedagogical system will blanket, and may negate, the specific intercultural lessons.'

(1954: 511; emphasis in original)

The determination to challenge sexism and racism, then, demands the radical reappraisal of all aspects of education to ensure that they are ideologically consistent with the imperatives of antisexist and antiracist principles. It also impels the development of a context in which students may probe the manner by which sexism and racism rationalize and help perpetuate injustice and the differential power accorded to groups in society.

The relationship between these theoretical stances, the conceptions of 'equality', 'inequality', and 'equality of opportunity' which they advance and the strategies which are proposed is a matter which has been grasped more fully in feminist literature than in the debates on antiracist and multicultural education. Feminist theorists such as Maggie McFadden (1984), Gaby Weiner (1985), and Lyn Yates (1986) do not consider the positions as incompatible but as points on a continuum designated in terms of the rate and extent of change. Initiatives such as the GIST project, the removal of sexist teaching materials and textbooks, and the introduction of single-sex groupings in particular subjects are seen as short-term goals which are based on what Weiner labels 'egalitarian' principles. Their realization, how-ever, can achieve no more than 'liberalize access to an inadequate system' (Weiner 1985: 10). At the other end of the continuum stand what Weiner refers to as 'feminist' demands. Their goals are more long-term and, as we have seen, more radical; seeking to 'transform or abandon masculine systems' (McFadden 1984: 498).

This distinction is not as clear-cut in the literature about racism in education – although some would have us believe differently. At a superficial level, perhaps, the distinguishing of multicultural and antiracist educational goals might appear to parallel Weiner's egalitarian/feminist or McFadden's minimizer/maximizer polarities This is certainly the argument of Robin Grinter (1985). He has asserted that multiculturalists seek reforms within existing structures (thereby confirming the legitimacy of those structures) whereas anti-racists seek to transform them. But this is an oversimplified and dis-torted picture. Closer scrutiny of the themes and concerns of anti-racist education policy statements (including those of Berkshire and ILEA) reveals a continuity and commonality with earlier multi-cultural imperatives (Troyna and Williams 1986). The suggestion that current discussions about 'equality' and 'justice' have precipi-tated a shift from a preoccupation with 'fitting minority ethnic groups into the existing *system*' to issues which have 'implications for many aspects of educational *practice*' exemplifies this confusion and misapprehension (Willey 1984: 1; emphasis added). Where the dis-tinction between these two models is most sharply drawn is in the con-tributions from black writers such as Stuart Hall, Pratibha Parmar, Hazel Carby, Gus John, and Chris Mullard. Their work both informs and reflects the struggle against racism which members of the black community are engaged in. In this context, their work is easily dis-tinguishable from the multicultural education model, which con-tinues to draw its rationale, inspiration and support from white, middle-class, professional understandings of how the education system might best respond to the 'needs' and 'interests' of black students and their parents.

Structure of the book

The contributors to this book are united in their commitment to combating racial inequality in education and in delineating the extent and manner in which racism (and the practices it gives rise to) has embedded itself into institutional and socio-political structures in the UK. In the opening chapters, Gurnah, Oldman, and Foster-Carter point to the ways in which the state (through the articulations of official commissions) and the 'New Right' provide a legitimating gloss to the ideology of racism and the role of the education system in the production, maintenance, and reproduction of racial inequalities. Despite some differences in rhetoric, the intervention of Swann and Scarman, on the one hand, and Honeyford, Flew, and Scruton, on the other, confers respectability and legitimacy on an educational system which marginalizes black students, their knowledge and experiences. The chapters by Dorn and Hibbert, on Section 11 funding, and Gibson on 'consultation' exemplify two of the strategies used by the state in the 'management' of black resistance to racism in education. The following chapters by Tomlinson, Wright, and Wrench focus more intently on those processes within school and post-school training schemes which operate to promote and buttress the ideology and practice of racism. Finally, the chapters by Chevannes and Reeves, Carter and Williams, and Hatcher propose in both theoretical and practical terms some of the strategies through which the development of antiracist principles might be realized.

In all, the book is intended to show how racism operates at an ideological, structural, systemic, and interpersonal level within contemporary British society and the role of schooling in perpetuating a system of racial inequalities in education and beyond. It seems to me that the complex and pervasive influence of racism in education which the contributors draw attention to necessitates both short and long term *antiracist* strategies. 'If the alternative to incremental change is no change', writes Hochschild, 'then incremental politics is not conservative' (1984: 37). This may be so; but whilst recognizing that education can play only a limited role in combating the structural dimensions of inequality the time has surely arrived when reliance on manipulative means to tackle racism is no longer a sufficient strategy.

© *1987 Barry Troyna*

Notes

1 The empirical studies carried out by Halsey and his colleagues have rightly been criticized for a repeated neglect of gendered forms of inequality (see Purvis and Hales 1983).

2 It is salutary to compare these interpretations of 'equality' – often referred to because of their radical origins – with A. H. Halsey's definition, which is said to exemplify liberal principles: 'a society affords equality of educational opportunity if the proportion of people from different social, economic or ethnic categories at all levels and in all types of education are more or less the same as the proportion of these people in the population at large' (Halsey 1972: 8).

Acknowledgements

I am grateful to Jayne Mills, Bruce Carrington, Chris Skelton, and contributors to this book for their comments on my initial draft of this chapter.

References

Allport, G. (1954) *The Nature of Prejudice*. Reading, Mass: Addison Wesley.

Arnot, M. (ed.) (1985) *Race and Gender: Equal Opportunities Policies in Education*. Oxford: Pergamon Press.

Berkshire LEA (1983) *Education for Racial Equality: General Policy Paper*. Berkshire: Local Education Authority.

Birley High School (1980) *Multicultural Education in the 1980s*. Manchester: Local Education Authority.

Davies, B. (1986) *Threatening Youth: Towards a National Youth Policy*. Milton Keynes: Open University Press.

Department of Education and Science (1985) *The Curriculum from 5 to 16*. London: HMSO.

Grinter, R. (1985) Bridging the gulf: the need for antiracist multicultural education. *Multicultural Teaching* 3(2): 7–10.

Hall, S. (1983) Education in crisis. In Wolpe, A. M. and Donald, J. (eds) *Is There Anyone Here from Education?* London: Pluto Press.

Halsey, A. H. (1972) Political ends and educational means. In Halsey, A. H. (ed.) *Educational Priority* (Vol. 1). London: HMSO.

—— (1978) *Change in British Society*. Oxford: Oxford University Press.

Halsey, A. H., Heath, A. F., and Ridge, J. M. (1980) *Origins and Destinations*. Oxford: Clarendon Press.

Hochschild, J. (1984) *The New American Dilemma: Liberal Democracy and School Desegregation*. New Haven: Yale University Press.

Jewson, N. and Mason, D. (1986) The theory and practice of equal opportunities policies: liberal and radical approaches. *The Sociological Review* 34(2): 307–34.

McFadden, M. (1984) Anatomy of difference: toward a classification of feminist theory. *Women's Studies International Forum*. 7(8): 495–504.

Morrell, F. (1984) Policy for schools in Inner London. In Grace, G. (ed.) *Education and the City*. London: Routledge and Kegan Paul.

Purvis, J. and Hales, M. (eds) (1983) *Achievement and Inequality in Education*. London: Routledge and Kegan Paul.

Troyna, B. (1987) Beyond multiculturalism: towards the enactment of antiracist education in policy, provision and pedagogy. *Oxford Review of Education*. 13(3): 307–320.

Troyna, B. and Williams, J. (1986) *Racism, Education, and the State: The Racialisation of Education Policy*. Beckenham: Croom Helm.

Weiner, G. (1985) Equal opportunities, feminism, and girls' education: introduction. In Weiner, G. (ed.) *Just a Bunch of Girls?* Milton Keynes: Open University Press.

Whyte, J. (1986) *Girls into Science and Technology*. London: Routledge and Kegan Paul.

Willey, R. (1984) *Race, Equality and Schools*. London: Methuen.

Yates, L. (1986) Theorizing inequality today. *British Journal of Sociology of Education* 7(2): 119–34.

2 Gatekeepers and caretakers: Swann, Scarman, and the social policy of containment

Ahmed Gurnah

'When the devil wants nothing done, s/he appoints a committee.'

Norwegian proverb

In this article I want to argue that figures like Swann and Scarman are gatekeepers and caretakers of the complex state functions and policies. In these roles, they are not merely functionaries of the ruling class, but synthesisers of establishment objectives (which they share) and the 'popular' will. The caretaking is being most successfully realized through their social policy of containment. As such, their deliberations are neither necessarily disinterested nor must they innocently be thought to be defending black interests. Thus, black people and their supporters cannot safely ignore them; they need to develop alternative (and collective) strategies for action in education and for coping with the racist legal system.

For hundreds of years the British State has used Royal Commissions, Committees of Inquiry, and Judicial Reviews to settle administrative grievances or resolve social crises at home or in its occupied lands. Their work has played an important role in both ensuring the survival of the old aristocracy and in the development of social democracy. Lords Swann's and Scarman's inquiries are therefore modern versions of a time-honoured tradition. The Commissioners invariably share the State's objectives and are by inclination at home with the State bureaucratic procedures, but also seek to represent popular grievances. In that role they converge State interests and popular perceptions into a programme for moderate change. Swann was required to diffuse black parents' and pupils' protest and resentment towards the education system, and Scarman to explain and lower the tension that provoked black young people to rebel against the State and their conditions.

11

As a document, the Sheffield CRE finds the Swann report 'patchy and inconsistent'. They rescue bits of it only in order to 'focus attention on deep-seated concerns of Afro-Caribbean and Asian communities' (Sheffield CRE/LEA 1985: 3). Sheila Patterson thinks it worth rescuing because 'like Little Jack Horner's Christmas pie' it is full of plums, the juiciest one being *Education for all* (Patterson 1985: 239). Alfred Jowett is grateful for the endorsement of multifaith religious education (Jowett 1985: 467), and Bikhu Parekh that Swann concedes that racism exists, is created by white people, even in education, and is responsible for underachievement (Parekh 1985: 1).

People have tried to rescue Scarman too. Comparing him to a 'social democratic rock upon which the strong waves of the law and order continue to break', Martin Kettle is impressed by the way he persisted in his 'investigations of social economic issues', when Margaret Thatcher, John Fraser (Labour), and Jim Wellbeloved were talking of criminal indiscipline, family breakdown, and lack of decent authority (Kettle 1981: 404). Overseen by a minister of the Home Office, John Benyon and his colleagues (most of whom are State representatives and workers) seek to *implement* Scarman's recommendations (Benyon 1982: 119–21). They issue Britain a challenge which links 'solutions' to Scarman; either we take 'vigorous action' and implement him, or we 'procrastinate' and ignore what 'will long rank as one of the most important post-war investigations' (Benyon 1984: 242).

The rescue of Swann is clearly not what pickets outside a Brent school had in mind when they tried to stop people from conferring on the report. They thought it irrelevant, because black people's protest against racism and the failure of schools to educate their children have never been heeded. They want action not more words and reports. These issues, some would say, do not need either Scarman or Swann, for there is ample political and academic evidence to support black parents' complaints (Dhondy *et al* 1982; Bridges 1981/82; Giles 1977; Stone 1981; Coard 1971). For its own reasons, the British State has not chosen to bestow on black citizens their legitimate rights of entry, residence, education, and protection from official and individual harassment.

The source of the problem is greater than just State racism, it is connected with the working of the system as a whole. Formal plebiscitary democracy has failed to involve the public *in situ* in the process of policy development or delivery of services. The State paternally bars ordinary citizens from participating in educational and legal policy development. When the public is brought into affairs of State, the devolution of power is carefully regulated through class, gender, and racial matriculation; this is the crux of our problem.

The educational system in a liberal democratic State has not enabled working-class parents to organize politically in order to prioritize their children's needs and contribute towards educational policy. The notion of 'public opinion' obscures the fact that 'representative' views tend to be those of articulate middle-class individuals who sit on governing bodies or teach, or the views of middle-class groups who have access to the media. The educational world of middle-class values becomes *professionally* insulated from the demands of working-class parents and pupils. Black parents remain outside this world and, since Swann has not addressed these issues, his report remains largely irrelevant to them. Those teachers who seek to end black oppression must therefore distance themselves from the rationale of the system which turns them into inaccessible 'professional' and thus minor State custodians, and instead make meaningful alliances with black communities.

The legal system is even worse in this regard. A sanctified independence from political and community accountability is given to aloof, middle-aged, ill-informed white judges. They have licence to moralize with their conservative upper-middle-class male views, on any subject they choose without recourse. They are serviced by and recruited from a self-selecting profession that is only accountable to its own association. Similarly, the police exercise enormous powers of arrest, prosecution, of directing physical violence towards any recalcitrant groups without much public accountability. Since the State allows even less public involvement *in situ* here, the legal system is even more insulated from the public than the education one.

Thus, as members and custodians of this Establishment matrix, it is naive to assume that any of us can meaningfully rescue Swann and Scarman to serve black people. Since on the face of it, despite their interest in 'public opinion' and 'moderate' resolution of social conflict, the inclination and brief from the State is to produce social policies in keeping with the existing order, it would be imprudent for black people to trust their judgment or integrity. The crucial strategic question then becomes, how are we to relate to State-sponsored inquiries when they are carried out by its honoured custodians? Should we rescue those parts which are not contradictory or racist, or only criticize them constructively, but refuse to have anything to do with them formally? Alternatively, are we to join with the Brent pickets and have nothing to do with them, or should we scrutinize them for what the State proposes for black people, and then construct alternative strategies? In my opinion, clarity about these questions will contribute towards the success of black struggles in Britain.

I shall argue that these reports cannot be rescued, because their 'hidden' brief is not open to question and their agenda is often in competition with our own. But to ignore them, as would the Brent pickets, will not do either, for we need to study them in order firstly to have a strategic response to them, and secondly to construct an alternative strategy.

But given the class and ideological differences between us, it may be unrealistic, or even undesirable, to expect all black people and their supporters to agree on a common response to the reports, or to construct a single alternative strategy. Clearly an unemployed young black will respond differently to Swann or Scarman from a black polytechnic lecturer who may well stand to gain from them. Their response will depend partly on their class, cultural, gender, racial or national standpoints, and maybe even if they share these, there is no guarantee that individuals will agree.

If a little overdetermined by functionalism, these are fair reflections. But if it is difficult to find a common response, political realities make it *absolutely necessary* that we at least narrow our options, for how else can black people and their supporters dismantle institutionalized State racism? But this does not meet the above objections, it merely indicates why they must be met. What obviously, brings black people and their supporters together, is their experience of and opposition to racism. But more significantly (as it happened in anticolonial movements) it is their *opposition* to the historical and structural *role* of the commissions which may unite them. Each one will then work out his or her structural relationship to the commissioners. Even if it is merely to pursue personal gain, all will then maintain a universal pressure for transformation on the State. That universal pressure will form a basis for a response to the reports and an alternative strategy. It is to that end that I commit the efforts of this piece.

My aim is not primarily to show the inadequacies of these reports via textual analysis. It is rather to clarify their *role*, in the belief that clarity on that will prepare us better for what we should do with them. I shall proceed by outlining black grievances in education and the legal system and show how the inquirers responded to them. Then, I shall examine the inquirers' role as State policy developers – as gatekeepers and caretakers – at three levels: by examining who they are, where they come from, and what they do. That should allow me to conclude with some comments on an alternative strategy.

Black grievances in education

While fully appreciating the work of individuals and groups in odd enlightened schools and authorities, black parents are convinced that schools 'underachieve' their children, for the following reasons.

Firstly, they believe that a lot of teachers hold stereotypes of their children which not only divide them from the white children, but also from children of other black communities. This view is not only supported by academic research, but also by Rampton who linked the reasons for failure to inadequate provision at a preschool stage, lack of dialect appreciation, teacher expectations, and inappropriate curricula and examinations. In short, he linked black children's failure to 'bad teaching, a lack of responsiveness, and bad practice' (Rampton 1981: 11). For him, racism 'intentionally and unintentionally has a *direct* and important bearing' on black children's examination performance (1981: 12). As part of this unintentional racism, many teachers still function with culturally implicit biological deterministic categories. It is the assumption of these categories and not the disgraceful stereotypes adduced by the Swann Committee which explain the differential examination passes between Afro-Caribbean and Asian children. The problem is compounded by teacher educators' failure to recruit more black student teachers or seriously re-examine their curricula. But to create an equal opportunity environment in the lecture room, black people would say, teachers will not only need to retrain themselves and recruit black lecturers, but also consult with and take advice from the black community at all levels of education.

Thus, *secondly*, black parents have not found schools sufficiently friendly to wish to get involved in them as parents or governors. But the importance of black parent involvement is underlined by Len Scott's remarkable conversion of Swann's averages of 6 per cent Afro-Caribbean and 17 per cent Asian passes, into 71 per cent black passes, at Parkland High School.[1] It is in schools that children first learn how to fail or pass. There they either come across for the first time, or reinforce, culturally specific implicit meanings. If those are racist, some of them will be reproduced in public institutions and personal relations in adult life.

Thirdly, the school curriculum has tended to be epistemologically narrow and exclusively Eurocentred. When Third World material is introduced in that setting, it is often unhelpful. It is only recently that the importance of the mother tongue has been recognized.

Fourthly, there is a relative absence of good quality action and academic research on black educational needs in teacher training

15

departments. The over-preoccupation with cultural exoticism does not focus on black needs and is partly responsible for the often inappropriate curriculum.

By identifying their grievances as such, black people are not setting out to make scapegoats of the already beleaguered teachers. They are identifying the roots and causes of their oppression. For when we examine Swann's attitudes on these issues, we find little reason for encouragement. I shall concentrate on the first grievance to show that Swann in fact retreats from Rampton, and has to be persuaded that racism exists (Parekh 1985: 1), but not sufficiently for him to mention it even once in his guide to the report. Using language befitting a Trotskyist rather than an Establishment figure, he argues that black grievances are simply more acute versions of working-class ones (Swann 1985: 2). But then he contradicts himself by insisting that 'prejudice and discrimination' are 'the major obstacles to the employment and advancement' of black teachers (Swann 1985: 10). Soon enough, however, he implies that no bias of any kind exists in schools. Since the war the education of black children has been 'marked [by] good intentions' and a powerful commitment by schools and teachers to 'see children as individuals' (Swann 1985: 3). Even his own description (Chapter 4) of bussing, dispersal, assimilation, and suspensions would indicate a differential and racist treatment of black children.

In a rambling chapter called 'Racism: theory and practice', the aim of his committee appears to be the wish to play down the notion of racism. Here racism is not accounted for in historical and structural terms of colonial, imperial, and capitalist dimensions, but is redefined in psychological and personal terms of prejudice. Racism becomes 'the ethnic minority dimension of prejudice', 'a pernicious form of it' (DES 1985: 12 and 14). Roots of racism are astonishingly linked to white natives' legitimate reaction to refugees and to the economic success of blacks (DES 1985: 18–19). The earlier motive of explaining 'underachievement' in terms of prejudice and socio-economic status now becomes completely clear. For it not only justifies white prejudice, but also denies 'white racism'; which the report believes to be 'misconceived' (DES 1985: 27). After all, black people too are prejudiced against each other. The committee purports to have observed Chinese, Vietnamese, and Asian children being 'racist' towards 'black' children, while Afro-Caribbean children both dislike Africans and join white children to attack Asians.

Thus, by ignoring historical and structural causes for contemporary white racism in capitalist societies, the committee is able to lump together all forms of cultural and national antipathies (many of which were *caused* by British occupation of their countries) and call them racist. Consequently, if racism causes 'underachievement', blacks must accept part responsibility for their children's failure. The committee, therefore, follows Scarman in 'vigorously' rejecting 'black racialism' (DES 1985: 27–28), and subsequently *also* reaffirms racist stereotypes of black people, which blame black people for racism.

The notion of institutionalized racism too is deemed 'confused and confusing'. State institutions are 'in no way racist in intent' (DES 1985: 28), just by accident. The best way of stopping the State from enacting all the racist legislation, it would seem, is by changing individual attitudes (DES 1985: 29 and 37. See Gurnah 1984). Thus, the only possible reason for underachievement (they guess) is 'socio-economic status' (DES 1985: 58–9, 78–79, 81–2). So contradicting Rampton, the committee removes the responsibility for under-achievement from the teachers, schools, LEAs, DES, and the State and gives it back to black parents. But since Asians who have the same socio-economic status get better results, and they do not acknowledge that some teachers hold biological deterministic assumptions, they are then forced to turn to what they admit are racist stereotypes. That is, firstly, Asians 'keep their heads down' and Afro-Caribbeans 'protest' a lot. Secondly, overturning a 1960s stereotype, the com-mittee proposes that rather than slow them down, the tight knit of Asian communities and families helps the children to do well (DES 1985: 86). Apart from being racist, in my experience these stereotypes are not even true. The conclusions of Chapters 2 and 3 are that Afro-Caribbeans are themselves (after all) responsible for the failure of the school system. Since parents do not use existing facilities, the local authorities should make them aware of the preschool facilities, and help them 'appreciate the contribution which they make to the progress of their child' (DES 1985: xix).

Swann's committee then similarly turns to 'recover' teacher education from Rampton. Their purpose seems to be to advise white majority teachers to get to know more about minorities. Being 'different from the *accepted* norm', they shoud learn about black people's cultural and linguistic peculiarities (DES 1985: 561. Emphasis added). Giving substance to the notion that black people are in a relationship of internal colonialism in Western capitalist societies, the report advises teachers to become what amounts to colonial urban anthropologists in order to find out what make blacks in their midst tick. Student teachers are advised to involve themselves in black activities 'beyond the school gates', thus making participa-tory colonial anthropology the real meaning of *Education for All* (DES 1985: 565). It is then not surprising that teaching institutions in white areas are advised to organize a new form of 'bussing' by starting a regular exchange of students with those in black areas to give them 'multiracial experience'.

Of course, no sensible person can be against anthropology or acquiring cultural knowledge of others, whether done for pedagogic or policy motives. It would be crass to admonish teachers for trying to find out more about black needs. For so long as those teachers *focus* on the historical causes of black oppression, seek the means to satisfy those needs, and keep clear of the highly dubious amateur cultural anthropology, they are bound to make a genuine contribution to black liberation. But the amateur focus on black culture to humanize and help white people revise their attitudes (DES 1985: 587) becomes highly dubious because it never seems to get round to addressing black oppression. I have argued elsewhere (Gurnah 1984) that understanding alone almost never leads to meaningful change. What multiculturalism seems to offer black people is yet another, and this time a particularly difficult, legitimized hurdle to scale over, every time they seek change. For now white colleagues either become 'experts' on their culture and therefore know what needs to be done, or they become infuriatingly 'understanding', but frustratingly slow to do something. Black parents have then to face not only school racism, but also cope with Swann's well meaning cultural experts.

Finally, towards the the end of Chapter 9, the committee deplores the 'low numbers' of black teachers 'in *our* schools', and asks for 'urgent attention and positive action' (DES 1985: 601). But for them positive action means neither 'positive discrimination' nor 'quotas' (DES 1985: 605 and 613); since both will lower standards and bypass the LEA's desire 'first and foremost' to appoint 'the best candidate for the job in terms of expertise, experience, and ability'. But these standards do not seem to be a problem when it comes to teaching black culture, language, and religion. Nevertheless, the committee still urges the CRE, the LEA and schools 'to devote far greater efforts in identifying and overcoming racist obstacles to employment and advancement' (DES 1985: 614), but without using effective techniques quite commonly employed by the Chancellor to control Government spending and the EEC to target policies and redistribute resources.

Summarily, the committee calls for more black employment, but bans *positive* steps for achieving it because it will lower standards. But apart from denying employers the use of an effective mechanism, its stance implies that black people are *rightly* not employed as teachers at the moment, not because of racism, but because they are no good. Insistence on professional standards is widely acknowledged to be one of the most common forms of institutional racism found in education and employment.

The trouble is this report strings together liberal educational *rhetoric* already known to have failed black pupils, with the *rhetoric* of cultural diversity, language appreciation, and religious tolerance. The coded message behind all the rhetoric is that the report accepts the failure of the school system *as part of the balance*. It blames and exonerates both teachers and black parents. The overwhelming implicit message is not 'Good education for all', for that would require more than they offer, but that except for a few hiccups in matters of attitudes, all *are* receiving good education now.

Black grievances in the legal system

Black criticisms of the legal system have since 1958 been regularly articulated by urban disenchantment. Black people have argued that the legal system finds its rationale in the matrix of institutionalized State racism: police structural racism, lack of accountability, and harassment of young blacks is but part of it. Immigration laws regularly infringe both incoming and resident black civic rights (see NCCL's *Rights!*). Race relations laws have at least partly outlawed positive action, while nationality and police laws have made black people vulnerable and provided an ideological rationale to deny black people political representation, employment, housing, and protection from harassment.

Though the causes for black rebellions have been understood for some time now, there is little acknowledgement of that in the Scarman Report. Even when he talks of urban deprivation, he talks about it in 1970s social democratic terms of the inner city, which as Lee Bridges has shown (1981/82) has little to do with responding to black needs. Like Swann, Scarman fails to make any real contribution and rather subverts, confuses, placates, and badly summarizes well known political demands and academic findings.

Scarman shows his hand from the beginning when he observes that '*British people* watched with horror and incredulity . . . scenes of violence and disorder in *their* capital city' (Scarman 1982: 13. Emphasis added). Contrary to Kettle, and like Margaret Thatcher, he condemns the rebellions from the outset as 'criminal behaviour' for which no unfavourable social condition must provide an 'excuse' (Scarman 1982: 14, 33–4). His tone is not that of an investigator searching for reasons that explain particular events, but of a moral custodian of the State. He thus greatly reduces the distance between himself and those other, self-appointed moral guardians of our democracy, the tabloid headlines.

Furthermore, Scarman does not believe Britain is 'institutionally racist . . . knowingly, as a matter of policy, discriminating against black people' (Scarman 1982: 28). Apparently unaware of racist legislation, he insists that public racism is unwitting (Scarman 1982: 24). Contradicting his own evidence, he insists that the police do not criminalize or harass black young people, that that is just a remour spread by the latter (Scarman 1982: 99, 106). He concedes that at Brixton the police were brutal and aggressive, used illegal weapons, 'improper use of dogs, shields, and truncheons . . . unnecessary force . . . undesirable tactics' and over-saturation. But he still 'totally and unequivocally rejects the attack made upon the integrity and impartiality' of senior officers. They are not racists, but lack 'imagination and flexibility' (Scarman 1982: 101, 105). The few racists in the force only appear irregularly and are usually 'young, inexperienced, and frightened' against whom black people overreact (Scarman 1982: 80, 105).

Thus, the police do not 'criminalize' young black people; the latter bring it upon themselves by mixing with criminals in the 'seedy, commercially-run clubs of Brixton.' Their street life brings them into contact with the 'visible symbols of the authority (police) of the society which has failed them' (Scarman 1982: 29). As exemplified by Brixton and Southall, Afro-Caribbean, and Asian young people are far too ready to mistrust and attack the police and take the law into their own hands (Scarman 1982: 30).

In this masterly rewrite of black complaints, State racism becomes unwitting, while the criminalization and harassment of young black people by the police and the National Front (in Southall) is blamed on the former. The rebellions are then not due to institutional racism, but are connected to inner city deprivation, 'vigorous' law enforcement, a lack of consultation (Scarman 1982: 79, 97–8) and criminality. The various studies which prove police misconduct or that they cook its crime statistics become inadmissible (80, 84). Government inaction is not due to institutional racism, but to the fear of 'backlash' (208). No new laws are required, better use of old ones and 'a positive effort by all', especially the Community Relations Council, should suffice. Blacks must refrain from being racialists (172–3) and be persuaded to 'take their share of general provisions' (170).

So why does the State bring in such people to confuse, subvert, placate, and misrepresent black grievances? The answer lies in the tradition of conducting social policy through containment. Such commissions help the State manage dissatisfaction, diffuse crises, and prevent the growth of popular movements; or where they already exist, limit their effectiveness.

Social policy of containment

John N. Young attributes to Swann 'an attempt once and for all to replace the notion of "good will" with that of justice' (Young 1985: 235). Quite the opposite would seem to be the case: the committee fails to present critical accounts of events, and those which are critical pertain to institutional incompetence and not to their inappropriateness.

To explain what I mean by social policy of containment, I shall approach the issue at three levels by examining who the commissioners are, where they come from, and what they do.

In the first place the policy is suggested by the kind of people who are chosen to chair and participate in commissions of inquiries. Regardless of which party is in power, they are invariably Law Lords, knights, retired civil servants, Privy Councillors, or an odd former chair of the BBC. They are usually well known public figures, often with reputations for independence, objectivity, and impartiality. As senior and competent Establishment figures with considerable communication skills, they also tend to command a great deal of authority. The State requires that the public should recognize their integrity, trust the facts they find, and acknowledge their humanity and sense of responsibility. Sir Roy Welensky in his blunt Southern African colonial way tell us what all this really means. As the Prime Minister of the white-dominated Federation of Central Africa, he finally accepted Macmillan's choice of Lord Monckton to go and adjudicate on the African claims for majority rule and the session from the white-ruled federation. He was assured that Monckton was not so much a politician as a wise, experienced, tactful man who knew about constitutions. He was also one of Macmillan's 'oldest and closest friends'. They met at Oxford, served together 'with distinction and gallantry' in the First World War, and were both in Churchill's Coalition in the Second World War and in his post-war administration. 'Mr Macmillan told me that he had absolute confidence in his friend's judgement' (Welensky 1964: 151).

The whole tenor of the character reference is to reassure Welensky that Monckton was a 'sound man'. There was no mention at all about whether he knew anything about, or had any commitment to African welfare. Swann is quite frank about this aspect. The offer to chair this committee 'came as a complete surprise' to him. As a scientist, a former principal of 'an ancient Scottish university', and the chair of the BBC 'I had little knowledge of the needs of Britain's ethnic minority citizens' (Swann 1985: 1–2). But even so, the State does not appoint people from this class background primarily to predetermine the findings, since that would only discredit the inquiry. Besides, the commissioners are not just class representatives or State lackeys, rather they are independent *partners* in the State system (and many value this aspect highly), who see it as their *duty* not to defend a particular class or State agency, but to serve the State and the system *as a whole*. They are celebrated members of the British Establishment and hardly its mere functionaries. Indeed, to appoint a publicly self-confessed ideologue to conduct such inquiries would be counter-productive for the State. Instead, the State counts on these people's professional and class instincts not to serve a particular government but to continue State legitimacy. Though their significance is rarely discussed openly, it is of considerable constitutional importance to the State. Their knowledge and links with the bureaucratic and 'old-tie' network ensures the continuation of established overall values and social relations. Their involvement reassures the public that import-ant issues are being addressed, and wrongdoers censured, without dis-ruption or extra cost to 'the tax payer'. Their strategy is to ensure stability by introducing gradual change.

Secondly, in order to explain what is meant by social policy of containment, I shall briefly examine the workings of this tradition by concentrating on its pattern in British-occupied lands. As I suggest in the conclusion, that will not only situate Swann and Scarman, but also teach us three lessons learnt from them: success only comes in the relative absence of sectarian squabbling; mass action triumphs in the end; persistence pays off.

The same broad formula was used in British colonies as is used here: the same personnel, to achieve the same aims. Picking out a few such in-quiries at random, of the six people heading constitutional inquiries Moyne (1938) in the West Indies, Donoughmore (1927) Ceylon, Simon (1927), Monckton (1960) and Blood (1960) Zanzibar, four are Lords and two are knights and all fit perfectly the profile drawn up by Welensky. Like Swann and Scarman also, none of the Commissions knew much about or sympathized with the people whose political future they were going to adjudicate on. It was very rare that local political rep-resentatives were included on those committees and when they were, they either had no influence or were chosen carefully. In the same way as the State here neither requires knowledgeable black people to chair their inquiries nor pays much attention to the black community's griev-ances, so it was in the colonies. The reasons are pretty similar to those given by the frank Welensky for co-opting two Africans onto the Execu-tive Council: 'To assure Africans that they were sharing in the process of government and thus diminish their desire for secession' (Welensky 1964: 152). The colonial State usually achieved that through co-opting its corrupt counterpart of the local ruling classes. It would seem to me that the desire by Swann and Scarman to absorb black people into a liberal democratic consensus without meeting their needs, has the same logic as the colonial situation: to diffuse the crisis by containment. The 1972 Pearce Commission will illustrate my point.

In 1972 Pearce was sent to Rhodesia (now Zimbabwe) by the British State to continue the 1960s policy of rescuing Smith's reactionary white government from internal and external Black African pressure to overthrow it. In the face of State intimidation and bribery, it was only the resolute African 'no' which undermined Lord Pearce's mission. The issues were quite clear. They did not need a seventy-year-old law lord to unravel them: Africans wanted universal suffrage and their land back, and the British State was unwilling to support those claims. At this time African leaders were in prison, repressive laws were pushed through by Smith, political meetings were not allowed, and fifteen Africans were machine-gunned in Umtali because they refused to disperse before representing their views to Pearce. Pearce vindicated Smith's action and the only change he was after was that which would ensure the continuity of the *status quo*. The crucial lesson to be learnt here is that black Zimbabweans refused to accept any of the State's attempts to saddle them with anything less than a one person, one vote administration, and resisted its commissioner's attempt to diffuse their struggles. They succeeded because they did not cooperate with the State-sponsored inquiries, and persisted in their claims, which were informed by an alternative strategy.

So, thirdly, we come to what I mean by containment. The State has contained political demands when it has convinced citizens that their grievances are seriously considered, under difficult conditions responded to, at very little cost to the public purse, without much disruption of the existing system. By the time the commissioners have successfully finished their work, the public morale should be reassured, a few misfits identified and condemned, 'difficult' problems genuinely addressed, and major debates initiated. The most important thing about these reports is that they *must not* be read for the *content*, but for their hidden symbolic *meanings*. That is, the very existence of such reports signifies the *realization* of a balanced, fair, democratic, and open society. Thus they 'contain' public opinion by placating, reassuring, diffusing, confusing, legitimizing, manipulating it, and save the public money.

The commissioners are therefore prepared to recommend limited political or financial reform to avert crises. They address all the interests involved and they apportion blame and exonerate all of them: the police, young blacks, and State institutions. They play down disharmony and leave groups with something to rescue and argue over from the report, for at least five years or so. In short, the commissioners both satisfy and manipulate the public and at the same time diffuse, redefine, and absorb black grievances. They are not brought in to meet demands, and increase public representation, but to renegotiate and redefine a new balance. They do not resolve grievances, they lubricate them. They incorporate and handle the grievances.

Their job is therefore broader than simply to defend a capitalist State and class, although that is part of it. They are defending *their* established system with all its traditions. They are defending the feudal customs and rights of property as much as the City and capital/labour relations. They are defending the Queen, Home Counties, and the Courts as much as competition and Japanese business. They are defending capitalism, it is true, but they are also defending England, and the idea of it: it is their duty to do so. They are defending the system, its roots as well as its future. They defend a way of life.

Containment, therefore, is not only the defence of capitalism, the ruling class and *its* State. *Firstly*, because there is no one class or State 'view' of events, there are several. There are racist, imperial views, as well as professional, liberal ones. These views may reflect the parliamentary-meritocratic-bureaucratic complex or the aristocratic-financial-public school traditions. In short, the Establishment constitutes not just one class or ideology, but a band of interlocking and competing vested interests, subtly inclined to defend the survival of the system *as a whole*, if not any particular aspect of it. But, *secondly*, even if there were a single recognizable interest and view, a crass manipulation of working people would not only give the game away, but as a number of aristocratic wets have pointed out to Margaret Thatcher, it would in the long term also increase resistance. But, *thirdly*, even if such repression and manipulation were possible without recourse, the Establishment is aware of too many other groups, representing their own interests, whose cooperation is crucial if the system is to remain intact. This would at different times include teachers, lawyers, parents, as well as working people. The State must find ways of at least partially satisfying them all. This is what constitutes the real success of liberal democratic containment; and its most successful custodians are the commissioners.

While Swann and Scarman at some level acknowledge black grievances, and partly advise the state to heed them, they also redefine them. At the same time, therefore, inquiries help State institutions to update their language and avoid giving constant offence: Coloureds become black, and prejudice begins to give way to racism. The educational and legal institutions, which for so long stonewalled any black criticisms, are asked to accept them and *do* something about them so long as that will not disrupt things too much, cost a lot, or threaten the system as a whole. Furthermore, their reports provide us with text which will legitimize racist State policies and keep teachers and sociologists occupied for years to come, mostly trying to find out what they mean.

Conclusion and comment

I conclude that as State gatekeepers and caretakers, Swann and Scarman help continue the fiction that Britain has a balanced, liberal education system and an equitable legal one. But to say this does not suggest that their role is just to manipulate the working class on behalf of the ruling class, although that is part of it, it is also to bring flexibility into, and 'aid' State management. As part of that task, the inquirers have transformed a traditional paternalistic management technique previously used to contain colonial and British white working-class people, into one more appropriate for diffusing the action of rebellious young working-class blacks in Britain. It is as a testament to the fiction they spread, that it is not they, but humanists and socialists who *rightly* find themselves defending critical education and liberal laws against State encroachment. Instead, the Commissioners blame racism on blacks, turn white teachers into amateur colonial anthropologists, and disapprove of those who meaningfully work with black people. They defend racist 'professional standards', deny the existence of institutional racism, and explain racist police action in terms of black criminality. There seems to be little point for black people to rescue such reports, particularly when we remember that their aim is to introduce the above as part of the new balance.

It would be folly, however, to respond to these reports with noble but ignorant distance. For without well informed counter strategies at our disposal, the State is bound to achieve its aims. When we are not actually, as often happens, blundering into the inquirer's frame of reference, our opposition will be reduced to reactive attempts that limit the damage. I have already suggested the basis upon which a common response can be launched, but for a counter strategy to succeed, we also need to know more about the State's own intentions.

The basis for a counter strategy, I believe, lies in the assumption that just as the inquirer's work increases the system's flexibility, it also exposes the system's Achilles' Heel. Notwithstanding recent police action, British liberal democracy avoids polarization and turns to extreme violence only when pushed to the limit. The slack between containment and violence provides a large area which well organized black groups can productively exploit and there would be nothing that the State can do about. For as long as the safety of the system has priority over a few concessions to black people, the State will avoid precipitating unnecessary crises and try not to upset middle-class vested interests. As I don't believe that grabbing concessions from the State is a 'sell-out', what is needed is better organization. But should such opportunities go past untapped, the State resolve hardens on the recognition of this absence of political willingness to make sustained demands. Concessions which had been previously won from the State, may even be withdrawn. Thus, this alternative strategy will require three elements: the end of sectarian posturing, mass action, and persistence; all of which were learnt from the colonial struggles against the British State.

Posturing over details of ideological differences which immobilize black action must come to an end. The futility of such political self importance is well illustrated by the failure of such groups to influence any radical events. In the Third World it was the populist, anti-colonial movement, in Britain CND and ANL, and in France a group of school children (SOS Racisme), who successfully mobilized mass action and not these ideological pedants. Fully recognizing colonial State motives, Third World popular movements refused to cooperate with Commissioners, and instead persistently reasserted their own coherent alternative. That coherence also exists in black British demands. It requires firm and persistent restatement from nationally organized groups, regardless of the country of origin of their participants. To avoid giving ammunition to the Commissioners who will mercilessly exploit it to show divisions between black people, participants must avoid unnecessary public disagreements. Nor can we any longer tolerate *macho* political intervention from isolated sectarian groups, which *wrongly* believe that nobody but themselves understands the contradictions of capitalism and with their exception, everyone else is on a 'sell-out'. With such coordinated and supported black action, I am convinced, instead of the State logic of containment working against us and always predetermining our working practices, it will concede to us to avoid precipitating a crisis.

I therefore conclude that for teachers, policy makers, and social analysts — black or white — to be part of our struggle they must distance themselves from State custodians, 'ethnicity' experts, or professional 'radicals'. They should join us in trying to find our legitimacy, rationale, and programme for action in the black communities themselves. It is to this satisfaction of community needs we should turn our energies, and not allow other vested interests to translate the plurality of those needs into divisions and confusions. Like any other oppressed group, our differences and confusions do not obscure what we want, diminish our case or call for its suspension. We will be thus disembodied only if we ignore the Norwegian proverb, heed the messages of the committees of State custodians, and fail to develop independent strategies.

© *1987 Ahmed Gurnah*

Note

1 Len Scott's work is part of research work he has been conducting with colleagues in Lancaster University.

Acknowledgements

I want to thank Alan Scott for his usual advice and support and Peter Gibbon for initially planting this notion in my mind some five years ago. I also want to thank Chris Searle and Robin Smith for their comments on the manuscript, which I know for sure, bless them, have stopped me from making the usual unnecessary blunders.

References

Benyon, J. (1982) Swann and After. *New Community* 10(1): 115–21.
—— (ed.) (1984) *Scarman and After*. Oxford: Pergamon Press.
Bridges, L. (1981/82) Rebellion and Repression. *Race and Class*, 23 (2 and 3).
Coard, B. (1971) *How the West Indian Child is Made Educationally Sub-normal in the British School System*. London: New Beacon Books.
Department of Education and Science (1985) *Education for All: The Report of the Committee of Inquiry into the Education of Children from Ethnic Minority Groups*, Cmnd 9543. London: HMSO.
Dhondy, F., Beese, B., and Hassan, L. *The Black Explosion in British Schools*. London: Race Today Publications.
Giles, R. (1977) *The West Indian Experience in British Schools*. London: HEB.
Gurnah, A. (1984) 'The politics of racism awareness training'. *Critical Social Policy* 11 (Winter): 6–20.
Jowett, A. (1985) Swann on religion. *New Community* 12(3): 464–9.
Kettle, M. (1981) The evolution of an explanation. *New Society*, 3 December: 404–406.
Parekh, B. (1985) *Report of the Conference 'Swann – a Black Community Response'*. Brent: Copland School.
Patterson, S. (1985) Random samplings from Swann. *New Community* 12(2): 239–48.

Rampton, A. (1981) *West Indian Children in our School.* London: HMSO.
Scarman, Lord (1982) *The Brixton Disorders: 10–12 April 1981.* Harmondsworth: Penguin.
Sheffield CRE/LEA (1985) Conference on the Swann Report (October).
Stone, M. (1981) *The Education of Black Children in Britain.* London: Fontana.
Swann, Lord (1985) *Education For All: a Brief Guide.* London: HMSO.
Young, J. N. (1985) Education for all: from 'good will' to 'justice'. *New Community* 12(2): 235–8.
Welensky, R. (1964) *Welensky's 4000 Days.* London: Collins.

3 Plain speaking and pseudo-science: the 'New Right' attack on antiracism

David Oldman

Any reader sympathetic to the concerns of this book, and wanting to explore current thinking on the amelioration or eradication of racial inequality in education, may wonder why valuable space is being used to look at the views of those who are implacably opposed to any form of affirmative action at community or state level. This chapter, which tries to explain some of the 'New Right' diatribes against antiracist education, has to start by persuading most readers that pronouncements which may appear to them as either transparently wrong, or crassly polemical, are a serious attempt to shape the form of discourse in which future argument about access to education, control over education and the content of education will be framed.

Since the time of the last Labour government's 'Great Debate', we have been confronted with demands not only for a *qualified* population, but also for a *disciplined* population, one that will accept the existing structures of power, authority, and wealth, and will compete in orderly fashion for the ever-decreasing opportunities for employment. In this climate, the Black Paper writers of the 1960s and the 1970s and their successors are not just capturing the middle ground of educational politics but are approaching the summit. Mrs Thatcher recently invited several of them, including Ray Honeyford (the subject of a separate chapter in this volume) to a private lunch in 10 Downing Street. Even if this is an exaggeration of their influence, their concern with the question of who controls education makes them especially important to those of us who want to see antiracism established within the education system, because we too see the issue as one of control. We share with our right-wing opponents the emphasis on *popular* control over education. The slogan, 'power to the people', is the prize sought by both sides.

The element of populism in right-wing educational discourse is at once its most interesting and its most pernicious quality. One form it takes, is the highlighting of 'plain speaking' as a virtue. 'Plain speaking' is my own term to describe a particular view of language and its functions that seems to me to be characteristic of many of the writers whose works I shall describe from here on as 'authoritarian'. One thing 'plain speaking' is not, is a reverence for demotic or colloquial speech. What it is most clearly is a three-pronged attack on, first, neologisms that they assume to be ephemeral (the 'trendy phrase'), second, on the 'jargon' of social science (often equated with 'trendiness'), and third, the 'dilution' of 'standard' English by those for whom it was not, or is not, their native tongue.

Karl Popper hit exactly the right-wing view of the relation of language to society when he said,

'Some of the famous leaders of German sociology who do their intellectual best, and do it with the best conscience in the world, are nevertheless, I believe, simply talking trivialities in high-sounding language, as they were taught. They teach this to their students, who are dissatisfied, yet who do the same. In fact the genuine and general feeling of dissatisfaction which is manifest in their hostility to the society in which they live is, I think, a reflection of the unconscious dissatisfaction with the sterility of their own activities.'

(Popper 1970: 296)

'Plain speaking', then, can protect us (all) from the machinations of critics who are hostile to the society in which we live!

'Plain speaking' is, however, not so plain. By insisting on the *correctness* of standard English, and linking it with the qualities to be found in the classics of English literature, 'plain speaking' moves very far from the speech of 'everyone'. 'Plain speaking' is the speech and writing of those particularly favoured, most obviously by having English as their parental and grandparental language, but also by having a family background already well 'enriched' by the appropriate literary currency.

The main plank of my argument in this chapter is that the authoritarian position on education is based on appeals to a common-sense philosophy of knowledge that is, in fact, nothing more than a crude empiricism of the sort that social scientists are wont to call somewhat rashly 'positivism'. In essence, the empiricism of the authoritarian is an appeal to 'what everyone knows' in the language that 'everyone can understand'. 'Plain speaking' and a 'respect for facts' are rhetorical appeals that allow them to hide their own political views, and their own selectivity of evidence, whilst accusing their enemies of 'bias' and 'distortion'.

In their study of the forms of discourse (deracialized or benignly racialized) that have characterized recent policies on race and education, Troyna and Williams (1986) adapt Edelman's (1964) notion of 'condensation symbols' which they define as '(having) deliberate political purposes; to create symbolic stereotypes and metaphors which reassure supporters that their interests have been considered. But the symbols have contradictory meanings so that the proposed solutions may also be contradictory or ambiguously related to the way supporters originally view the issue' (Troyna and Williams 1986: 100). This chapter is, in effect, a study of the condensation symbols 'captured' by the 'New Right'.

The chapter has three main sections. In the first, I identify the authoritarians and expose their main assumptions. In the second, I examine the issue of the relationship between politics and education as seen through the eyes of the authoritarians. In the third section, I look at their views on race, and the question of what is, and what is not, 'racism'.

The nature of authoritarianism, and its naive empiricism

The particular works on which I have drawn most heavily to illustrate the authoritarian position are *Education and Indoctrination* (Scruton *et al.* 1985), *The Wayward Curriculum* (O'Keeffe 1986), and two papers by Antony Flew, *Education, Race and Revolution* (1984) and *Power to the People* (1983) both published by the Centre for Policy Studies. Readers may be surprised that I make little reference to Ray Honeyford, whose writings on race and education in the *Salisbury Review* had the seal of approval from Scruton and Flew, but his attack on multicultural education is dealt with by Olivia Foster-Carter elsewhere in this volume. All the authors mentioned are linked by the favourable citations they make of each other's work, and their tendency to appear within the same covers.

In an earlier paper (Oldman 1985), I defined authoritarianism in the following terms:

1 an insistence on a clear distinction between those in authority and those subject to authority;

2 a belief that there is a consensual basis for authority in our society and that those who challenge this consensus are enemies of our society;

3 a belief that the basis for authority rests ultimately on the possession
   of qualities whose superiority is a matter of nature, and which
   cannot therefore be altered by human decisions.

I would now add that the legitimation of quality is not only by an
appeal to nature, but also by appeal to history or tradition where
these are seen as sequences of self-evident and corroborated events
about which no 'reasonable' person could disagree. It might be
argued that, for example, the authority of the teacher of literature
cannot depend upon qualities of literary analysis that are 'factually'
based, but the authoritarian will refer to the historical continuity of
the consensus as to the nature of literary quality. (Scruton *et al.*
1985: 36−7). In both the sciences and the humanities, an appeal to
the 'fact' of quality is made. Academic disciplines, each having their
own history, and their realization in school subjects, are therefore to
be self-directing. They cannot be guided or altered by human
concerns coming in from outside, and they cannot be directed in their
course by those who are mere neophytes in the respective traditions.
'Power to the people' does not include tampering with the curriculum, or the power to decide what is spurious and what is worthwhile within a given curriculum.

Here we have a particularly grandiose view of education. Naive
sociological observers, such as myself, might debate whether
education is an 'integrative sub-system' or an 'ideological state
apparatus' or some other concept that stresses the subservient and
conservative nature of education, but the authoritarian viewpoint
makes education the very flagship of society, with certain well-known
professors of philosophy as its admirals! Perhaps, 'pilot' is a better
term than 'admiral', because the direction of the educational flagship
is provided by a combination of science and tradition.

When we start to look at this philosophy in detail, the first feature
that strikes us is a surprisingly cavalier attitude towards forms of
expression. The empiricist position demands that the 'truth' of a
statement is determined by the state of the world that the statement
expresses, and has nothing to do with the language in which it is
expressed. Whilst there is obviously a lot of mileage in this principle,
it is unfortunately only a half-truth, and it is where it is wrong that
problems arise. Its main implication is that it seals off for ever any
possibility of analysing the political import of the 'condensation
symbols' in which 'factual' truths are expressed. Thus, in a *Times*
article where he castigates sociology for extending the term 'violence'
to cover all forms of power (he calls this 'spurious equivalence'),
Scruton justifies his criticism on the grounds that the sociology of

power is a 'hysterical and over-burdened boatload on the sea of pure opinion', that is, it is not based on facts. However, in the very same article he makes the following 'factual' statement:

> 'Recently several academic sociologists, speaking at the British Association for the Advancement of Science, staged what amounted to a show-trial of the "New Right", denouncing their colleagues who had departed from the fold of socialism as morally corrupted and intellectually void. Not one of these colleagues was invited to reply, and the authority of the British Association was used as a badge of office with which to consign to silence all those whose opinions offended the bigots.' (Scruton 1985: 14)

As one of the sociologists concerned, this puzzled me deeply! Here is a writer accusing his colleagues of bigotry and propaganda because they use the tricks of, first, conspiracy, and then the linguistic fraud of 'spurious equivalence'. Yet is it not the case that 'the authority of [*The Times*] was used as a badge of office' to insult, through the spurious equivalence of terms such as 'bigot', a group of colleagues who happened to share a common interest and who gave it a public, and well-advertised, airing!

This gargantuan paradox is very common in authoritarian writing. In *Education, Race and Revolution*, Flew accuses the proponents of antiracist education of wishing to censor text-books and curricula, and yet on the very next page he suggests that the CRE 'be directed on pain of dissolution to formulate its own redefinition' (Flew 1984: 12–13). Similarly, Honeyford scores a hole-in-one in the following sentence: '[There is] an influential group of black intellectuals of aggressive disposition, who know little of the British traditions of understatement, civilised discourse, and respect for reason' (Honeyford 1984: 32).

The only way I can resolve these paradoxes is to assume that the empiricism of the authoritarian standpoint gives them a confidence in the underlying truth of their factual assertions, regardless of the form of words used to describe the truth. They presumably distinguish their own polemics, which they would see as matters of style, from the 'biased' and 'politically loaded' *opinions* of their enemies. What we see here is that 'plain speaking' can descend to gratuitous insult without ever, apparently, affecting the 'truth' of the assertions made. Flew's double standard, too, is explicable if it is seen as merely the simplistic belief that truth and error are distinguishable as 'fact' and 'non-fact', and that censorship of the latter, but not the former, is therefore justified.

I, and most other social scientists surely, see this crude empiricism as dangerously simplistic. We would say that the material world has its facticity which allows us to see that some statements about it are manifestly wrong but, at the same time, the facticity of the material world does *not* set limits on what we *can* say about it. Those limits are set by whichever body of theory the factual statements are embedded in. The theory determines the language used, and affects the adequacy of the factual statements. 'The land is flat' is fine as a fact about travel conditions, but is hardly adequate as a geometrical statement. Moreover, the language of theory often involves the metaphorical use of language drawn from other theories, and it is here that crude empiricism runs into trouble. The indiscriminate use of metaphor in the expression of scientific truths has led, and will continue to lead, to quite bogus developments. The best current example is the so-called 'socio-biology' as applied to humans, where scientists have dressed the technical equations of evolutionary process in metaphors drawn from the cupidity and aggressiveness of their own shabby lives, and then have claimed these personal qualities to be justified by biology. (For a critique, see Sahlins 1977.)

This demotion of language to the superimposition of style upon fact, and the cult of 'plain speaking', allows what people actually say to be secondary to what they do, and what they do, of course, is expressed in the observer's linguistic style and not that of the actors in question. Empiricism leads to behaviourism and, most importantly, leads to a lack of interest in the words, feelings, reasons, and rationalities of the subjects of social scientific study. We see this in the Scruton paradox, illustrated above. He (a 'colleague') was complaining about the lack of opportunity to state his case, but we (the objects of his criticism) were attributed motives which belong only to Scruton's argument and nowhere else. Our actual states of mind seem irrelevant to his case against us. Just as, in another affair, the views of Bradford parents seem to be largely irrelevant to Honeyford's views on the superiority of educational tradition over family tradition (Honeyford 1984).

Education and indoctrination

The contributors to this book would, I think, all agree that antiracism constitutes a *programme* for education. The authoritarian position is that when education is driven by such a programme, it ceases to be education and becomes indoctrination. For them, indoctrination is characterized by a closing-down of argument, whereas education is an opening-up of possibilities. Scruton and his co-authors (Scruton *et al.* 1985) see indoctrination as identified by foregone conclusions, a hidden unity, a political programme, a closed system, and closed minds. Foregone conclusions and the hidden unity, in their turn, are signalled by loaded language, loaded questions, and loaded references.

Indoctrination in all its aspects is illustrated by an examination question they discovered which reads as follows: 'How does schooling reproduce racial inequality?' (quoted in Scruton *et al.* 1985: 18). This, apparently, is a loaded question. Of course, the question *is* loaded; it is loaded with meanings which will hopefully be apparent to those who have taken the course. But the critics see a 'foregone conclusion' in that the question assumes a role for schooling that the student is not expected to challenge. Let us now ask whether the following question is loaded: 'How does RNA reproduce proteins?' Is the student unwarrantedly prevented from querying whether ribonucleic acid does function in this way? Presumably not, on the very good grounds that the role of RNA in protein synthesis is taken for granted in undergraduate biochemistry, and the question is asking about the mechanisms involved. Similarly, several decades of sociological theorizing and research allow the 'foregone conclusion' that schooling (amongst other institutions) reproduces racial inequality (amongst other social states), and the question is testing the student's knowledge about how schools actually operate. What Scruton *et al.*, of course, are really saying is that the 'foregone conclusion' is unacceptable to them, not on the grounds of its factual inadequacy, but because, by a circularity of argument, education cannot and should not act in this way. What it boils down to is that the question, and the discipline from which it is drawn, upsets their view of the ideal society, in which inequality is justified as 'natural'. To what extent, then, does the question have a 'loaded' vocabulary?

'Among neo-Marxist terms the following are particularly important in slanting questions, and presupposing a neo-Marxist perspective upon them: "reproduction" . . . "schooling" . . . "social inequality". . . . A non-Marxist might reject the use of all these terms in the application here given to them. He [*sic?*] might say the following:

Social structures may be similar from one generation to another, but this does not mean that they are "reproduced", for that implies a mechanism directed to the production of such an outcome. Marxists do indeed accept that there is such a mechanism, but others do not.' (Scruton *et al.* 1985: 21)

Again, the glaring paradox! Of course, particular terms belong to particular perspectives and part of the process of 'reading' the question is to recognize the perspective, or range of perspectives, involved. But Parsons, Bourdieu, and Bernstein, to mention at least three famous non-Marxists, have written at great length on the reproductive function of schooling and, incidentally, did not or do not see the mechanism as directed. What could be more 'loaded', in the sense of deliberately trying to narrow down the focus of the reader's mind, than the use of the term 'Marxist' in this passage? And to what end, it must be asked? Nothing more than an attempt at an anti-Marxist pogrom.

As it happens, I do not believe that Scruton and his co-authors are being deliberately dishonest, nor do I believe that they are so stupid that they cannot see the paradox in their position that is so apparent from within the sociological tradition. Again, it comes back to their distinction between what can be seen as fact, regardless of the terminology in which it is expressed, and what is mere opinion. Their empiricist stance, and this is the real paradox, blinds them to any statement of fact, when reported from outside the world of sciences that are cocooned within an authoritarian education system. Something of the gulf between the authoritarians and critical social science, as to what is and what is not reliable fact, can be seen in the following quote from John Marks' criticism of the Brent enquiry into its secondary schools:

'the methods used were unlikely to lead researchers nearer to the truth. Much time and effort was devoted to seeking and taking evidence from self-selected groups such as respondents to advertisements, attendees at meetings, pressure groups, and organizations. Sometimes such evidence had been solicited directly by informal approaches from members of the investigation.

However useful such evidence is in the formative stages of research and as a supplement to systematic studies it is no substitute for them. . . . There was no *adequate* survey of the views of a representative sample of parents, despite the terms of reference of the investigation specifically mentioning the concerns of parents.'

(Marks 1986: 217)

I do not know if the Brent enquiry was adequate or inadequate, but I do know that if one were to reverse the positions of the social survey and the solicited opinions in the above passage, one would arrive at something that reads very like the methodological prescriptions in the best textbooks of social anthropology. Blundering, with pseudo-anonymity, into complex and conflict-ridden scenes armed with a clipboard and a list of preselected questions, has been shown over and over again to produce nothing but 'safe' responses from the subjects filtered through the prejudices of the interviewer. Objectivity is a far, far more complex matter than crude empiricism would have it, and it is unobtainable without recognition of, and sensitivity to, the politics of data collection.

My conclusion is this: authoritarian empiricism simply buries the political import of all scientific and cultural questions under the carpet of a self-serving and insular notion of objectivity.

Finally, if education has no programme, it is hard to see why authoritarians are so concerned about the education standards attained by the consumers of education. After all, if education is, by definition, self-directing and self-justifying, its standards are independent of its consumers. In fact, of course, education *has* a programme, even for authoritarians, and that programme is the efficient selection of persons to fill the more elite positions in a stratified society, and to discipline all its consumers into accepting the *status quo*. The authoritarian programme is *precisely* the 'reproductive' function that its proponents have professed to query. The charges of 'indoctrination' and 'closure' begin to look suspiciously like the defence of a position that is in danger of being 'sussed out'.

Race and culture

To the extent that antiracist policies constitute a programme for education, they are seen by the authoritarians as indoctrination which hides its political purpose behind loose definition. Flew (1984), and Marks (1986), insist on a distinction between 'race' and 'culture', and accuse the proponents of antiracism of using the former label when they mean the latter, thereby broadening the scope of racism to include differentiations that the authoritarians would see as justifiable. Since 'racism' to Flew can only mean discriminatory beliefs and practices applied to 'race', objectively defined from within biological science, it is not surprising that he and his colleague claim, first, that the evidence for racism is poor and, second, that it is essential to debate the 'evidence' that might justify inegalitarian outcomes. Further to this line of argument, they would say that whether or not 'biological' racism is found, 'cultural' racism is a contradiction in terms, but in so far as unequal treatment of different cultures is implied then this may very well be justified on the grounds that there is a hierarchy of cultures in terms of their suitability for coping with life in Britain. On all counts, antiracist programmes are held to ignore the evidence of how both 'race' and 'culture' affect educational attainment.

To attempt to separate the biological from the cultural as the authoritarians do has two consequences. First, it invites their readers to see racial inequality as 'natural' and, second, it obscures the most salient fact of 'minority' cultures in a racist society, that they are constituted, at least in part, as responses to the 'common-sense' reductionist thinking of the majority who insist on seeing minorities as defined by their biology. It is this latter point which the authoritarians refuse to grasp, and which is central to the definition of racism that so offends them. Marks takes issue with the following passage from a paper by Chris Mullard:

> 'we can speak of racism, as both a structural and ideological form, in terms of a race relations structure in which the inequalities and differentiation inherent in the wider social structure are related to physical and cultural criteria of an ascriptive kind and are rationalized in terms of deterministic belief systems which tend to make reference to biological science.'
>
> (Mullard 1980, quoted in O'Keefe 1986: 216)

and Marks responds in paradigmatic 'plain speaking':

> 'This vague, jargon-ridden definition is functionally useless. It also confuses two separate definitions of "racism" (discriminatory behaviour, and belief in generic inferiority).'
>
> (O'Keefe 1986: 216)

Now, it is manifestly clear to me, as a professional sociologist, that Mullard's statement, whilst technical (and therefore requiring some education to be understood), is precise, functional in that it does indeed provide the starting-point for an antiracist policy, and deals adequately with the two meanings of racism by pointing out that discriminatory behaviour is frequently justified by reference to beliefs about generic inferiority. Marks' 'plain speaking' diverts the well-intentioned reader away from the import of Mullard's writing, and would prevent any study of the political power of mundane biologistic reasoning about race. Precisely because racist thinking lumps a wide range of peoples together and labels them 'black', a proper study of, and policy against, racism has to take this point on board, as Mullard explains:

> 'many of us would prefer to see ourselves as *blacks* rather than as West Indians, Asians, or Africans, for this not only accentuates our common experience in Britain, but it also points to a set of explanations that cannot be presented as ethnically specific.'
>
> (Mullard 1982, quoted in O'Keefe 1986: 215)

Marks sees this as 'extremely dubious sociology in that it seeks to deny many real differences which many of those involved would like to

The 'New Right' attack on antiracism

maintain. And it also has the clearly stated intention of ruling out, *a priori*, any explanation based on such differences.'

(Marks 1986: 215)

The bulk of earlier literature on positive discrimination and multi-cultural education, characterized by what Troyna and Williams (1986) call 'deracialised discourse', makes much of ethnic differences in educational attainment. What this work did, and much of it was valuable, was to seek the kinds of explanation that Marks advocates. But, as we now know, this explanatory framework offered too narrow a focus on the grosser patterns of discrimination to which all defined as 'ethnic' were subject. Antiracist educational policy starts from the premise that discrimination in Britain does not make, nor is it felt to make by those subject to it, the distinctions that Marks wishes to preserve and study as a matter for science. Here again, we see in the authoritarian stance a refusal to accept the definitions of the situation provided by those who constitute the focus of study.

The reduction of complex social processes to a pseudo-biology is very much a feature of everyday explanation. At various times, and to various degrees, madness, criminality, 'abnormal' sexual lifestyles, and excesses of temperament have all been reduced to some unspeci-fied operations within the brain that relate the constitution of the body to its behaviour. In spite of the repeated warnings from neuro-biology that the necessary theories are simply nonexistent, correla-tional evidence that links the morphology of the body to the content of thought and action is still used as 'proof' that such mechanisms (however philosophically implausible) must exist. The seductiveness of such reasoning lies in its simplicity, and the fact that it appears to absolve us all from any responsibility for the problem. When Flew says:

'Whether there are in fact average phenotypical or geno-typical differences between different races or racial groups, either in intel-ligence as technically defined, or in intelligence in the ordinary sense, or in any other kind of inclination or capacity are all scientific questions.'

(Flew 1976: 63)

he is half right, but unfortunately he picks the wrong science. They are social-scientific questions. 'Intelligence' is not and never has been a biological concept; the identification of human intelligence depends upon judgements being made about actions where both judgements and actions can only be defined and described from within a culture. And this, by the way, is a far more fundamental point than saying that intelligence tests are culturally loaded. 'Race', on the other hand, has been used both as a biological and as a cultural concept, but it can only be theoretically linked to intelligence in its latter capacity. The literature is full of studies, both from the US and Britain, which explore in detail the operation of various kinds of stereotyping used by teachers, social workers, child psychologists, or whoever, that routinely produce the lower intelligence and attainment measures in children perceived by those who are processing them as 'black'. These 'chalk-face' processes constitute, of course, only a small part of the systematic denigration of people whose appearance invites the application of simplistic theories of inferiority. But, even so, crude empiricism decides to ignore all the detailed work done in this area, and demands that good, honest-to-God prejudices be turned into the content of a biological science. A final consequence of the separation of 'race' and 'culture' is that it allows the authoritarians to argue that even if we do not know (science not yet being ready) whether some races (defined biologically) are inferior, we can at least be sure that some cultures are inferior. Flew argues for a distinction between valuing a culture for its own sake (itself a value judgement) and valuing a culture for what it can achieve (which is a matter of fact once the ends are defined).

> 'Once this distinction is made, it becomes obviously preposterous to maintain that no culture may be said in any respect, or with regard to any possible objective, to be either superior or inferior to any other.' (Flew 1986: 158)

Once again, his empiricism rejects any social or political purpose in valuing cultures for their own sake, which might well be an essential part of any antiracist education, and instead we are forced onto the back foot to argue about the instrumental value of cultures. Leaving aside the point I stressed earlier, that most 'minority' cultures have adapted to racism and therefore have their own well-developed 'instrumentality', we are left with the charge that some cultures are ill-suited for equipping children to gain access to the particularly insular culture of the education system. An obvious riposte would be that the morally correct response to differential access is to alter the curricula and selection systems of the educational system itself, and this, indeed, is part of any antiracist programme. But the authoritarian argument is that standard English has become the necessary medium for the understanding of school subjects, by *force majeure*. There is, of course, a trivial sense in which their claim is true. If English remains the sole medium of instruction in British schools then clearly those who do not have English as a first and family language will be disadvantaged. However the authoritarians take it further; their argument against a multilingual medium within schools is that standard English, as guarded by education, is to be the badge of membership for British society.

> 'Nevertheless, [no] speculative historical linguistics has the slightest tendency to show as things in fact have been and now are, that it is not imperative for anyone proposing to make their home and their career in the United Kingdom to master English, and standard English, rather than Urdu or Creole.'   (Flew 1984: 18)

If Flew needs an example of discriminatory practice, he need look no further than his own article! The children who might benefit from multilingual education are not, of course, those 'proposing to make their home and career' in the UK, but those who are already doing so, through no choice of their own, and who would like to be treated as the Britons they are. The fact that they speak, as do most Britons, nonstandard varieties of English, and possibly other languages as well, is their birthright, and must surely be recognized by any education system that claims to be British.

Concluding remarks

Antiracist policies challenge the existing cultural hierarchies, and the modes of access to them, by proposing to teach children about what is happening to them, by offering them alternative cultural hierarchies, and by giving them some indication of how these might be used to oppose the discrimination they will experience, or that they will collude in. The authoritarian attack on antiracism proceeds along two fronts. The first justifies the self-isolating dynamic of education, arguing that the authority of educational hierarchies stems from a combination of 'nature' and 'tradition', and by denying that education can be linked to any kind of political programme. The second line of attack has been to pick up the 'common sense' theorizing of the inhabitants of a discriminatory and unequal society, and to demand a scientific status for it. Both these lines of attack are defended by reference to 'facts', but the factual nature of their assertions is founded upon a simple-minded empiricism which allows them to dissociate their 'facts' from the language in which they are expressed. Whilst they demand clear conceptual distinctions, they seem indifferent to the words used to make these distinctions, extolling the virtue of 'plain speaking', but refusing to hear the plain speaking of those subject to authority. Thus 'facts' can be dressed up in rhetoric, polemic, or insult without their being called into question, whilst the attempts of social science to evolve new forms of theorizing with appropriately new terminologies are dismissed as mere jargon.

Any challenge to these lines of argument is attributed to ulterior political motives stemming from an unholy desire to reduce variety to sameness. The problem for the authoritarians is that they seem unable to conceptualize egalitarianism in anything but empiricist terms. Thus, Flew:

> 'we are going sooner or later to be asked to condemn or abandon anything and everything the actual effects of which are that the racial distribution in any social group is substantially different from that in the population as a whole. . . . Anything, but anything, that stands in the way of this proposed ideal is to be denounced and execrated. It has to be, by definition, racist.'
>
> (Flew 1984: 11)

This quote nicely summarizes the incomprehension of crude empiricism when faced with policy-oriented social science. How does one break through the barrier to persuade the authoritarians that the issue behind egalitarianism is not numbers but power? Or rather that the issue of power is not a choice between control by state bureaucrats engineering statistical equality, and protection of legitimate inequality by 'free' academics. What is not even remotely apprehended in the authoritarian writings is the idea of communities shaping their children's education in ways that *they* feel to be valuable, even if this happens to contradict the traditions of existing curricula. They are adamant that education must direct itself according to its own traditions, and they assume that this is both accepted and valued by the bulk of the population, whose only power is then to dip into their pockets and use hard-earned private resources to buy some competitive edge over their neighbours, or, if this is impossible, to trade their 'vouchers' in whichever educational 'supermarket' appears to be offering value for money.

In the final analysis, the poverty of the authoritarian position lies not so much in its pseudo-scientific justification of an unequal and discriminatory society, but that its attempt to capture the world of everyday educational discourse by 'plain speaking' can only succeed in alienating those whose very real discontent with present schooling is simply not heard by the likes of Scruton and Flew. I am well aware that discussions of education in most newspapers have established a concern with 'standards' that overrides all other issues, and, like the authoritarians, they put the blame for declining standards on 'trendy', left-wing or, more recently, greedy teachers. However, public opinion polls show, and here I too will be crudely empiricist for a moment, that people see low standards in terms of crumbling buildings and lack of books and, in the case of black communities, it is not hard for them to see this as yet more evidence of discrimination. Certainly, few people want, or are able, to buy their own way in. Educational vouchers will not help black communities to eliminate the racism they currently have to face. The sad thing is that, at the end of the day, if the authoritarians have their way, this is all that they will be offered.

© *1987 David Oldman*

References

Edelman, M. (1964) *The Symbolic Uses of Politics*. Urbana: University of Illinois Press.

Flew, A. (1976) *Sociology, Equality and Education*. London: Macmillan.

—— (1983) *Power to the People*. London: Centre for Policy Studies.

—— (1984) *Education, Race and Revolution*. London: Centre for Policy Studies.

—— (1986) Education against racism. In D. O'Keefe (ed.) *The Wayward Curriculum: A Cause for Parents' Concern?* London: The Social Affairs Unit.

Honeyford, R. (1984) Education and race – an alternative view. *Salisbury Review* (Winter): 30–2.

Marks, J. (1986) Educational policies on race – a case study. In D. O'Keefe (ed.) *The Wayward Curriculum*. London: The Social Affairs Unit.

Mullard, C. (1980) *Racism in Society and Schools: History, Politics and Practice*. London: University of London Institute of Education.

—— (1982) The educational management and demanagement of racism. *Educational Policy Bulletin* 10(1): 21–40.

O'Keeffe, D. (1986) (ed.) *The Wayward Curriculum: A Cause for Parents' Concern?* London: The Social Affairs Unit.

Oldman, D (1985) The rise and fall of the concept of educational opportunity. Paper presented to The British Association for the Advancement of Science (Sept.).

Popper, K. (1970) Reason or revolution. In T. W. Adorno (ed.) *The Positivist Dispute in German Sociology*. London: Heinemann.

Sahlins, M. (1977) *The Use and Abuse of Biology*. London: Tavistock.

Scruton, R. (1985) Who will cure this social disease? *The Times* (8 Oct): 14.

Scruton, R., Ellis-Jones, A., and O'Keeffe, D. (1985) *Education and Indoctrination*. Harrow: Educational Research Centre.

Troyna, B. and Williams, J. (1986) *Racism, Education and the State: The Racialisation of Educational Policy*. Beckenham: Croom Helm.

4 The Honeyford affair: political and policy implications

Olivia Foster-Carter

The context of the campaign

The Asian community in Bradford numbers 50,000, more than ten per cent of the city's population. The majority are from the Mirpur district of Kashmir in Pakistan and Muslim by religion. They came to Bradford mainly to work in the textile industry in the poorly paid jobs that were rejected by white people. Bradford industry has benefited from the influx of cheap labour. Most of the Asian community inhabits inner city areas and makes little claim on education, housing, and public services. Unemployment in Bradford is now 50 per cent and the Asian population is badly affected by this.

Recent boundary reorganization gave the Conservatives the advantage over other parties in Bradford, which was once a city of Labour majorities. The policy of dispersal ('bussing') was introduced in 1964. This aimed at limiting the number of Asian pupils to ten per cent of a school's population. The figure was later changed to thirty per cent. The system of bussing was attacked in the late 1970s. Those on the right were concerned about its financial implications. Those on the left pointed out that it was formally discriminatory in the light of the Race Relations Act of 1976. In Bradford, bussing ended in 1980 under pressure from Asian community groups and the Commission for Racial Equality. They preferred neighbourhood schools. Now, 19 schools in Bradford consist of more than 70 per cent Asian pupils (see Carling *et al.* 1984).

In November 1982, halal (or ritually slaughtered) meat was introduced into the school meals service. Animal rights campaigners, supported by a racist fringe, objected to it in 1983. They claimed that the method of slaughtering was inhumane. Eighty to 90 per cent of Asian pupils went on strike and 3,000 people demonstrated in support of halal meat on 6 March, 1984, when the Council was going to vote

44

on the issue; 59 voted for halal meat and 15 against (see Morris, Hussain, and Aura 1984).

There was an attempt in January 1983 by the Muslim Parents Association (MPA) to purchase five schools with a majority of Asian pupils and to run them as separate schools with one school for Muslim girls. The MPA was concerned about the existing school system and wanted to pass on their religion and culture to their children in the same way as the Jewish people or Roman Catholics had in the past.

In this climate the Director of Education's guidelines on multi-racial, multicultural education were given to headteachers. The policies were agreed by all political parties. The Council committed itself to promoting racial equality and to bringing about the conditions where good race relations are best able to flourish both locally and nationally. Two sets of guidelines were introduced: Local Authority Memorandum (LAM) 2/82 and LAM 6/83. They attempt to recognize the religious, linguistic, cultural differences, and variety which exists in Bradford and accord each equality of esteem, respect, and understanding. These guidelines included statements on the choice of religious jewellery and dress for girls (Muslim girls may wear shalwar kameez, or trousers); nonreligious assembly; the taking of religious holidays; and the monitoring by the employer and head-teacher of racial prejudice, discrimination, and racist incidents. The guidelines were a response to the idea of segregated schools and were in opposition to the beginning of educational apartheid in Bradford (Morris *et al* 1984).

Controversy about the guidelines attracted national attention with the opposition mounted by one local headteacher, Raymond Honey-ford. It is with the nature of the subsequent struggle between anti-racists in Bradford and Honeyford that this article is concerned.

The article

Towards the end of the campaign Honeyford himself spoke out in his own defence, claiming that he was wholly in favour of the preservation of mother cultures. His problem was how to combine a respect for the mother culture with a knowledge of the English culture: 'I have been represented as a kind of proto-Fascist trying to turn children into good, little Englanders.'

When Mr Honeyford was taken to court on 5 September 1985, certain accusations were made against him. These were that he was professionally irresponsible and that serious errors of judgement over his written articles had destroyed the trust and faith of parents and the local community.

Mr Honeyford's main defence was his right to freedom of speech. Alex Fellowes, Head of Drummond Language Centre responded by saying:

'Surely, it is wrong and irresponsible for anyone to suggest that headteachers have an unrestricted right to express publicly their own personal view regardless of the effect on the community in which their schools are an integral part. Negative and hostile views and attitudes to the community, particularly if it is multiracial in character, are sowing the seeds of social division and racial tension.'
(*Bradford Telegraph and Argus*, 28 October 1985)

Councillor Riaz, Labour Councillor for the University Ward, joined in this tangential debate about freedom of speech with the statement that freedom does not enable one to abuse the culture and religion of others. Freedom demands respecting the rights and freedom of others and not inciting hatred between fellow human beings. He added that Mr Honeyford's role should be promoting and strengthening harmony and unity, rather than one of dividing the communities in Bradford and turning one against the other.

Mr Honeyford's views reproduced in the January 1984 *Salisbury Review*, and entitled 'Education and race, an alternative view' are worth outlining, to explain why they became so controversial. Because of his articles, he has been likened by some to Enoch Powell (see Seidel 1985). Parts of this article were simply abusive, immoderate, inflammatory, and extreme. It contained gratuitous insults and negative statements. For example, Mr Honeyford described a local Community Relations Officer as a 'half-educated and volatile Sikh'. He wrote that 'aggressive, black intellectuals in the area of multiracial education know little of the British traditions of understatement, civilised discourse, and respect for reason'. He described the parents' religious beliefs as a 'purdah mentality'. An article in *The Times Educational Supplement* similarly caricatured parents. He described one as a figure straight out of Kipling bearing down on him: 'His English sounds like a Peter Sellers' Indian doctor on an off day' (*The Times Educational Supplement* 2 September 1983).

More than 90 per cent of Mr Honeyford's 530 pupils were ethnic minorities, mainly from Pakistan. Two out of the 27 teachers were Asian, yet he described their country of origin as obstinately backward and unable to cope with democracy. He wrote of the 'hysterical political temperament of the Indian subcontinent'. Mr Honeyford also believed that Asians are responsible for the increase in heroin addiction in British cities. Yet, in reality, there is no more a drug problem in Bradford than there is in Brighton where there are considerably fewer Asians (see Singh 1984, for discussion of this point).

Mr Honeyford complained about the habit of many Asian parents of sending their children abroad for long periods in term time, as this disrupts their children's education and has obvious and harmful effects on standards of achievement. He failed to point out that the Asian families in the inner city area of Bradford where he worked could only afford to send their children to the Indian subcontinent perhaps once in their school careers. To challenge the process, by which links with different generations and different members of the family on the subcontinent were maintained, was racist. In any case it is strange that Mr Honeyford did not describe these trips as educational and enriching. The Education Advisors' Report (see below) points out that the children on these trips abroad may miss formal schooling but they learn from wider experiences. What is more, most of these visits take place in the Christmas holidays. Criticism of them makes the relationships with the parents difficult. All of the children, who have been taken back into the school, have been accommodated in their original sets.

In brief, Mr Honeyford was critical of the culture, religious practices, and family structures of ethnic minorities. He was also critical of the English parents of children in his school. He described them as lower working class, and lacking the ability to articulate their educational concerns and anxieties. Further, according to Mr Honeyford, people of West Indian origin make unfit, noisy, unreasonable neighbours. Their music is an 'ear splitting cacophony'. Minority languages described as 'creole pidgin', and other nonstandard variants are not equally good. They do not 'have the same power, subtlety, and capacity for expressing five shades of meaning and for tolerating uncertainty, ambiguity, and irony as standard English', according to Mr Honeyford. There is a debate about the use of language and dialect in schools in the social sciences. Most people would agree, however, that education which makes use of the linguistic and other skills which the child brings to the classroom is better for the child.

Mr Honeyford's core point is about the plight of white children. His principal claim is that white children's educational standards are lowered because of the dominant presence of a black majority in the schools. He claims that state schools are failing the children of the dispossessed, indigenous parents as the direct result of multiracial education. He rejects the claims that black pupil failure is the result of 'teacher prejudice or an alien curriculum'. He writes: 'It is no more than common sense that if a school contains a disproportionate number of children for whom English is a second language (true of all Asian children, even those born here) or children from homes where educational ambition and the values to support it are conspicuously absent (i.e. the vast majority of West Indian homes, a disproportionate number of which are fatherless), then academic standards are bound to suffer' (Honeyford, 1984b).

The media tended to portray Mr Honeyford as fighting against poor educational policies and for white children. One man, George Kelly, accepted the media's portrayal and gathered petitions and displayed a banner which read 'Let's defend Honeyford, he's defending us'. In fact, Councillor Riaz stressed that Mr Honeyford's statement that white working-class parents are not articulate or clever enough to realize or fight for their rights is an insult to the integrity and intellectual capacity of the white working class.

Those teachers who disagreed with Mr Honeyford were described by him as misguided and radical with political motives, or professional opportunists, a race relations lobby who perceive the professional advantages of supporting multiculturalism and not really concerned with ethnic minority children. Ethnic minority children are not incapable of being educated, indeed educational research has found completely the opposite. National research evidence shows that children of Asian origin actually achieve slightly better than other children (see Alex Fellowes, *Bradford Telegraph and Argus*, 22 March 1984) whilst Driver (1980) found similar results locally.

Most headteachers shared Mr Honeyford's views. Out of 167 headteachers in Bradford, 163 gave unqualified support to him. However, other schools in Bradford became worried about the good work that they had achieved. St Andrews School in Keighley, with 90 per cent of pupils who were black, found no evidence to support the view that the minority, who were white, suffered in this context. What is more, bilingual children are often more advanced conceptually than children who can only speak one language. Mr Honeyford's stereotypes about West Indian families are exaggerations and distortions. In any case, as almost one sixth of white British families are now female headed, prejudices against such families will have to change.

Mr Honeyford lacked judgement, prudence, wisdom, and sensitivity throughout the campaign. He showed disloyalty to his employers. The Council's own advisory team stated firmly that white children as a group were not underachieving in Mr Honeyford's multi-ethnic school. Also, Asians and West Indians were not responsible for the poor achievement of white children. What is more, their summary was that more could, and should, be done by the school to use the children's experiences and acknowledge their home cultures. The teachers at Drummond Middle

School needed to foster self-respect and confidence in the children as members of a variety of linguistic and cultural groups.

In general, Mr Honeyford's article is ethnocentric in expressing the opinion that black and working-class children are culturally deprived. The Council's advisory team point to the effect of the underestimation of the potential of pupils and a stress on their weakness, or deficiencies. They state that the underestimation of black and working-class pupils' potential ability (which was evident in the school as a whole) would ultimately lower expectation and consequent performance. Similarly, an R. Thompson wrote to the *Bradford Telegraph and Argus* on 22 October that education is about drawing out the value that children have, extending their knowledge and skill and deepening their self-esteem. 'By denigrating [*sic*] the communities from which many of his children came in his articles, Mr Ray Honeyford has achieved the opposite.'

Jenny Woodward, Chairperson of the Drummond Parents Action Committee (DPAC) summarized the committee's opposition to Mr Honeyford's views, in the following terms:

'Firstly, if the headteacher has genuine concern about the educational welfare of all children in his care, then why publish these concerns in a journal which has carried support for the repatriation/deportation of black, British citizens?

Secondly, why did the headteacher relate the education of children in a Bradford school to the political and socio-economic factors supposedly prevalant in Pakistan?

Thirdly, what connection has the serious problem of the heroin trade to do with the education of middle school children – likewise, the issue of single parent families which, incidentally, are not solely to be found among the West Indian community?'

The DPAC concluded that:

'the implementation of Bradford's policies on multicultural education would be seriously hindered in Drummond Middle School due to the opinions of the headteacher and to the detriment of the school as a whole.

The notion of multicultural education is to us an essential component of our children's education . . . (it) recognizes in a positive way that Britain is now and has been for many years a multi-racial nation. . . .

West Indian, Asian, and white parents at the school are grossly offended by what Mr Honeyford said about them.'

(*Bradford Telegraph and Argus*, 26 November 1985)

Parents and children belonging to the different ethnic groups that are represented at Mr Honeyford's school were categorized along the narrow stereotypes of race and class. The *Salisbury Review* article on education completely ignored structural factors, social deprivation and institutional racism. Children at this and other inner city schools, whether they be Afro-Caribbean, white, or Asian, face poor housing, inadequate nurseries, the lack of resources, jobs, or school facilities, and overcrowded classes. Mr Honeyford makes scapegoats of children for what is wrong with education as a whole. Like other schools, Drummond Middle School is understaffed, underequipped, and underfinanced as Max Madden, then Labour MP for Bradford West, pointed out in an article for the *Bradford Telegraph and Argus* (8 May 1984).

Alex Fellowes (Head of Drummond Language Centre) questioned whether Mr Honeyford's alternative to a multiracial, multicultural school was enforced integration where children from Asian, or Afro-Caribbean origin, or background, are compelled to accept the majority white culture. He was concerned that Mr Honeyford's division of the community into black and white was sectarianism and could have the same tragic effects in the future as in Northern Ireland (Fellowes 1984).

Mr Honeyford received written warnings from the Department of Education in 1982 and 1984. However, he gained much support in the local and national press. Stanley Garnett, former head of Delph Hill Middle School in Bradford called on Professors Eysenck, Jensen, and Herrnstein (who claim that blacks are genetically inferior to whites in intelligence) in Honeyford's defence. He wrote that the culture of the indigenous population should be inviolate and that it should be reinforced in the schools. Garnett also supported the educational apartheid of separate Muslim schools (*Bradford Telegraph and Argus*, 4 April 1984).

Max Madden, however, strongly opposed Mr Honeyford, insisting that Mr Honeyford had caused racial tension, given respectability to racist views and encouragement to racists. He concluded that the views expressed by Mr Honeyford exploited freedom of speech to confuse and mislead people.

The campaign against Mr Honeyford

The Drummond Parents Action Committee (the DPAC) was formed in March, 1984, in response to Honeyford's article on 'Education and race'. Its campaign was geared towards Mr Honeyford's removal as headteacher of his school. On 8 May 1984 the *Bradford Telegraph and Argus* reported that 400 demonstrators marched from Drummond Middle School to the Bradford Council Offices. The demonstrators included representatives from the Bradford West Indian Parents' Association, Council for Mosques, Al Falah, the Islamic Youth Movement, Bangladeshi People's Association Asian Youth Movement, and Mothers Against Racism.

A deputation handed in a petition with 600 signatures that demanded of the education director, Mr Richard Knight, that Mr Honeyford be sacked for his alleged racist stance. Ms Jenny Woodward, Chairperson of the DPAC stated, 'Mr Honeyford's views are not compatible with a multiracial school and we want the Council to stick by the guidelines laid down on race in schools' (*Bradford Telegraph and Argus*, 5 May 1984).

In June 1984, the Shadow Chairman of the Education Committee, Councillor John Lambert, wrote a four page letter to the Director of Education denouncing Mr Honeyford, demanding his immediate suspension, and the setting up of an inquiry into how he ran his school. As a result of all the controversy, a team of ten inspectors from the Education Authority's Advisory Service was sent into Drummond Middle School to carry out a two week investigation. They studied various features of the school from its standard of work to its community life and racial issues. Despite his apparent commitment to intellectual freedom, Honeyford, at this stage threatened Councillor Lambert and Jenny Woodward with legal action for their opposition.

To show the extent of the support for the Drummond Parents Action Committee, a school strike was organized during the inspectors' visit. Only 145 pupils out of 530 turned up for lessons on Tuesday 12 July 1984. Tim Whitfield, a senior Community Relations Officer in Bradford, stated:

> 'The fact that more than half the parents have taken the grave step of keeping their children away shows strong opposition to Mr Honeyford continuing as Headteacher and that, so far, the Education Authority's assessment of the parents' feelings has been out of touch.' (*Bradford Telegraph and Argus*, 12 June 1984).

This clearly indicated that Mr Honeyford was dividing the community rather than fostering good race relations.

In July 1984 Jenny Woodward, Chairperson of the DPAC, was elected onto the Board of Governors of the School. The strength of support for the DPAC's stance was shown when Ms Woodward polled 205 votes to her nearest rival's 48 votes. On 19 September 1984, 230 parents, half the parents at Drummond Middle School, wrote to the Director of Education to say that they wanted their children to be transferred as a group from Drummond Middle School if Mr Honeyford was not removed. The DPAC stated that the request for pupils to be moved was inpracticable. The real demand was for one person to be moved, Mr Honeyford.

The advisers' report

As a result of the school governors' meeting on 16 October 1984, and a later meeting of the Bradford Council's education subcommittee on 22 October, Mr Honeyford had been given six months to overhaul his school and restore the confidence of parents who wanted him sacked. He was accused by the DPAC of lacking understanding and remorse over the controversy caused by the writing of the alleged offensive, racist article. The Council's advisers' report of October 1984 had concluded: 'The situation as it has emerged must raise serious questions as to whether it will be possible for the school to continue to function effectively unless the headteacher is able to regain the trust and confidence of a significant proportion of the parents'.

At the meeting on 22 October in the City Hall, set up to discuss the advisers' report, Councillor Barry Thorne (Labour) expressed the fears of many about the Honeyford affair. He stated: 'Unless the Committee takes action tonight, I can foresee large sections of the community, Muslims, in particular, withdrawing from the Council's educational system. Social and cultural apartheid will become Bradford's normal way of life. We will step back ten years' (*Bradford Telegraph and Argus*, 23 October 1984).

Seven governors, who opposed Mr Honeyford, stormed out of the October school governors' meeting in the City Hall, complaining that it was a special meeting, not a routine one, and that Mr Honeyford should not have been present. The meeting was picketed by the Asian Youth Movement, the DPAC, and rank and file teachers.

Eight Council officers, from advisers to the Director of Education, carried out checks on Drummond School. One monitored what Mr Honeyford wrote. (He had previously been admonished for bringing both the officers and the Authority's multiracial education policies into disrepute).

A small team was set up to implement the forty-four recommendations in the report on the school by the education advisers. These included the suggestion that more could be done to interpret the spirit of the Authority's LAMS dealing with minority ethnic groups and racism, and to convey a welcoming of diversity. It also noted that there was a need to recognize similarities and understand differences and diversity in Bradford.

Mr Honeyford was also given six tasks to carry out by Easter 1985, some of which were in line with the Council's educational policy with regard to ethnic minorities. They were:

1 A plan to welcome and involve parents in the school and the school in the local community.

2 A review of how the school communicated with parents. The advisers' report had stated that Mr Honeyford needed to consider the effect of his writings on his relationships with parents and the life of the school.

3 A review of methods of teaching and testing children. Tasks given to the children were often low level, including copying, colouring, or demonstrated techniques rather than problem solving, reading, analysing, creating, or imagining.

4 A review of teaching materials in the school. The report had also stressed that the multiracial, multicultural community should be more evident in classrooms and in the communal areas of the school for parents to feel welcome. The school should show, through the curriculum and material it used, that children's experience and cultural traditions are valued and used.

5 Monitoring what was being taught at the school and how this reflected the experience of the pupils. In particular to seek an equity of respect for the integrity of other religous communities.

6 A review of the aims of the school.

The Drummond Parents Action Committee was convinced that the trust and confidence of parents in the headmaster was irrevocably lost. They proposed to start an alternative school if Mr Honeyford was not sacked soon. However, they were loath to take this step until they had exhausted all lines of discussion through legal and bureaucratic channels.

In March 1985, a rival school was set up by parents. The idea of an 'antiracist school' was an exciting venture. The many teachers, parents, and ancilliary staff had to settle their differences in definitions of multiculturalism, antiracism, and even 'alternative education'. Discussions ranged widely: antiracist maths could be taught using, for example, illustrations such as salary differences in South Africa. Art, geography, economics, and so on, could be made multicultural or antiracist, beginning for example with the variety of vegetables found in Bradford's cosmopolitan shops. At the end of the week Drummond Middle School was felt to be in perilous disequilibrium due to Mr Honeyford and he was suspended on full pay.

He returned in September 1985 to a school boycotted by most of the parents.

Another novel aspect of this campaign was the crossing of the existing boundaries of religion, politics, class, union, and gender. This was clear when the black organizations added their support to the DPAC in demonstrations, pickets, and so on. However, the NUT's strongest statement was to fine teachers who supported one of the days of action against Mr Honeyford. The National Association of Headteachers supported Mr Honeyford throughout. The media were flummoxed by this. The usual stereotypes, 'Trotskyite left-wingers' (Eric Sunderland, *Bradford Telegraph and Argus*, 30 November 1985), 'a mafia of Imams' (David Selbourne, *Guardian*, 21 October 1985), the 'white left' supported by one minority group (*Panorama*, March 1984) etc., were all inaccurate descriptions. Perhaps the only stereotypical box that described almost everyone on the campaign was that of 'antiracists'.

How could the situation be resolved? Bradford Council's chief executive, Gordon Moore, stated that a number of options were being explored. One way of resolving the situation was that if Mr Honeyford decided to relinquish his post, there would be some measure of compensation. At this stage, the outrageous figure of £250,000 compensation was mentioned (*Bradford Telegraph and Argus*, 19 November 1984). An alternative suggestion was that he should be sacked. Transferring to another school was another option. However, the DPAC was concerned that Mr Honeyford's views should not spread to other schools. There was no easy solution to the Honeyford affair!

In September 1985, the Drummond Middle School governors sat for four days to consider the case. Four anti-Honeyford governors boycotted the meeting. Eight out of the remaining fifteen demanded his reinstatement. This was one of the first occasions on which Mr Honeyford's actual statements were discussed by this body.

The position held by the local authority was expressed by Mr Roper, the Assistant Education Director, who argued that the Council was party to Mr Honeyford's employment and should have a say in his suspension or dismissal. A case was taken to the High Court. There were important implications in this issue for other teachers. The judge, Simon Brown, ruled that the governors' decision exhausted the disciplinary process.

A few months later, the constitution of governing bodies began to change nationally. Three anti-Honeyford governors were elected at Drummond Middle School. Mr Naqui, Mr Rahmann, and Mr Farukh each gained more than 200 votes. Reuben Goldberg, elected as the Labour Party representative, spoke for them all when he said: 'As new governors we want good education for our children — that is all.' The results suggested that the majority of Drummond parents did not want Mr Honeyford in charge of their children.

Despite the hopes that the organization of the new governing bodies would increase parental control, in reality the staff representatives could potentially be influenced by the headteacher. Also, the selection of community representatives by the elected governors meant that, in effect, Mr Honeyford could have used a casting vote on his own behalf.

On 3 October 1985, what has been described as an 'inept invitation' (*Bradford Telegraph and Argus*) from 10 Downing Street did not help to control the strained race relations in Bradford. Mr Honeyford was greeted in London with boos, protests, and cries of 'racist'. This invitation was criticized by one demonstrator as giving Mr Honeyford false credibility. It suggested that he was an eminent educationalist who should be advising the Prime Minister on multiculturalism. Progressive educationalists in this area were worried that much good work would be undone.

On 13 November 1985, the power of local authorities nationally was felt to have been upheld. The Council won the right to take disciplinary action against Mr Honeyford if it so wished. The High Court judgement was overturned. The implication of this was that the local education authority was given the ultimate responsibility for the education of children.

Lord Justice Lawton was not concerned with the correctness, or otherwise, of Mr Honeyford's views on education in a racially mixed community or whether his views were expressed wisely or temperately. The decision was that the local education authority had the power to dismiss Mr Honeyford despite the school governors' recommendation. The costs were awarded against Mr Honeyford and the NAHT who had supported him.

Many local education authorities had articles of government which were similar to those of Bradford Council, based on the 1944 Education Act, suggesting that the decision to remove headteachers could only be made by school governors. As a result of the High Court judgement many authorities changed their articles to define the power of headteachers, governors, and local authorities more precisely. Perhaps partly as an effect of the Honeyford campaign, education authorities employing teachers began to question whether they were sound in the authority's 'antiracist and equal opportunity strategies'.

'Party games'

Throughout the campaign the views of representatives of political parties differed publicly in Bradford. Eric Pickles, Conservative

Chair of Education, was calling for Mr Honcyford's reinstatement, while the Labour Party leader, Councillor Philip Beeley, stated that the damage to the school would be horrific if Mr Honeyford was reinstated. The Lord Mayor, Councillor Ajeeb, was inundated with hate mail for supporting Mr Honeyford's suspension. Councillor John Lambert of the Labour Party stated: 'In rushing to defend the rights of one individual to offend a whole community, the Tory group had denied the rights of that community who found the actions of one man unacceptable.'

Bradford was a 'hung' council at this stage with the Conservatives holding 43 seats, Labour 41 seats, and the Liberals 6. In March 1985, Eric Pickles offered Mr Honeyford £90,000 as one solution to the issue. Kath Greenwood, the leader of the Liberals, refused to agree. In May, Mr Honeyford turned down an £8000 a year pension and a £27,000 lump sum.

There were increasing complaints at the lack of prompt and appropriate action by the Council. Community leaders, such as Choudry Khan, of the Bradford Council for Mosques, warned that racial tensions in the city were becoming intolerable as the conflict dragged on. There was a general fear of street violence. A solution, agreed by all parties involved, was essential.

At one point a group of black people in the *Caribbean Times* suggested that: 'All teachers, especially those like Mr Honeyford, should be compelled to attend massive inservice training to bring them up to date with modern educational theory and practice and purge them of their racist outlook and ideology'. This was no solution. The Bradford Race Awareness Trainers refused to take Mr Honeyford onto a course as he was a 'known racist'. This led to questions about its value. It was clear that they believed that they could not raise the consciousness of an adult with a lifetime of specific educational and socialization experiences in a short course (cf. Gurnah 1984; Sivanandan 1984).

In December 1985, a £71,000 pay-off was offered to Mr Honeyford by Bradford Council. The final figure was negotiated by Gordon Moore, the Chief Executive, who reported back to an all-party committee. Approximately this amount was accepted by Mr Honeyford.

Conclusion

Gill Seidel (1985) has linked Mr Honeyford's images with those of the 'New Right' in general. She points out that Mr Honeyford does not say that cultures are different but that they are inferior (see also Barker 1981). Like Enoch Powell and Margaret Thatcher, Ray Honeyford reinforces the irrational fears that the superior 'culture' of white, British people could be 'swamped' by alien cultures.

The main problem with the Honeyford campaign was that the careful consideration of multicultural, or antiracist strategies in education was lost in the debate about whether one was for Mr Honeyford and his views, or against them. Mr Honeyford concluded his *Salisbury Review* article of Winter 1984, with the words 'I am no longer convinced that the British genius for compromise, for muddling through, and for good-natured tolerance will be sufficient to resolve the inevitable tension' (Honeyford 1984b). The 'Honeyford affair' had the national repercussions that I have pointed out. The effects continue. Whatever the final implications of the campaign the conclusions should support those of the Swann Report. No one is a 'cultural police officer'. In order to reduce racial disadvantage and discrimination we need the sensitive provision of services in education to all as individuals and not as cultural, class, gender, or racial categories.

© *1987 Olivia Foster-Carter*

Acknowledgements

The author would like to thank J. W., M. S., and the Independent Black Collective for help in compiling this summary, and L. H., P. D., M. S., and G. B. for constant background support. As always, thanks to my sons for their admirable patience.

References

Barker, M. (1981) *The New Racism*. London: Junction Books.
Bradford Council (1981) Race relations in Bradford policy statement. Bradford.
—— (1983) Local authority memorandum 6/1983. Bradford.
—— (1984) Advisers' report (22nd October). Bradford.
Brown, A. (1985) *Trials of Honeyford*. London: Centre for Policy Studies.
Carling, A., Husband, C., and Palmer, S. (1984) A clash of view on Bradford, *New Society*, 10 May: 241.
Driver, G. (1980) *Beyond Underachievement: Case Studies of English, West Indian, and Asian School Leavers*. London: C. R. E. Publications.
Fellowes, A. (1984) A divisive view which can only hurt children. *Bradford Telegraph and Argus*, 22 March.
Foster-Carter, O. (1984) Racism in Bradford. *The Times Educational Supplement*, 4 May: 20.
—— (1985a) The struggle at Drummond Middle School, Bradford. *Critical Social Policy* 12: 74–8.

—— (1985b) Parents take a stand, *National Childcare Campaign Newsletter* Nov./Dec: 4.

—— (1985c) Honeyford, bias, and the media, *Free Press* 32: 23.

Gurnah, A. (1984) The politics of racism awareness training. *Critical Social Policy* 11: 6–20.

Honeyford, R. (1983a) Multi-ethnic intolerance. *Salisbury Review* Summer: 12–13.

—— (1983b) When east is west. *The Times Educational Supplement* 2 September: 19.

—— (1984) Education and race – an alternative view. *Salisbury Review* Winter: 30–2.

Hugill, B. (1985) Multicultural row comes to a head. *New Statesman* 15 March: 14–15.

Morris, G., Hussain, A., and Aura, T. (1984) Schooling crisis in Bradford. *Race Today* August: 8–11.

Seidel, G. (1985) Culture, nation and 'race' in the British and French New Right. In R. Levitas (ed.) *The Ideology of the New Right*. Oxford: Polity/Blackwell.

Singh, M. (1984) Education and race: A reply to Mr Honeyford (March). Bradford.

Sivanandan, A. (1985) RAT and the degradation of black struggle. *Race and Class* 26(4): 1–33.

5 A comedy of errors: Section 11 funding and education

Andrew Dorn and Paul Hibbert

The long-running saga of Section 11 funding exhibits many of the characteristics of a television soap opera. Tragedy, farce, pathos, melodrama, and a script in which the actors appear unable to control the world around them. Unlike the fantasy world of 'Dallas' and 'Dynasty', however, the bizarre world of Section 11 is for real, as are the people and money involved.

Section 11 (S11) refers to that section of the Local Government Act 1966 that empowers the Home Secretary to make payments to local authorities 'who in his opinion are required to make special provision in the exercise of any of their functions in consequence of the presence within their areas of substantial numbers of immigrants from the Commonwealth whose language or customs differ from those of the community.'

The sums involved are not inconsiderable. In 1984/85 total S11 expenditure was £98 m and in 1985/86 estimated to be £110 m, the bulk of this going to local education authorities (LEAs) (£80 m and £88 m respectively). Looked at from a local perspective the sums are also substantial. For instance, it was estimated that the Inner London Education Authority (ILEA) claimed £17,352,320 from S11 funds in 1985/86, whilst Birmingham, Bradford, and Brent each claimed over £4 m that year. Amongst the shire counties the biggest claimants were Avon (£2.5 m), Bedfordshire (£1.5 m), Lancashire (£3 m), and Leicestershire (£2.5 m).

Our purpose in what follows is to try to dispel some of the myths and uncertainties surrounding Section 11 by describing the history of its use and application and drawing out its implications for educational provision in a multiracial society.

Simply put, our argument is that S11 represents an anachronistic form of provision when compared with other trends and developments in multiracial education and 'race relations' policy. S11

59

is firmly rooted in a policy tradition that prefers voluntarism to compulsion, inexplicitness to explicitness, assimilation to antiracism, marginal rather than mainstream spending, and is preoccupied with racial disadvantage rather than racial discrimination.

S11 is very much a child of the 1960s and its current problems and persistent contradictions must be seen as emanating from the race relations policy ideologies that prevailed at that time. Whereas other policies and practices regarding 'race' and education have evolved (albeit painfully and partially) from assimilation to antiracism, S11 itself has remained relatively static in its conception and application.

Origins

The origins of Section 11 can be traced back to the Labour Party's *volte face* on immigration and race relations policy in the mid 1960s. The pragmatic appreciation of anti-immigrant feeling in the country (exampled by shock Labour defeats at Smethwick and Leyton in 1965) plus lobbying from local authorities seeking compensation for the alleged financial burden placed on local services by the presence of immigrants in their areas led to the development of a dualistic policy as set out in the 1965 White Paper, *Immigration from the Commonwealth* (Home Office 1965). This document, described as 'possibly the most logically incoherent Government paper ever produced (Dummett and Dummett 1982: 105), promised a judicious mix of increased immigration control and measures to assist assimilation and integration. The prescription sounded deceptively simple:

'this policy has two aspects: one relating to control on the entry of immigrants so that it does not outrun Britain's capacity to absorb them; the other relating to positive measures designed to secure for the immigrants and their children their rightful place in our society, and to assist local authorities . . . in areas of high immigration in dealing with certain problems which have arisen.'

(Home Office 1965: 2)

The causes and consequences of this contradictory policy, encapsulated in Roy Hattersley's infamous equation 'without integration limitation is inexcusable, without limitation integration is impossible', has been well documented elsewhere and need not detain us (see, for instance, Foot 1965). What is important here is that it is in this race relations climate that S11 emerged as part of the remedial side of the coin to cope with the disadvantages experienced by those blacks (and their children) who were already here.

If race policy in general was dualistic, so too was that specifically aimed towards racial disadvantage and the plight of immigrants. On the one hand it was said that there were disadvantages experienced as a result of discrimination and prejudice and which were to be legislated against by a succession of Race Relations Acts (1965, 1968 and 1976). On the other it was said that there were disadvantages associated with the very cultural and linguistic characteristics of the immigrants themselves; problems that they brought with them.

The perceived role of immigrant language and customs as a cause of disadvantage and an obstacle to assimilation was well expressed, again by Hattersley, in the parliamentary debate on the Local Government Bill that included Section 11:

'I hope that, when the money under S11 is distributed, the Secretary of State will bear in mind, that as well as providing smaller classes in which English can be adequately taught, as well as providing extra visitors to remind parents of their new obligations in Britain, it is essential to teach these children basic British customs, basic British habits and, if one likes, basic British prejudices – all those things which they need to know if they are to live happily and successfully in an integrated way in this community.'

(Hansard 1966, col. 1336)

Indeed the notion of the disadvantaging consequences of cultural difference was enshrined in the very wording of the legislation itself. Though subsequent Home Office Circulars have surreptitiously inserted the phrase '*rest* of the community' the original legislation (still unamended) refers to immigrants whose 'language or customs differ from those of *the community*'. In other words 'immigrants' are not part of the community and will languish as outsiders until such time as their distinctiveness has been removed; when in Rome. . . .

Of course S11 was not the only aspect of educational policy characterized by the ideology of assimiliation and cultural disadvantage: DES Circular 7/65, *The Education of Immigrants*, for instance advocated the dispersal of immigrant pupils by 'bussing' where they constituted 30 per cent of a school population. The point is that while other assimilationist policies were gradually rejected, S11 has remained tainted by this original perspective. Thus as much as ten years later, Alex Lyon, a former Home Office minister responsible for race relations was able to assert that though an immigrant was likely to suffer greater disadvantages than a similar white the reason: 'it is not his colour, it is cultural arising from the newness of his family in our society, and his consequential unfamiliarity with our customs' (McCrudden 1982: 340).

In this chapter we attempt to bring out this, and other features of S11, by reference to the relevant Home Office Circulars and research, conducted in selected LEAs, on the actual use and application of S11 funds.

Administration 1967 to 1982

In February 1967 the Home Office issued Circular 15/1967, *Commonwealth Immigrants*, setting out the details and conditions under which S11 grants were to be paid. Originally grant aid was set at 50 per cent of 'approved expenditure' (the rest made up by the local authority itself) but, following the introduction of the Urban Programme in 1969, this was raised to 75 per cent. There was (and still remains) no limit to the amount a local authority could claim but the payment was to be retrospective. Furthermore local authorities were not compelled to apply for funds; the scheme was to be voluntary.

For the purposes of grant aid the 1967 Circular outlined three main criteria which local authorities had to meet in order to qualify for funding. Firstly, grant was payable only in respect of 'Commonwealth immigrants' defined as: 'a person, adult or child, born in another country of the Commonwealth who has been ordinarily resident in the United Kingdom for less than ten years and the child of such a person.'

This definition came to be known as the 'ten year rule' and carried with it the assumption that after a decade the problems faced by immigrants would simply vanish, presumably because, as one DES official later put it, 'their newness had worn off and the alchemy of assimilation had done its work' (Personal communication).

Secondly, the 'substantial numbers' refered to in the Act were operationally defined as meaning 2 per cent or more of the entire school population of the area calculated from the DES's 'Annual School Returns' (Form 7i); in fact a rather crude teacher-administered head count. Under this '2 per cent rule' the Circular listed 51 local authorities as having a *prima facie* case for claiming the grant; in subsequent years others were approved and in 1985/86 103 authorities claimed the grant.

Thirdly, local authorities could only submit claims in respect of staff who represented 'special provision'. Apart from the assumption that special needs arose with work attributable to differences in language or customs the circular (astonishingly) failed to specify what this special provision might be. However (as we note below) the link made in the original legislation, and continued in Circular 15/1967, between special provision and the mere presence of immigrants made it possible for LEAs to claim grant simply because 'the blacks are here'. The distinction between providing for special needs and 'compensating' local authorities for the immigrant burden was blurred from the outset and has remained a major source of contradiction.

This situation was compounded by the Circular's definition of the scope of S11. Although a grant was payable only in respect of local authority staff the choice of what type of staff was left to the discretion of individual local authorities. LEA discretion was further enhanced by the Circular's acceptance that while most posts would be identifiable, there would nonetheless be some posts where it would not be possible (or desirable) to identify 'individual officers as being specially employed to deal with extra pressures created by differences of language or customs' (1967: para 10).

In respect of unidentifiable education posts the 1967 Circular only asked that LEAs make a 'reasonable assessment' of the proportion of staff involved in work arising from the linguistic or cultural differences of Commonwealth immigrants, or of the expenditure incurred in employing such staff. The long-term effect of this clause was to allow LEAs to employ large numbers of unidentifiable teachers with no specific brief beyond that of ostensibly being an addition to the staffing complement of 'immigrant schools'.

As might be expected LEAs were not slow to exploit paragraph 10 of the Circular. Several notable education authorities quickly made what can only be described as secret 'gentlemen's agreements' with the Home Office for unidentifiable teaching staff based on idiosyncratic notional assessments of additional costs. For example, ILEA in 1981/82 received an S11 grant for over 1000 unidentifiable teaching posts based on Educational Priority Area (EPA) social deprivation indices. Similarly, Walsall based its claim on a crude formula that calculated the additional cost to the education service caused by the mere presence of 'immigrant children'. By making the maximum use of paragraph 10, and with the exception of ESL provision, LEAs were able to satisfy their desire for 'compensation' (because the blacks are here) rather than directly and explicitly meet any special needs. Section 11 was a pushover, a *quid pro quo* for the black presence.

Criticisms

As the House of Commons Home Affairs Committee noted: 'there is no single aspect of Section 11 which has escaped criticism' (House of Commons 1981). Generally speaking, and up to 1982, criticisms of the grant focused on two broad sets of issues: those relating to its scope and administrative criteria as determined by the Home Office, and those relating to its actual use by LEAs. Thus the definition of Commonwealth immigrant and the ten year and 2 per cent rules were criticized for their assimilationist assumptions and restrictive consequences (effectively excluding Liverpool blacks for instance).

It was noted too that in the absence of national statistics and with the abandonment by the DES in 1974 of school ethnic records the possibility of a reliable data base for S11 distribution was undermined.

The limitation of the grant to local authority staff (i.e. excluding capital costs and grants direct to community groups) and the level and retrospective payment of monies were also criticized. Furthermore the absence of any monitoring or promotional role by the Home Office, the reactive and precedent-bound nature of Home Office management of the grant, and the absence of any consistent coordination between the Home Office and other relevant departments (for example the DES) were among the many problems that were laid at the door of central government and the ambiguities and inexplicitness of the 1967 Circular.

In the case of LEA usage of S11, criticisms have highlighted: the unevenness of grant take up in relation to the size of the local Commonwealth population; the reluctance of some authorities to claim at all; the narrowness of utilization; the unidentifiability of posts; and the tendency of some LEAs to see S11 as a 'pump-primer' for mainstream provision in multi-ethnic schools and as a way of improving pupil-teacher ratios. Finally from the point of view of many black and ethnic minority groups the most significant failing of S11 was that LEAs were able to use it without any consultation with its supposed beneficiaries (Bakhsh and Walker 1980; NUT 1978).

Put simply, the criticisms of S11 boiled down to the fact that it was an irresponsible, unaccountable form of funding unrelated to the real needs of the black communities. As Paul Boateng rhetorically asked: 'why is Section 11 like an iceberg? Because there's a lot of it around, you can't see much of it, and it's very, very white' (1984: 5).

Government responses and reforms

In 1979 the then Labour Government attempted to respond to the mounting criticisms of Section 11 by replacing it with new legislation in the form of the Local Government Grants (Ethnic Groups) Bill.

This Bill, in line with the 1975 White Paper, *Racial Discrimination*, and the Race Relations Act of 1976, continued Labour's dualistic policy which defined 'racial disadvantage' as: 'a complex of problems deriving not only from newness and differences of culture but also from disproportionate material and environmental deprivation accentuated by racial discrimination and occurring principally in an urban context' (1978: 1).

Most significantly the Bill recognized that such disadvantage could be experienced by *any* ethnic minority (not just those from the Commonwealth) and that such problems extended beyond the short term needs of the first generation. Further the Bill proposed that grant aid be utilized in a wide range of services and extended to include capital projects, non staff costs, and voluntary organizations. In the event this first attempt at reform fell with the Conservative election victory in May 1979.

The new Government's response to Section 11 problems and criticisms was deliberately limited to a Home Office review of the grant's administrative procedures. This review proceeded fitfully until 1982 when, against the backdrop of the uprisings and continued parliamentary criticism, the Home Office outlined the future plans for S11 in its response to the House of Commons Home Affairs Committee's report *Racial Disadvantage* (Home Office 1982). Though that report called for fresh legislation to remove S11's restriction to Commonwealth immigrants the Government argued that administrative changes to S11 would be sufficient to: 'go some way towards making it more relevant to present day needs and overcome some of the anomalies of its operation' (Home Office 1982: 10).

These changes were detailed in Circulars 97/1982 and 94/1983. The first set out the revised administrative procedures for application and payment of grant for 'new' posts (i.e. claims made after 1 January 1983) and the second outlined the arrangements for a review of existing posts already funded under previous circulars. In considering these two Circulars we need to ask whether they have been successful in countering the various criticisms and contradictions we have noted.

Circular 97/1982 introduced five main changes in the operation of Section 11. Firstly the 'ten year rule' was abolished and the definition of Commonwealth immigrant extended to include those from Pakistan born there before it left the Commonwealth in 1972, and children aged twenty or less. Though these changes were generally welcomed, they continued to exclude non-Commonwealth immigrants.

Furthermore, it was noted that the limitation to children of immigrants aged twenty or less perpetuated the assimilationist assumptions of the 1960s and flew in the face of research which had established the long-term nature of racial disadvantage; too little too late was the general verdict.

Secondly the '2 per cent rule' was abolished and instead local authorities were instructed to supply information (from the 1981 Census) on Commonwealth immigrants in their areas and the term 'substantial numbers' was intentionally left undefined. Authorities were also allowed to submit claims for small or localized Commonwealth immigrant populations (based on local electoral wards). For its part the Home Office indicated that it would exercise 'maximum flexibility' in considering new applications. Superficially this change appears as an encouragement to wider S11 use; in reality the 2 per cent rule had been totally redundant anyway since the abandonment of ethnic statistics in 1974, by the DES.

Thirdly, grant aid would only be made available for applications that satisfied certain criteria which included:

1 Applications must be for posts expressly designed to meet the needs of Commonwealth immigrants whose language or culture differ from those of the rest of the community.

2 The post holder must be readily identifiable and his/her duties specified.

3 The post must represent 'special provision'.

4 The needs which the post(s) are designed to meet must either be different in kind from or the same as but proportionately greater than those of the rest of the community.

The Circular also informed authorities that new applications would not be admissible if the post holder commenced duties before the application was made to the Home Office.

Though these new criteria went some way to ensuring that future S11 posts would be identifiable and locatable, the Circular singularly failed to provide any clear guidance as to what was meant by 'special provision' and 'special needs'. Indeed the Circular only added further ambiguity to what was already a confused and contentious situation.

On the one hand local authorities were informed that special provision was restricted to Commonwealth immigrants with linguistic or cultural differences, and yet on the other hand that the 'needs' that this provision met were broadly defined to include not only those which were different in kind, but also those that were the 'same as but proportionately greater' than the rest of the community. Effectively, then, the definition of special needs/provision was left to the discretion of individual authorities. In the hands of an imaginative LEA, concerned about discrimination and inequality, this might have been of positive merit. On the whole, however, it permitted the continued use of S11 to meet a narrow and anachronistically defined range of (language) needs and, conversely, the marginalization of *anything* to do with ethnic minorities under S11 rather than its incorporation into mainstream spending. Whereas this failure to define basic concepts and scope might normally be thought bizarre, in the case of Section 11 it was very much par for the course.

Fourthly, local authorities were asked to show that they had consulted with local immigrant communities or Community Relations Councils about proposed posts. Wherever this was done the Home Office recommended that consultation be located within the context of other provision funded through S11 and the authority's 'general strategy' in relation to ethnic minorities. Again the Circular created the impression that action was being taken to resolve the past problems of S11. In fact this was far from the case. Local authorities were given no guidance as to how this consultation should be undertaken and, crucially, the extent to which they should take notice of the ethnic minority groups' own expressed perceptions of their special needs (which might be very different from those of the LEA or Home Office). The publicly expressed interpretation of consultation held by the Home Office was that it would be wholly inappropriate for them to impose a central model of consultation on local authorities.

On the issue of framing consultation within the context of a 'general strategy' the Circular again failed to give clear guidance and, moreover, omitted any reference to LEAs' responsibilities under Section 71 of the 1976 Race Relations Act to 'eliminate unlawful discrimination and promote equality of opportunity'. An optimistic interpretation of the Circular's reference to 'general strategy' would be that it was an attempt by the Home Office to get authorities to develop such policy statements. However, research suggests that even where these policies exist they tend to be limited in scope and content, are usually based on vague multicultural (if not assimilationist) philosophies and encounter considerable resistance at the implementation stage (Troyna and Ball 1985; Mullard *et al.* 1983). Put simply, even where general strategies existed there was no guarantee that they could be clearly related to the operation of S11 posts.

Finally the Circular asked local authorities to show how they proposed to monitor the effectiveness of 'new' S11 posts and were informed that they would be subject to a three-yearly review. Superficially the requirement to monitor appeared to resolve the problem of LEAs not knowing where their S11 appointments were or what exactly they were doing. However in the absence of any Home Office guidance as to how monitoring should or could be undertaken the Circular's recommendations had a familiar hollow ring. Methods of staff assessment not only vary across the country, but there is often also deep local resistance to monitoring. Consequently by merely asking local authorities to indicate their proposals for monitoring the Home Office not only failed to give a clearer definition of what it meant by monitoring but also provided a loophole for those authorities who did not wish to monitor.

In conclusion, and concentrating on the main changes introduced by Circular 97/1982, it is our view that the procedures for new posts represented a cosmetic exercise designed to remove the patently anachronistic features of the original Circular 15/1967. Because of this, and because the language of the Circular still echoed the assimilationist and voluntaristic ethos of the 1960s, several commentators concluded that the past problems of S11 remained (Hibbert 1982; Kapur 1984). Turning to the review of existing posts (i.e. those funded before 1982) the Home Office in Circular 94/1983 stated that: 'The main aim of the proposed review is to monitor the expenditure incurred under Section 11 and to ensure that the funds in question continue to be spent in meeting the special needs of the intended beneficiaries' (1983: para 2).

To achieve this aim the review of existing provision was to be conducted over a seven-month period (August 1983 to March 1984) and in two stages.

First, local authorities were asked to reassess their need for existing posts and inform the Home Office whether, in their opinion, such provision now met the new funding criteria outlined in Circular 97/1982. In undertaking their review local authorities were again asked to examine provision within the context of their 'general strategy' and were 'strongly encouraged' to consult with their Commonwealth immigrant communities and the local Community Relations Council. The Home Office also indicated that where existing posts failed to satisfy the funding criteria 'replacement bids' could be made. In submitting their review reports, local authorities were asked to set out the objectives the posts were designed to meet and the extent to which those objectives had been met. Furthermore, all S11 posts were to be accounted for in terms of the total number of posts, their location and specific job descriptions. Authorities were also asked to consider making their review reports publicly available.

Second, and after receiving the review reports, the Home Office would assess the case for continued funding. The Department noted that, in the majority of cases, the information contained in the report would be sufficient to make a positive response to an authority's review. However where there was any doubt about 'particular posts or blocks of provision', the Home Office would seek further information. Circular 94/1983 further warned local authorities that where there were any doubts about review reports Home Office officials might also visit the local authority to discuss the review further. Finally, all existing posts were to be brought into the three year review cycle introduced by Circular 97/1982.

Although Circular 94/1983 outlined a review process which, at first glance, appeared to have the potential to correct the past misuses of Section 11, commentators were not slow to point out that the document contained ambiguities and fundamental weaknesses. In particular it was noted that the ambiguities surrounding the funding criteria outlined in Circular 97/1982 remained; that there was a danger that local authorities would be unwilling to fulfil their responsibilities in respect of the review; that the nature and extent of consultation was left entirely to the discretion of the local authorities, and that the capacity of the Home Office to coordinate the review remained open to question. The general verdict was that the review of existing provision would be problematic and possibly ineffectual.

For its part the Home Office, during 1983, remained supremely optimistic. Department officials were confident that local authorities would cooperate and undertake the review. Moreover if any problems did arise they could be resolved, as one senior Home Office official put it, 'in discussions conducted in the spirit of partnership that is the hallmark of Home Office relations with local authorities' (personal communication). These confident sentiments were reiterated at Home Office meetings with Community Relations Councils and at local authority conferences organized by the Home Office and the DES.

Despite this confidence and the Home Office's attempts to explain the mechanics of the review to local authorities the review itself was characterized by confusion, equivocation, frustration, and obfuscation. To the many critics of Section 11 the experience of the Home Office and local authority administration of the review was no more than long overdue chickens coming home to roost.

In their report, Crispin and Hibbert (1986) examined the consequences of Circular 94/1983 for the Home Office's administration and looked in detail at the response of seven selected LEAs to the Circular. Their report does not make for happy reading but lends further evidence to our contention that Section 11 represents an anachronistic, unaccountable, and inefficient form of provision.

Crispin and Hibbert identified a number of problems associated with the Home Office aspects of the review. They pointed out that the Home Office exhibited an inability to provide clear and consistent advice to local authorities in respect of the implications of Circular 94/1983 thereby resulting in varying and contradictory interpretations by local authorities. They also noted how Home Office Officials appeared to continue to subscribe to an assimilationist perspective when interpreting the new funding criteria, particularly as regards the concept of 'special needs'. As one senior offical put it: 'In the Section 11 context, when we are talking about special needs, we are talking about needs that wouldn't be there if not for the presence of people whose language and backgrounds are not British . . . not English . . . not white Anglo-Saxon' (personal communication).

Crispin and Hibbert also reported an inadequate level of staffing within that section of the Home Office responsible for Section 11 (7.5 persons) resulting in an extremely slow response rate by the Department to the flood of enquiries arising from the review.

And finally there was a reluctance on the part of the Home Office to visit local authorities to ensure that the terms of Circular 94/1983 were being complied with. In part this was due to the fact that officials were virtually 'house bound' due to the workload created by the review. But it was also the case that Home Office officials became aware that LEAs could (and did) engineer visits so as to show only those parts which clearly met funding criteria. For instance, in one LEA visited by the Home Office, a senior education official admitted that the LEA had orchestrated the Home Office visitation so as to include only the 'shining examples' of S11 use in the borough. As part of the department's attempt to castrate the Home Office's visit officials were taken to youth centres where the presence of 'surly black lads' would convince them that the money was being well spent (personal communication).

At the local authority level a similarly depressing picture emerges from Crispin and Hibbert's study (1986). To begin with, they found a lack of appreciation and comprehension by local authority officers about the nature and scale of the tasks arising from Circular 94/1983, which resulted in most of the LEAs failing to submit their review reports on time. There was also a continued reluctance to consider S11 funded posts as a special or strategic resource to meet Commonwealth immigrant needs rather than as a general compensation and means of improving pupil-teacher ratios.

Thirdly, and indicative of the lack of strategic thinking on the part of LEA officers, there was a general dependency on the part of local authorities to rely on Heads, Principals, and other managers to draft job descriptions. Often this was done without any training or explanation and resulted in review reports that were, at best, disjointed and contradictory bundles of paper and, at worst, masterpieces of fiction.

Finally, and perhaps most significantly of all, in all but one of the LEAs studied, consultation had been either nonexistent or perfunctory. For instance out of the seven LEAs looked at by Crispin and

Hibbert only four bothered to consult at all on the review. In one of these the researchers found that the LEA, despite its recognition of 150 ethnic minority organizations, only consulted with eight, who were given less than two weeks in which to respond to a 200 page document. In another authority the review document used for consultation was significantly different from that submitted to the Home Office.

From the research, and from other informal local reports, it is difficult not to conclude that the reviews stemming from Circular 94/1983 were no more than cynical exercises designed to retain funding rather than confront the real problems of existing S11 provision.

The final episode?

Following the failure of the above administrative measures to modify the more obvious abuses of Section 11 (let alone resolve its basic contradications) the Home Office decided, in April 1986, to revise, once again, its guidelines on S11 use. The failure of previous reforms is tacitly admitted in the new guideline's opening statement that: 'The Home Secretary has now decided that further adjustments are required to the administration of the grant to improve the targeting of Section 11 grant to those areas and those types of provision where it will be most effective in meeting special needs' (1986: para 1).

At the time of writing (September 1986) these guidelines were still in draft and their final form cannot be certain.[1] Nonetheless, some speculative comments on the main features of this complex, opaque, and intriguing document are called for.

The 1986 draft Circular starts by redefining 'Commonwealth immigrant' as: 'all those born in another country of the Commonwealth (or Pakistan before it left the Commonwealth, before 1972) however long they have been resident in the UK, and their immediate descendants'. Despite certain improvements this simplified definition perpetuates the deficiencies of the original legislation. The Swann Report's recommendation that S11 should be extended to all ethnic minority groups (DES 1985: 358–60) is routinely ignored (presumably on the grounds that it would involve amending the original legislation). Furthermore the term 'immediate descendants' is ambiguous and appears to exclude the third generation; a growing proportion of the ethnic minority population will therefore be excluded from S11 because they are only of immigrant origin.

With regard to application procedures and grant payment the new Circular introduces several changes. The Home Office says that it will be sympathetic towards applications in respect of posts which no longer qualify for funding under other Government schemes (Urban Programme, Education Support Grants, MSC) but which local authorities may wish to retain. Though this could be seen as an attempt to allow local authorities to continue important race relations initiatives it might also be viewed as a loophole by which they can off-set (marginalize) the cost of those initiatives

Authorities will also now be required annually to supply the Home Office with a list of approved posts indicating whether they are occupied and to report immediately of any changes in such posts; failure to do so may result in withdrawal of grant aid. Though presumably introduced to improve Home Office monitoring these requirements will impose additional administrative burdens on local authorities which may have consequences for the level of grant take-up.

Though the criteria for grant aid remain essentially the same as those of 1982 (with all its ambiguities and limitations) the draft Circular introduces a number of intriguing modifications. To begin with, new applications (bids made after October 1986) must contain an analysis of the needs which have been identified for each post to meet, how they have been identified, and how this relates to the location (e.g. school) of the post holder. Moreover the post holder's job description and activities must be explicitly related to this analysis of need. Furthermore local authorities are informed that it is 'important' that S11 posts be part of their 'general strategy' regarding local Commonwealth immigrants' special needs and for fulfilling their duties under Section 71 of the Race Relations Act. Local authorities are also required to show that they have consulted with the local CRC and with a 'cross section of the community concerned'. Importantly, such consultation should be conducted prior to application to the Home Office and on the basis of 'sufficient information for the communities to see the purpose of the post and the context in which it will operate'.

Finally, regarding criteria, the new Circular states that the Secretary of State may from time to time decide that particular needs should receive priority funding and that local authority applications will be considered in the light of these Home Office priorities.

Though these revisions to the funding criteria are long overdue and to be welcomed doubts must remain as to the extent to which they will be implemented. Quite apart from local authorities' willingness to respond positively (and again there are administrative burdens), the Home Office's ability to evaluate the extent to which LEAs have complied adequately with the new criteria remains an open question. This is particularly true as regards the inadequately defined 'consultation', 'general strategies' and S71 duties (under the 1976 Race Relations Act) but is even more pronounced in terms of the Home Office's own 'priorities'.

The most unexpected innovation of the 1986 guidelines is its reference to Section 5 of the Race Relations Act. This section of the Act permits an employer (including an LEA) to specify that an employee should be of a particular racial group where being a member of that group constitutes a 'genuine occupational qualification'. However S5 is severely restricted by its limited application to posts providing a 'personal service' to persons of a particular racial group. Thus LEAs could not appeal to S5 as a means of correcting historical inequalities or ensuring that their teaching force more accurately reflected the ethnic composition of the local population. There is also the danger that LEAs might be tempted to use S5 in conjunction with S11 as a means of increasing the number of black teachers but only in marginalized rather than mainstream posts.

Finally the new Circular addresses itself to the complex and contentious issues of the monitoring and review of posts. In terms of monitoring the Circular says that when applying for new posts the LEA will have to state the objectives of the post for the next twelve months and the 'output measures' or 'performance indicators' they intend to use to monitor the posts' effectiveness on a yearly basis. Though these will be for the authority to decide, grant approval will depend on 'satisfactory arrangements being made'.

At first reading these new arrangements for monitoring performance appearance appear to be useful remedies to past malpractices. In reality they present a number of practical and political problems. In common with other features of the Circular, administrative burdens will again be considerable. More intractable however will be the back door teacher appraisal implied by the obscure terms 'output measures' and 'performance indicators' which have already provoked teacher union opposition; monitoring the performance of S11 teachers may place them in an inferior position *vis à vis* other teachers regarding conditions of service.

In terms of reviewing posts the new Circular completely changes the previous arrangements and in its place introduces a three tier structure. Now local authorities will have to report on the results of their first twelve months' monitoring of new posts and inform the Home Office of the objectives set for the next year. The renewal of the grant for these posts will depend on a justifiable case being made to the Home Office. The Home Office expects monitoring arrangements to remain in force and, from time to time, will call for annual reports on selected posts.

Secondly, at an as yet unspecified date, the Home Office will begin a 'rolling programme' of spot checks on selected LEAs to look in detail at their S11 provision.

Thirdly, all 'existing posts' (including those funded previously under Circulars 97/1982 and 94/1983) will be brought into the above review system and authorities will be expected to develop objectives and 'output measures' or 'performance indicators' as per the monitoring of new posts.

The problematic nature of this cumbersome review procedure must be obvious. Yet again the administrative burden placed on authorities will be considerable and the Home Office's own ability, given its level of staffing and expertise, to undertake the type of review proposed is suspect. Additionally, however, as with the monitoring of performance, the new review procedures will reinforce the marginality of S11 staff and their feelings of insecurity because they are being scrutinized in a way that other teachers are not.

Conclusion

In assessing the latest Circular's likely impact, and the current state of play regarding Section 11, we are forced to come to pessimistic conclusions. Any attempt to redirect S11 monies to antiracist objectives 'compensating' black people for the problems of racism rather than compensating LEAs for the 'problems' of immigrants would be welcome. But there is nothing in the 1986 Circular, nor those of 1982 and 1983, to suggest that. Quite the contrary. It appears to us that the mandarins at the Home Office have at last managed to square the proverbial circle.

The Home Office Circulars, in answering some of the past criticisms of S11 have done so in a way that will be interpreted by LEAs as a reactivation of an assimilationist perspective and a narrow definition of special needs. At the same time, the byzantine administrative framework, ostensibly created to check abuse will probably have the effect of curtailing antiracist developments and reducing the overall level of spending. As a senior LEA officer explained to one of the authors: 'the new guidelines are an attempt by the Home Office to make us (LEAs) jump through smaller and smaller hoops leaving us little room to develop the type of initiatives which we know must be developed. I think that the complexity of the new guidelines will also be a major disincentive to future take-up' (personal communication).

The final contradiction of Section 11 becomes clear. With each successive reform of procedures and arrangements for grant aid we are forced back to the originating and anachronistic notions of the problem of 'immigrants' and their 'special needs'. These remain unchanged and rooted in 1960s race relations ideology – Catch 22?

© *1987 Andrew Dorn and Paul Hibbert*

Note

1 Circular 72/86 was issued in October 1986 and is virtually identical to the draft circular discussed in this chapter.

References

Bakhsh, Q. and Walker, N. (1980) *Unrealized Potential: A case for Additional Resources Under Section 11*. Gravesend: Gravesend and District Community Relations Council.

Crispin, A. and Hibbert, P. (1986) Education funding for ethnic minorities: a case study of Section 11 (Unpublished report submitted to ESRC). London: Economic and Social Research Council.

Department of Education and Science (1985) *Education for All: The Report of the Committee of Inquiry into the Education of Children from Ethnic Minority Groups*, Cmnd 9543. London: HMSO.

Dorn, A. (1983) LEA policies on multiracial education. *Multi-Ethnic Education Review* 2(2): 3–5.

Dummett, M. and Dummet, A. (1985) The role of government in Britain's racial crisis. In Husband, C. (ed.) *'Race' in Britain: Continuity and Change*. London: Hutchinson.

Foot, P. (1965) *Immigration and Race in British Politics*. Harmondsworth: Penguin.

Greater London Council (1984) *The Role of Section 11 Workers*. London: GLC.

Hibbert, P. (1982) Funding inexplicitness. *Multiracial Education* 11(1): 11–16.

Home Office (1965) *Immigration from the Commonwealth*. London: HMSO.

—— (1978) *Proposals for Replacing Section 11 (Consultative Document)*. London: HMSO.

—— (1982) *Government Reply to the Fifth Report of the House of Commons Home Affairs Committee: Racial Disadvantage*. London: HMSO.

House of Commons (1981) *Fifth Report from the Home Affairs Committee Session 1980–1981: Racial Disadvantage*, Vol. 1.

Kapur, S. (1984) *Section 11 Posts: Review or More of the Same?* Leicester: Indian Workers' Association.

McCrudden, C. (1982) Institutional discrimination. *Oxford Journal of Legal Studies* 2(3): 303–69.

Mullard, C. *et al.* (1983) *Racial Policy and Practice: A Letter Survey.* London: Race Relations Policy and Practice Research Unit, Institute of Education.

Sivanandan, A. (1982) Race, class, and the state. In *A Different Hunger.* London: Pluto Press.

Troyna, B. and Ball, W. (1985) *Views from the Chalk Face: School Responses to an LEA's Policy on Multicultural Education.* Warwick: Centre for Research in Ethnic Relations, University of Warwick.

6 Hearing and listening: a case study of the 'consultation' process undertaken by a local education department and black groups

David Gibson

The aim of this chapter will be to present an analysis of the consultation process undertaken by the 'Milltown'[1] Education Department with some of the local black groups. Other contributors to this book have emphasized the increasing involvement of central government in decisions concerning the curriculum in schools, the reduction in resources of local education authorities (LEAs), and the continued take-over of education by the Manpower Services Commission (MSC). While I consider it is only possible and reasonable to support analyses which emphasize the mode of State interference in the education system, it is also the case that central government agencies have, belatedly, lent support to the requirement that local education officers should 'consult' with members of black groups. As Dorn and Hibbert's chapter in this volume shows, revised guidelines on the administration of Section 11 of the 1966 Local Government Act issued to LEAs by the Home Office require, without precisely defining what is intended, that local authorities will demonstrate that they 'have consulted the local Commonwealth immigrant community or the local community relations councils about the proposed post' (Home Office 1982: Para 9 (vi)). Similar exhortations to 'consult' are included in *Better Schools* (DES 1985) and *Education For All* (The Swann Report (1985)). Furthermore, there has been a marked increase in the number of LEAs adopting multicultural and antiracist policies. As Troyna and Ball suggest:

> 'on the grounds of the recent increase in LEA multicultural and antiracist policies, the establishment of consultative structures between LEA administrators and local black organizations . . . one might be tempted to conclude that important gains have already been secured.'
> (Troyna and Ball 1986: 39)

This study will examine first the question: Have important gains already been secured within the education services of Milltown? An analysis of the consultation process itself has been required in order to demonstrate the different models used by officers. In the next section I shall give some consideration to theories of public participation, consultation, and social control, and outline the seven different models of consultation used by the education officers. It will then be possible to examine in more detail examples of the outcomes of the Milltown consultation procedures.

Public participation–consultation: social control?

The argument that public participation can be used as a form of social control is not a new one. Indeed Bridges (1975) argued that the Community Development Projects (CDPs) had university-based research teams appointed to them in order to ensure the efficient 'feedback' of intelligence on the urban poor to the Home Office. The CDPs, modelled along the lines of the American Poverty Program, helped to provide such feedback to both local and national states, but also as Cockburn stressed: 'had a "clear-cut" element of social control, the management of unrest' (1977: 125).

As Dearlove (1979) recorded in the report of the Ditchley Park Conference, called to discuss CDP and Inner Area Studies, the Chief Inspector of the Children's Department admitted that in the initiatives there appeared to be an element of looking for a new method of social control. In considering the US experience of community participation and comparing it with subsequent developments in England, Marris and Rein highlighted the fact that: 'both sets of projects arose partly out of concern with the assimilation of newcomers to the city and in both initiatives came from national agencies in which the implementation and control is local' (Marris and Rein 1972: xvi).

Marris and Rein also stress that a system can have the *appearance* of being democratic but that the essence is whether or not a genuine attempt is made to redress the balance of power between government and citizen. This latter point was emphasized and an 'official' warning sounded, in the Skeffington Report which claimed that participation would require the devolution of power which could not be conceded by the government without sacrificing the integrity of its own planning.

The requirement for the transfer of power from the consultors to the consulted is crucial within any genuine consultation process, or indeed one which is not seeking merely to maintain its own integrity.

For if the State appears to offer some semblance of power to the consulted, it can be argued that there are considerable dangers, because by legitimizing the status of the group involved in such a consultation process, the State, by carefully ensuring it is only a semblance of power being made available, can within that relationship subordinate the group involved. This issue is confronted in an interview with the convenor of the local Black Parents' Organization who argues that to be a part of the consultation process whilst being offered a 'semblance of power' is in fact a loss of power; it is debilitating, for the locus of the power should be independent of the local state and thus this organization has deliberately decided that: 'We are an independent political organization which believes in the principle of independent parents' power and independent students' power and we stress very much our independence . . .' (personal communication 1985).

The crucial question to be faced is whether, when considering local authorities' consultation procedures, the process has to be such that only 'a semblance of power' is transferred. Certainly Ouseley *et al.*, in the analysis of the approaches adopted by Lambeth Council, pointed out it was evident that

'Blacks were outside the decision-making processes: no Black councillors, no Black chief officers, very few Blacks in key management positions. Some consultations did take place with the CCRL or the odd Black group, but even they viewed these arrangements with enormous dissatisfaction.'

They went on to say that

'In practice, what consultation was perceived by many people in the community to mean was having a *fait accompli* presented to them. Problems were seen as having already been diagnosed by officers and members with solutions, policies, and programmes virtually ready for implementation. The consultation process then became a rubber stamping operation. This meant that participation was confined to reaction rather than the community being involved at the earliest stages of problem identification, suggesting solutions, and contributing to devising policies and programmes.'

(Ouseley *et al.* 1982: 32)

Whilst it needs to be noted that Ouseley's work did not include education, other writers such as Young and Connelly (1981) and Ben-Tovim *et al.* (1981; 1986) have argued that education is a part of the local state, which as Corrigan (1979) observed, is an important arena for the battle of democracy. Certainly Ben-Tovim *et al.* note that

'For those Left organizations and groups in Liverpool and Wolver-hampton it is initially at the local level that real participatory intrusion into the State will be made, and from local struggles that popular movements will emerge. The materialization of race ideologies in local state practices has developed unevenly and sub-ject to a series of local restraints: community ideologies, economic, demographic, political.' (Ben-Tovim *et al.* 1981: 158).

These writers clearly include education within the provision of the local state but as they themselves stress there are local restraints and indeed differences. When considering Milltown's education depart-ment, it is necessary to consider such differences in more detail as well as seeking to analyse the outcomes, whether positive or negative, of the consultation meetings held.

Models of consultation

To assist in the analysis of the outcomes of those consultation meet-ings, I have devised a typology of different models of consultation using some sociological theories of public participation and consulta-tion, the data collected from interviews with representatives of the black groups and education officers in Milltown, and the work of several writers including Ben-Tovim *et al.* (1981; 1986), Ouseley *et al.* (1982), and Collett (1985). The degree of validity of the consultation process should, I maintain, be assessed by the willingness or ability of those who maintain the power to transfer such power to those for whom they provide the service. Thus the success or otherwise of the Milltown education officers' consultation meetings with the representatives of Milltown's black groups should be based on the extent to which officers are prepared to alter radically their relation-ships with black groups, so that there is a significant shift in status which currently can be described as being between a superordinate group (the professional) and a subordinate group (the black groups). Unless there is a commitment to enable black groups to determine and/or influence proceedings and outcomes, the consultation process is destined to achieve little more than an improved information resources gathering, constitute no more than an increased social control mechanism, or remain as something of a cosmetic exercise dealing mostly with the need to obtain 'rubber-stamping' approval for policies devised and presented by officers.

Table 6.1 Models of local authority consultation

Model title	Nature of meeting	Officers' aims	Outcomes of meetings	Power shift: from local authority officers
1 Control	Formal: arranged by officers	Gain information feedback	Information gained assists social control	Nil: power retained
2 Illusion	Formal or informal: arranged by officers	Create illusion of involvement/decision making	Status quo maintained	Nil: power retained
3 Post-event	Formal or informal: arranged by officers	Provide minimal restricted involvement Presentation of fait accompli	Rubber-stamping requested from black groups	Minimal shift of power to black groups
4 Advisory	Informal: arranged by individual officers	Obtain 'black perspective' on planned policies and strategies	Individual officers better advised: no certainty recommended actions implemented	Slight shift to black groups possible
5 Pragmatic	Formal or informal: arranged by officers	Solve particular problem: meet specific black group demand	Specific demands expressed and either acceded to or considered further	Sufficient power shift to enable solution to problem identified to be achieved
6 Empowerment	Formal or informal: arranged by groups	Full involvement of black groups in identification of needs and examination of possible policy and strategy changes	Policies and strategies altered to meet demands and needs of black groups	Power shared
7 Confrontation	Formal: arranged by groups	To defend themselves and 'consider' changes of policies, strategies, and practices	Significant changes in policies, strategies, or practices achieved	Power taken by black groups

1 *Control Model:* Meetings are called by officers with the purpose of increasing their information and understanding. There is no benefit to the black groups and the information gathered by officers can be used to check out reactions of the representatives and to inform officers so that they do not need to give concessions when it is not essential.

2 *Illusion model:* Again, officers call the meetings and while they may make every effort to suggest that the black representatives are being involved in the decision-making process, there is no power transferred and no policy changes made.

3 *Post-event model:* Once more officers call the meetings and regulate the amount of information given to the representatives. Often the amount of information given is partial and sufficient only to enable officers to obtain agreement to their previous actions. A modicum of power could be transferred in so far as it is possible that representatives could refuse to agree to provide the requested 'rubber-stamping'. According to my research in Milltown, however, this power was rarely exercised.

4 *Advisory model:* Generally this is requested by officers who are doubtful or anxious about a planned policy or strategy, and wish to obtain views of members of the black communities. A slight shift of power is possible for the views given could be strong enough to persuade officers to amend or even cease to pursue the discussed changes.

5 *Pragmatic model:* Meetings again arranged by officers in order to seek to find a solution to a particular difficulty or problem. Alternatively, if the black groups are making specific demands it provides a method by which officers can judge the extent of the demands and decide the degree to which it would be necessary to accede. Power can in this way be transferred to the black groups.

6 *Empowerment model:* Such meetings may be called by either officers or the groups. For the empowerment model to be applicable the groups must be given extensive information and be involved at the earliest stages so that they are in a position to identify the needs and be involved in the planning of strategies designed to meet such needs. In these circumstances the groups are fully involved and the power is shared.

7 *Confrontation model:* The group calls the meetings, makes its specific complaints and demands known, and insists on these demands being met. In this way previously implemented policies,

strategies or practices are altered and the group takes the power from the officers.

These seven models of local authority consultation can be used to analyse the consultation meetings held between officers of the education department and black groups over an eighteen month period. The following are examples of the product (or lack of it) from these meetings.

SECTION 11 REVIEW REPORT

The procedure for discussing this long report which gave details of all Section 11 funded posts in the education department, was unsatisfactory, for the members of the black groups had not been presented with the report prior to the meeting. Nonetheless, they were requested to approve it at the meeting.

Dissatisfaction was expressed by representatives of black groups who complained that there was a vast amount of information, which had not been circulated before the meeting and that it was impossible to examine the information simply by hearing an officer reading through it. Further, it became evident that the reply, or lack of replies, to the following question, posed by a member of one group, gave cause for considerable anxiety:

'the local authority has carried out the review of existing posts. The new regulations apply to new posts.

How were the previous Section 11 posts evaluated and arrived at, and do these posts serve the needs of the ethnic minorities?'

(Minutes of a Consultative Meeting 1984)

No reply to the last question was recorded in the minutes. Members of the group were presented with the essential information in a manner which made it impossible for them to examine the report. They were given the officers' views and asked to rubber-stamp the report. This provides an example of the Post-event model.

A GUIDE FOR PARENTS

Despite considerable support from members of the groups for the publication of a guide for parents about the rules and regulations adopted by local schools and for the need for such a document to be printed in several languages, no draft had been circulated to groups, some thirty months after the initial request was made, despite the fact that copies of a similar document produced by the Bradford Local Education Authority were obtained. This would seem to typify the Illusion model, for although members of the different groups had been asked whether such a publication would be of assistance, there had been no progress made, despite their expressed wish for this.

RELIGIOUS EDUCATION CONFERENCE

The decision to consult widely on the production of a new religious education syllabus is a requirement on officers of Milltown LEA. However, on this occasion the actual proposed consultation process agreed with the consulted black groups had been (and is proceeding with) each of the groups and with many nonconsulted groups sending representatives to the various workshops undertaking the tasks. Regular reports are being fed back to the groups. This process can be defined within the Pragmatic model as every effort has been made to obtain views and opinions and all the reports back including those of the representatives attending, indicates that their views continue to be fully expressed and incorporated into the syllabus.

PUPILS' ABSENCE FROM SCHOOLS TO COUNTRY OF ORIGIN

This item was raised as a consequence of officer concern. It had been agreed amongst officers that they should draft a letter requesting parents to ensure that headteachers were informed of such impending absences and stating that the school places of children involved could not be guaranteed in the same school. One group supported this view and agreed to provide a translation of the proposed draft letter. No debate occurred about whether the same school places should be reserved. Again this was an information-giving exercise, with the added benefit of free translations, and falls within the Control model.

Items placed on the agendas by officers

An evaluation of the outcomes of all items placed on the agendas by the education officers and those put forward by the secretaries of the eight black groups serves to demonstrate the control element of the officers choosing the items for those agendas. I now want to consider the way in which agenda-setting, and outcomes, might be explained in terms of the typology.

Fifteen items were placed on the agendas by officers and of those, eight involved either the Control or Illusion models which involve no shift of power from officers to representatives. Three are the Post-event model where although possible for a shift in power to have taken place (by representatives refusing to endorse a policy) this was not the case in these instances. In all, eleven out of the fifteen items realized no shift in power in the relationship between officers and representatives. The remaining four items involved either the Advisory or Pragmatic models where the shift of power from consultors to consulted was minimal.

Items placed on the agenda by representatives

When the items placed on the agendas by representatives were examined, there were more examples of models of consultation being used which involved some shift of power from officers to representatives. When we look at the twenty-two items which representatives placed on the agenda of meetings with officers, we find that in seven instances there was no shift of power evident. In those cases, the Illusion model prevails. Of the remaining items (fifteen), ten were the Advisory model and four could be characterized in terms of the Pragmatic model. However, as the typology indicates the one model which has clearly demonstrated a process in which the group took power, has been the Confrontation model. In the only example of this model case considered representatives ensured that teaching materials which in their opinions were unsuitable were taken out of use in local schools. As Ben-Tovim *et al.* (1986) and Collett (1985) noted, a shift of power from consultors to consulted is required if a genuine process of consultation is being undertaken. There would seem to be quite reasonable evidence from this work that some shift of power is more likely to be achieved when the representatives select those items to be discussed at their consultation meetings with education officers.

In this work I have assessed the applicable models of consultation by considering the process involved when items were placed on the consultation agendas by officers and by the black representatives. Overall there is only little evidence of any shift of power from officers to those representatives. For the items placed on the agenda by officers there is evidence of the effects of the fundamental belief of officers that the meetings are, and should be, concerned with information exchange. Information gathering and exchange involves no *power* exchange. Such processes are seen as being unproductive by the representatives, however. In contrast, there is some evidence that when the representatives themselves select the agenda items there are *occasions* when there is a genuine power sharing, and one particular item when the representatives wrested the power from officers and achieved their desired outcome. If the consultation meetings are to continue (and it is the wish of some officers that they are genuine attempts to involve fully the representatives in the decision making processes) then there seems no doubt that representatives should be given the information required to make them aware of current policies and planned changes in practice and that representatives should have more say in the choice of items which they wish to discuss and the order in which they appear. This would ensure that there is ample opportunity for the representatives to examine the items which are of concern to them.

Transfer of power

The central concern in any professionally honest consultation process must be the need to transfer power from the officer to the representative. The evidence from Milltown suggests that any such transfer has been relatively small. The extent and nature of the inequalities between officers and representatives have been recorded but Milltown is certainly not unique in this failing; for as Ben-Tovim *et al.* noted from their work in Wolverhampton and Liverpool:

> 'The reality of consultation, however, in our view can hardly be said to represent a significant advance in terms of an extension of local democracy. On the contrary, and almost without exception, the variety of consultation measures in which we have been involved or have observed close at hand have served to emphasize inequalities between consultors and consulted. This has been the case irrespective of consultation measure.'   (Ben-Tovim *et al.* 1986: 7)

Such inequalities will continue unless it is the intention of officers to release power and reorganize the current structure which does, in itself, help to maintain the inequalities. It is essential, therefore, to consider an alternative structure which will radically alter this power relationship.

Power to the representatives

As Collett (1985) argued, any process of consultation concerning education departments and black groups will be meaningless without a transfer of power, but in Milltown this transfer has been realized only at a minimal level. Representatives of the black groups, including those who are and are not consulted, share a concept of successful consultation which comprises a shift of power as well as a clear definition of the purpose of the consultation process. For example, one representative of a nonconsulted group observed:

> 'The problem is the key word, consultation. Would it be consultation after the event or before the event and would there be any power in it? I think that's what you're talking about − power. To

consult after an event is no consultation, but you can still put it down on paper as consultation.' (personal communication 1985)

The view that a consultation process can appear to be valuable, genuine and worthwhile is one readily identified by Ben-Tovim *et al.* (1986), Greenberg (1969), and Marris and Rein (1972) as well as by Collett who, when considering current efforts by education department staff to consult black groups about Section 11 funding, poses the question: 'Is it being cynical to suspect that the word "consultation" in public affairs has taken on overtones at least patronizing, and at worst, totally cosmetic?' (Collett 1985: 19).

The exercise of power by officers within Milltown Education Department's consultation meetings is extensive. As demonstrated earlier the transfer of power to the representatives does not necessarily include the ability to effect immediate changes to a system of education within a capitalist society. However, such a transfer of power can be assessed in the terms of conditions which can enable its effective exercise by those who are consulted, as Ben-Tovim *et al.* note: '(as we) have suggested above, that power in social relations could be analysed in the first instance in terms of those conditions which create the potential for its effective exercise' (Ben-Tovim *et al.* 1986: 13). The current conditions in Milltown only afford the black representatives limited opportunities to effect change because of the extent of the power retained by the officers.

Power of the officers

The loci of power retained by officers include the power:

1 of the chair to control and direct debate

2 of the minute-taker to record fully and accurately (or otherwise) the debate and all different views concerning the matters discussed and requests for future action

3 of the person who prepares the agenda which requires him/her not only to consult groups about agenda items they wish to have included, but also to order the agenda in such a way as to ensure equal priority is given to the groups' items in discussion time

4 to arrange and agree the attendance of officers so that there is some continuity and groups are not regularly forced to meet new and different sets of officers

5 to retain information or to limit the availability of that information:

(i) there is a need for officers to bear the responsibility for sharing information, with sufficient copies for all representatives and in reasonable time to allow representatives to acquaint themselves with the contents of frequently long, and often jargon-loaded reports

(ii) to provide time, as appropriate, for translations to be made

(iii) to provide all relevant information. Furthermore, it is, not least of all because of the cost of official reports, necessary for the officers to provide copies or at least a précis of such vital reports as the *West Indian Children In Our Schools* (DES 1981) – the interim report of the Committee of Inquiry into the Education of Children from Ethnic Minority Groups – and *Education For All* – the final report of that committee (DES 1985).

(iv) to bring to the attention of groups all committee reports which are likely to affect the representatives, their children, and those whom such group members are seeking to represent

6 to maintain, as Young and Connelly (1981) stressed, those strategies which can and have been used to inhibit initiatives aimed at promoting racial equality. As Ben-Tovim *et al.* note, such strategies include;

> 'it's [the administration's] capacity to pursue traditional bureaucratic traits of perceived self-interest, inertia, and defensiveness [which] can pose a formidable array of obstacles in the way of effective intervention from below.'
>
> (Ben-Tovim *et al.* 1985: 17)

7 to share or not to share the views, requests for action and so forth received by officers with other officers and with Council Members of the appropriate committees.

A political structure for consultation meetings

Milltown's consultation meetings have not taken place within a structure which links them to the local politicians. There are no formal reports to committees detailing the anxieties or requests reported at the consultation meetings nor do any of the other reports include any clear outline of the views of the various black groups. Any process which excludes the politicians is, at best, likely to achieve little. The politicians control the resources and take a keen interest in policy change and developments in Milltown.

An education department structure for consultation meetings

Again there is no readily agreed, well publicized, system for the dissemination of information concerning the wishes or complaints of the representatives, either within the central education office (for example, to subject inspectors or staff involved in the processing of urban aid grants) or to those in charge of, or working within, Milltown's schools, training units, colleges, and so forth.

The black groups consulted

There is no publicly advertized structure by which black groups can arrange to participate in the consultation process. While, as previously indicated, there are groups who have no desire whatsoever to be involved, there are others who are not aware that the process exists so that they could, if they chose, be part of that process.

Implementation of actions agreed in consultation meetings

On many issues there continue to be instances reported to the officers at consultation meetings when the agreed guidelines or procedures appear not to have been followed in the education institutions. Examples of these failures have been reported by many of the consulted groups. The following example refers to the occasion when a representative's complaint appeared in the minutes of the meeting as:

> 'A case which had happened at "a" school was then related where one of the school governors said that a child was suspended for a simple thing and when the triviality of the incident was brought to the teacher's notice, the teacher said there was no way he would have that child in class. When the headmaster was asked to intervene the headmaster said his hands were tied and that he could do nothing about it.' (Minutes of a consultation meeting 1984)

There seems little doubt that there are differences in whether or not, and in which ways, headteachers implement and interpret Committee and the Chief Education Officer's guidelines and instructions.

Restrictions of consulting formally organized groups only

Representatives maintained that they regularly debated the issues discussed with officers, with others in their communities. However, the ability of any representative to undertake a systematic and thorough 'sounding-out' operation with large numbers is seriously limited especially when s/he has his/her own job and/or personal and social repsonsibilities to perform. These limitations are further emphasized if the group have no facilities to photocopy reports and other documents. However, there are considerable dangers in the question of how representative are the representatives.

Whilst it must be a reasonable and proper expectation that representatives can demonstrate that they are accountable to those whom they claim to represent, it must also be clearly acknowledged that it is for the communities to decide if they are satisfied with such forms of accountability.

Conclusion

From this examination of the consultation procedures in Milltown, it is evident that despite the LEA's multicultural and antiracist policies, and their apparent agreement to participate in the recommended consultation with black groups, the current consultation processes have achieved only limited results. The locus of power has clearly remained with the professionals despite the radical rhetoric. Until such a time that this power is indeed shared, any other alterations or improvements in the procedures will be cosmetic. Hearing and listening are indeed not the same thing.

© *1987 David Gibson*

Note

1 'Milltown' was the pseudonym which Troyna and Ball (1985; 1986) used in the publication of their research carried out in this LEA.

References

Ben-Tovim, G., Gabriel, J., Law, I., and Stredder, K. (1981) Race, left strategies and the state. In *Politics and Power* (3). London: Routledge and Kegan Paul.
—— (1986) A political analysis of local struggles for racial equality. In J. Rex and D. Mason (eds) *Theories of Race and Ethnic Relations*. Cambridge: Cambridge University Press.
Bridges, L. (1975) The Ministry of Internal Security: British urban social policy. *Race and Class* 16(4): 375–86.
Cockburn, C. (1977) *The Local State*. London: Pluto Press.
Collett, R. (1985) Consultation: participation and control. *Multicultural Teaching* Spring III (2): 19–20.

Department of Education and Science (1981) *West Indian Children in our Schools*. London: HMSO.

—— (1985) *Education for All: The Report of the Committee of Inquiry into the Education of Children from Ethnic Minority Groups*, Cmnd 9543. London: HMSO.

Corrigan, P. (1979) The welfare state as an arena of class struggle. *Marxism Today* 21.

Dearlove, J. (1979) *The Reorganization of British Local Government*. London: Cambridge University Press.

Greenberg, J. (1969) *The Devil has Slippery Shoes*. London: Collier-Macmillan.

Marris, P. and Rein, M. (1972) *Dilemmas of Social Reform*. London: Routledge and Kegan Paul.

Ouseley, H., Silverstone, D., and Prashar, U. (1982) *The System*. London: Runnymede Trust and South London Equal Rights Consultancy.

Ouseley, H. (1985) The case for high priority equality. *Local Government Chronicle*, March: 362–3.

Troyna, B. and Ball, W. (1985) Styles of LEA policy intervention in multi-cultural/antiracist education. *Educational Review* 37(2): 165–73.

—— (1986) 'Partnership, consultation, and influence: State rhetoric in the struggle for racial equality. In Hartnett, A. and Naish, M. (eds) *Education and Society Today*. Lewes: Falmer Press.

Young, K. and Connelly, N. (1981) *Policy and Practice in the Multiracial City*. London: Policy Studies Institute.

7 Curriculum option choices in multi-ethnic schools

Sally Tomlinson

One way of examining racial and ethnic inequalities in education in Britain is to study those normal school processes, which have developed over a number of years without having the deliberate intention of disadvantaging particular groups of pupils, but which nevertheless have that effect. Option choice processes, which occur during pupils' third year at state secondary schools, when subjects are chosen and examination level placements made for the final two years of compulsory schooling, bear such an examination. The option allocation process is a crucial point in the school careers of most pupils. In terms of preparation for future employment or unemployment, income, status, and lifestyle, there is an awesome finality to decisions taken by teachers, parents, and pupils when the pupils are aged only 13 or 14.

Secondary schools, particularly during the third year, as Ryrie, Furst, and Lauder noted in 1979, perform the function of putting some pupils on the route to more favourable social positions and putting others on the route to low positions with little prospect of upward movement. With the increase in the importance of public examination success in the 1980s, the sorting of pupils into different curricula, and different examination levels at 13+, has taken on an added importance.

There is a large literature which suggests that option choice processes do disadvantage pupils of manual working class parentage (Ford 1969; Ryrie, Furst, and Lauder 1979; Ball 1981; Gray, McPherson, and Raffe 1983; Hargreaves 1984), and an even larger literature examining gender differences in subject choice at 13+ and subsequent disadvantages for girls. (DES 1975, 1979; Byrne 1978; Wardle 1978; Kelly 1979; Murphy 1980; Pratt, Bloomfield, and Seale; 1984). There is also a literature expressing concern that pupils designated as slow learners or of low ability have less choice at option time and a subsequent 'impoverished curriculum' (DES 1979). There are also hints in the literature that pupils perceived as having behaviour problems are less likely to be selected for high status subjects and higher level examinations (Hargreaves 1984).

Research and literature examining the effects of option choice processes on minority pupils is minimal at the moment, although there is some evidence that minority parents would like more research attention paid to this crucial year in their childrens' schooling. A report on educational standards in Brent in London, compiled at the request of the Black Parents Association for Educational Advance (Barrow *et al.* 1986) concluded that the selection processes for higher level examinations favour middle-class pupils and places both black and white working-class pupils at a disadvantage. The report noted that 'subsequent dissatisfaction with the (education) system, with pupils' progress, and with disciplinary difficulties, can very frequently be traced back to the period of options and the disappointment experienced at that time'. There are also suggestions in other literature that allocation to examinations at option choice time is one reason for the development of segregated black education. Roger Homan, describing the John Loughborough Seventh Day Adventist School in Tottenham, a virtually all-black independent school, notes that 'it is moving from a CSE to a GCE climate that many find to be the reward of John Loughborough schooling' (Homan 1986: 174). Black parents, and others, have also questioned whether it was appropriate for both the Rampton and Swann reports (DES 1981, 1985) to publish statistics on numbers of 'O' levels achieved by different minority groups, without some indication of the proportions of pupils actually entered for 'O' levels at 13+ and some explanation as to why entry proportions should be different.

However, given the intensity of the debate on the public examination performance of minorities (particularly those of Afro-Caribbean pupils) and the often vague or confidential nature of criteria for allocation to subjects and examination levels, it was likely that a debate would arise as to whether minority pupils were likely to be 'misplaced' into lower level examinations, on the basis of criteria other than their 'ability'. The interim report of the committee of inquiry into the education of children from ethnic minority groups included a section on 'channelling into CSE's, pointing out that many parents and pupils of West Indian origin felt that West Indian pupils were 'unfairly channelled into CSE rather than GCE examinations' (DES 1981: 38). The committee was not able to document examination entries for schools in detail, but they 'formed the impression' that West Indian pupils were over-represented in CSE streams, and quoted as evidence the school leavers survey in six LEAs, carried out by the DES for the committee, which found 46 per cent of West Indian pupils entered for CSE only, as against 33 per cent of all pupils nationally. There is certainly not sufficient research evidence available at the moment to be able to generalize widely on this issue, but one small study by Middleton (1983) investigating factors affecting the exam performance of Afro-Caribbean boys found that in the schools he studied the boys did tend to be allocated to lower bands and be less likely to be placed in 'O' level classes, even when measured ability did not justify lower placement. Teachers' perceptions of, and responses to, the behaviour of the boys seemed to explain this situation. However, in discussion with the boys, Middleton found them willing to admit to bad behaviour in the lower school, but they did not realize the effect that this had on their examination chances. Wright, in the project reported by Eggleston, Dunn, and Anjali (1985) (and in the following chapter) also suggested that assignment to 'O' level or 'CSE' classes in two schools she studied did tend to be based more on teacher perceptions of pupils' behaviour, than on ability as measured by school tests. Afro-Caribbean pupils whose marks in school examinations during the third year would seem to indicate placement in 'O' level classes were placed in CSE groups, and although Afro-Caribbean pupils had entered the two schools with reading ages on a par with white and Asian pupils, only one Afro-Caribbean child in each school, in the year of the research, obtained five or more 'O' levels. (Eggleston, Dunn, and Anjali 1985: 260). Wright also suggested that because black pupils believed the school organization worked against them, they saw little point in trying hard. She suggested a circular model in which school procedures, including option allocation procedures, become powerful determinants of pupil effort and performance.

This chapter uses evidence from a research study carried out in eighteen multi-ethnic schools in 1983/84,[1] and suggests that option choice procedures, as they have developed in comprehensive schools over the past twenty-five years, can have the effect of disadvantaging groups who are racially or ethnically different, although membership of such groups and any educational disadvantages, obviously overlaps with class and gender groupings and disadvantages. The chapter presents evidence of differences in subjects and examinations entered for by different ethnic groups, examines pupil satisfaction and dissatisfaction with the option choice process, and discusses how the processes can work to the disadvantage of minorities.

Option choice processes

The eighteen study schools were located in four LEAs in the North, the Midlands, and the South-east of England, and they had been originally chosen for their variety of ethnic mixes, social class profiles, and geographical locations. A good deal of information on the schools, pupils, and parents had been collected during a study of the pupils' first two years of schooling (1981/83) but during the third year teachers involved in the option processes were interviewed, option booklets and other literature collected. The pupils also filled out questionnaires, just after they had finalized their option choices, recording their perceptions of the subjects and examinations they would take in years four and five, and their views of the option process. The researchers also 'sat in' on fifty interviews of pupils and their parents, by teachers involved in the option choice process. Over 2000 pupils completed the questionnaire, of whom gender was established for 1839 and ethnic origin for 1678. Of these, 817 pupils were of UK/Eire origin, 159 Indian, 109 Pakistani, 94 Afro-Caribbean, 68 African-Asian, 64 Bangladeshi, 19 half Indian, half Pakistani, and 348 'mixed and other origins'.

All third year pupils in comprehensive schools are introduced to the idea that they will be expected to participate in a process of 'choosing' a part of their curriculum for their fourth and fifth year and are thereafter subject to a process of testing, guiding, and counselling by a variety of teachers. Most schools involve parents at this time, via parental evenings, triangular interviews with pupil–teacher–parent, option booklets for pupils and parents to study, and an option form of final subject choices, to be signed by parents. The length of option choice procedures varies between schools and can take between three and nine months.

Schools, understandably, wish to convey a notion of 'free choice' of subjects and levels of study which are 'right' for individual pupils, but the reality, as schools are aware, and pupils and parents made partially aware, is that there are considerable constraints on 'choice'. Schools are constrained, by their historical development and selective functions, to invest large amounts of teacher time in contructing an elaborate, examination-oriented curriculum for the fourth and fifth years and in offering pupils a choice within this curriculum. In fact, many pupils (and their parents), are guided or persuaded into taking subjects and examinations which the schools have already decided will be suitable for them. The process is presented as open, and although there is some room for negotiation, varying between schools, much of the process is prejudged. As one head of year in the research reported here remarked: 'Our idea is to let them feel they're choosing, when really they have no choice. We get our way in the end, but it's best for them too, some of them wouldn't survive on the courses they've chosen.' Certainly, during the whole option choice process, teachers and schools attempt to be as helpful and supportive as possible.

The subjects and examinations which pupils will take in their final two years of compulsory schooling are constrained mainly by the schools' views of the ability, motivation, and behaviour of pupils, and by staffing, timetabling, equipment, and other resources. Numbers of microcomputers and typewriters in a school are an obvious example of resource constraints.

Ability, however, is the major criterion which schools claim decides pupil option placements, and on one level this would appear sensible and unproblematic. When the eighteen schools were asked what was the actual basis for recommendation to subjects and levels of study, ability, as indicated in Table 7.1 emerged as most important. It is however, ability as measured by past-attainment, and those judged to be of 'low' ability do not have similar choices of subjects or levels of study.

'Ability' is, in fact, a much more ambiguous concept than it appears at first sight. Smith and Woodhouse, who studied option placements in four schools, concluded that 'measures of ability used are shifting and ambiguous' (1984: 17). For example, pupils are given 'cues' by teachers, and often assess their choices in the light of what they are told about their ability. Ability has also been considerably affected by school organization during the first three years of secondary schooling, by streaming, banding, setting, and so on, and by the quality and extent of teaching. Teachers' judgements about 'ability' can mean that the chance even to attempt to study or attain in a subject is denied to some pupils.

From the evidence provided by the interviews with pupils and their parents, it did appear that teachers are in a very powerful position at option time. In addition to judgements on ability, those involved in the guidance process can choose to divulge different amounts of information to pupils and their parents, they can apply a variety of techniques to persuade parents that 'it will be best for their child if . . .' and their decisions about the suitability of pupils for particular subjects and levels of study, remain more or less final.

It can readily be appreciated that if teachers do hold stereotyped views or 'low' expectations about pupils from a particular socio-economic, gender, or ethnic group, their decisions at option choice time could disadvantage pupils in those groups.

Table 7.1 *Ability as the basis of recommendation for options*

School	Main basis of recommendation	High and low ability have same choice	Ability tested in third year
1	ability/behaviour	No	No. But pupils ranked as suitable
2	ability/gender	No	Yes. Standardized tests
3	ability/pupil choice	No	No
4	ability	No	Yes. Subject exams
5	ability/behaviour	No	Yes. Subject exams in Eng/Maths/French/ Science
6	ability	No	Yes. Subject exams
7	ability	No	Yes. Subject exams
8	ability/behaviour	No	Yes. Exams plus continual assessment
9	ability/behaviour/effort	No	Yes. Exams and standardized tests
10	ability	No	Yes. Exams and standardized tests
11	ability	No	Yes. Exams and standardized tests
12	ability (level)/pupil choice (subject)	No	Yes. Subject exams
13	pupil choice	No	No exams
14	ability (level)/pupil choice (subject)	No	Yes. Subject exams
15	ability/resources	No	Yes. Standardized tests
16	ability/pupil choice	No	No. Assessment profiles made out
17	ability	No	Yes. Subject exams
18	ability	No	Yes. School exams: pupils ranked on marks and effort

Subject choices

The eighteen schools offered a wide range of subject choice at option choice time. All the schools required pupils to study a 'core' of 4 subjects on average: English, maths, and either PE, RE, or some variety of social and life skills, and, depending on the school, between 3 and 6 (usually 5) option subjects. Some 90 core and option subjects appeared on the final option forms of the eighteen schools, 20 of these being 'academic' in the traditional sense, the others being technical, practical, commercial, creative, physical, and remedial. In common with many comprehensive schools in the 1970s and 1980s, the schools had developed a number of subjects designed to hold the interest of the below-average pupil; for example, child-care, rural studies, motor vehicle engineering, and a variety of integrated science courses. Several subjects were relatively recent arrivals on the curriculum, notably computer studies and Asian languages. It is noteworthy that only 6 option subjects were common to all the schools: the three sciences (physics, chemistry, and biology), history, geography, and French. Pupils in different schools around the country can be offered a widely differentiated curriculum, and within any one school pupils can end up studying a vastly different curriculum.

Schools have attempted during the 1980s to offer a 'broad, balanced curriculum', and they all make much of this in option literature. The White Paper *Better Schools* (DES 1985) suggested that to achieve the aim of accommodating pupils' special interests and aptitudes, while still retaining breadth and balance, pupils in the fourth and fifth years of schooling:

> 'need to continue in these years with English, mathematics, science, and save in exceptional circumstances, with both physical education and games; should study elements drawn from both the humanities and the arts, and should take part in practical and technological work in a number of subjects. . . . Most pupils should also continue with a foreign language.'
> (DES 1985: 23)

It seemed opportune to analyse the curriculum the pupils reported that they would study in years four and five, for 'balance'. Although the majority of pupils would be studying a minimum core of English, maths, a science, and a humanity (but at different levels) very few pupils indeed would be studying a balanced curriculum in terms of the white paper. When a practical subject and a language were added to the above 4 subjects only 19 per cent of UK/Eire, Asian, and 'mixed and other' pupils and 13 per cent of Afro-Caribbean pupils would be studying such a balance. Pupils of Afro-Caribbean origin were not only less likely than other groups to be studying a minimum balanced curriculum, but also rather more likely to have chosen social studies instead of the separate history and geography, and rather more creative and practical subjects than other groups. Asian pupils, as an undifferentiated group, were as likely as UK/Eire pupils to be studying a minimum balance, and they were rather more likely to have chosen the separate (and higher status) sciences, than the integrated sciences. This was particularly so for Indian and African-Asian pupils. Bangladeshi pupils, who, in this research, were mostly girls attending one particular school were noticeably more likely to end up with a different curriculum from all the other pupils, having 'chosen' to study biology, typing, and a course in textiles, more than pupils in the other schools, and history, computing, French, home economics, and drama least. It was the African-Asian pupils who were most likely to have chosen what could be termed the 'highest status' curriculum, in traditional academic terms. It was very noticeable that there were considerable differences in curriculum choices in different areas and different schools, which was partially accounted for by resources or subjects actually offered. There were also social class differences in selection of subjects at option time. In common with previous research, this study indicated that pupils from lower socio-economic groups were more likely to have 'chosen' integrated sciences, commercial subjects, remedial, and English as a Second Language (ESL) courses and in general to have a more restricted curriculum. Integrated science is often perceived at present as of lower status, but the Government hopes to establish it as the norm for study to sixteen. Equally, the girls were more likely, as other studies of option choice and gender have found, to be studying subjects traditionally associated with girls' education: languages, commercial subjects, and domestic subjects.

Examination entry

The eighteen schools offered a variety of examinations, although it is fair to say that the majority were geared to lower level or vocational examinations rather than GCE. Eight of the schools had sixth forms, but it was not always the case that pupils in these schools were entered for more 'O' levels than schools without sixth forms. Apart from GCE, the schools offered exams at CSE (modes I, II, and III), Royal Society of Arts, Pitmans, City and Guilds, Cambridge Certificate of Proficiency in ESL and several local exams. A number of schools entered pupils for the 16+ examinations, and four schools entered for the National Association of Maternal and Child Welfare. Preparation for GCSE had not begun when this research was carried out. Some subjects (for example basic skills, remedial, and various 'lower status' subjects) were designated as non-exam, although it is worth noting the considerable pressure on schools now to develop some kind of exam or certificate for every course taken. An analysis of the eighteen option booklets given to parents and pupils by the schools demonstrated that all the schools stressed examination passes as *the* major goal of courses in years four and five. Several schools made it clear that a tripartite selection was being made, of pupils whose 'ability and effort' would indicate 'O' level, a 'good CSE', or a lower level CSE/non-exam course. One school opened its option booklet with a trendy message from the Rolling Stones 'Its my life and I'll do what I want', but followed this with the more sobering message that 'for many jobs, how well you do in 'O' levels and CSEs is more important than the subject'. This contrasted with the message from several other schools that 'enjoyment' was also a factor in option choice. Other schools taught some GCE/CSE courses together until the fifth year but gave out ambiguous messages as to how and when choices for exam level would actually be made. Teachers spoke about who was 'O' level or CSE 'material' citing criteria such as effort, motivation, and the 'right attitude'. Some parents were dissatisfied with the ambiguous nature of the criteria used to decide on examination levels and also with the limited information offered them on this issue. The schools were, however, at pains to stress to parents that CSE was a useful level of study, 'an intelligent citizen's guide to a subject' as one school put it. Over half the schools reported that 'parents insisted on their children doing exam work and certificated courses' and 'a major pressure is that parents want their children to do 'O' levels'. This would seem an unsurprising pressure from parents who know the crucial importance of qualifications, but schools had a variety of strategies to persuade parents and pupils that lower level exams were perhaps more appropriate. One way was to limit the amount of information that parents would need to be clear about exam levels and their relevance. It was noticeable from the analysis of option booklets that schools with a higher proportion of ethnic minority pupils were those which offered the least amount of serious information on exams.

There were considerable differences in the level of examinations pupils said they were entered for by areas, by schools, by gender, by ethnic origin, by socio-economic group, and by 'behaviour'. A variance components analysis carried out on the data indicated that while past attainment (as measured by tests) was the major factor in deciding the exam level a pupil would study for, ethnic origin and

Table 7.2 *Percentage of pupils taking one or more subjects at a given examination level. By ethnic origin*

	Non-exam	CSE/non-exam	CSE	CSE/0	16+	0	Other	
UK/Eire	45	7	64	49	29	47	15	
Asian	42	7	65	47	25	35	9	
West Indian	57	11	68	55	7	34	5	
Mixed and others	40	13	57	45	10	35	10	
								Total
(Numbers)	(737)	(140)	(1057)	(805)	(399)	(681)	(201)	(4020)

Table 7.3 *Percentage of pupils taking one or more subjects at a given examination level. By Asians in detail*

	Non-exam	CSE/non-exam	CSE	CSE/0	16+	0	Other	
Indian	42	6	58	43	37	44	6	
Pakistani	29	12	72	42	19	30	9	
Bangladeshi	63	6	73	70	0	17	16	
African/Asian	40	4	63	46	24	43	12	
Sub cont.	47	11	53	47	47	16	0	
								Total
(Numbers)	(174)	(29)	(271)	(199)	(105)	(146)	(38)	(962)

socio-economic group played a role, particularly in marginal cases.[2] It seemed to be the case that, depending on the school, the composite effect of socio-economic group and ethnic origin would result in some pupils with equal attainment scores, but with differing physical and social characteristics, being entered for examinations at different levels.

In this research, pupils of Pakistani, Bangladeshi, and Afro-Caribbean origin were less likely to say they were directly entered for 'O' levels than UK/Eire, East African-Asian, and Indian pupils. Indeed Tables 7.2 and 7.3 indicate that while it appears that in comparison with an 'Asian' category that the Afro-Caribbean pupils are less likely to be entered for any 'O' levels (and 16+ exams) and more likely to be entered for some non-exam classes, when 'Asians' are broken down in detail there are clear differences in examination entries between Indians and East African-Asian, 44 per cent and 43 per cent of whom said they were directly entered for some 'O' levels, and Pakistani pupils, who at 30 per cent were entered even less than the Afro-Caribbean pupils. Bangladeshi pupils were the least likely to be entered for any 'O' levels and most likely to be entered for non-exam classes. Although examination entries depend on LEA and school policies, resources, and teacher decisions, and other factors, it is worth noting that if the Rampton and Swann reports had recorded the entry and success rates of 'Asian' pupils by country of origin for the data they reported and which was widely used to claim that 'Asians did better than West Indians' (*The Times* 18 June 1981, for example) the 'success' rates of Pakistani and Bangladeshi pupils might have been shown to be on a par with or lower than West Indian pupils. Much of the stigma surrounding the achievement of West Indian pupils could then perhaps have been dissipated.

It was also clear in this research that the children of professional and white-collar workers were far more likely to be entered for 'O' levels than the children of manual workers. Girls were more likely to be entered directly for 'O' levels in English and European languages and less for science subjects, although Asian pupils were more likely to think science subjects suitable for girls. It is of interest to note that behaviour did emerge as a criterion for examination entry. In 1981 the pupils' primary school teachers had filled out a Rutter B2 behavioural questionnaire for all the pupils prior to their entry to secondary school An analysis of the exam entries showed that pupils rated as having 'poorer' behaviour on entry for secondary schools were less likely to be studying directly for 'O' levels than those rated as better behaved. Thus discussion of definitions and perceptions of good and bad behaviour of all pupils, particularly those from ethnic minorities, would seem an important issue for teachers to focus on at option time.

Pupils' views

Pupils do have their views on option choice processes, although they are not very often solicited. Some studies which included asking pupils the reasons for their choices and satisfaction or dissatisfaction are Reid *et al.* (1974), Hurman (1978), Ryrie, Furst, and Lauder (1979) and the Schools Council (1982). In these studies, the assumption that pupils are 'free' to make choices came under scrutiny, as did the ways pupils' perceptions of their choices were influenced and constrained by guidance processes and teacher expectations. There is little research soliciting the views of minority pupils, but as noted earlier Middleton (1983) and Wright, in Eggleston, Dunn, and Anjali (1985: 212) and in this volume both discussed placement in 'bands' and 'O' level groups with minority pupils. Wright reported that even some white pupils were of the opinion that black pupils with similar school marks to them were less likely to be placed in 'O' level classes.

In the eighteen schools pupils were asked whether they were happy with their subject choice and exam entry for their final two years of compulsory schooling, whether they would have liked to study more of particular subjects, why they thought they were unable to take certain subjects, and whether they thought their exam entry levels were 'right for them'.

All pupils, overall, thought they had 'a lot' or 'quite a lot' of subject choice, although Asian, particularly Pakistani, pupils were less likely to think this. Pupils' perceptions of the amount of choice they have, and their satisfaction with the process, is perhaps more complicated than might be expected, and varied considerably between the areas and the schools. Having 'a lot' of perceived choice does not necessarily lead to satisfaction with the intended curriculum. For example, Indian pupils tended to think they had more choice and were satisfied. African-Asian and Pakistani pupils thought they had rather less choice and were less satisfied, while Bangladeshi pupils thought they had least choice but were most satisfied! Afro-Caribbean pupils were as likely as UK/Eire to be satisfied with their option choices but less inclined to think they had much choice. However, when satisfaction with choices was analysed by gender, socio-economic group, and single parentage as well as ethnic group, it did appear that the 'white, male, middle-class pupil from the two-parent family' was the most satisfied client at option choice time. Those who study educational disadvantage might be tempted to ask whether we have been here before!

Pupils' views on subjects they would have liked to take, or take more of, and their reason for feeling debarred, were also quite complex. There is perhaps a message for curriculum planners and developers that *all* the pupils, of whatever gender, ethnic group, or socio-economic group, would have liked to study more separate sciences and humanities. This may have been the result of pupil observations that these were academic subjects usually regarded as of higher status, or it could have been, as one pupil explained because 'some things they give you, you can learn out of school but there's some that you can only learn in school'.

Racial inequality in education

It was noticeable that Asian pupils, who were actually rather more likely than other pupils to be taking the separate sciences, were anxious to study yet more of these, followed by the humanities (except for Bangladeshi pupils who wanted more creative subjects). Afro-Caribbean pupils also wanted to study more separate sciences and humanities most, but followed this by wanting more practical, creative, and commercial courses. The most frequent reason offered by pupils as to why they could not take a desired subject was ability, they thought they were 'not good enough'. It seem that schools do manage to convey this view to pupils quite successfully. They also convey the message that certain subjects are only for those of low ability. Pupils wanting to take particular subjects could be put off by being given this information. The third most popular reason was behavioural, some pupils thought that the teacher 'wouldn't accept me' or had debarred them because of bad behaviour. Asian pupils were most likely to ascribe their prohibition from certain subjects to a lack of ability in themselves, but were also over twice as likely as all other groups to avoid subjects they perceived as being only for those of low ability. They and the Afro-Caribbean pupils were most likely to find that 'the teacher wouldn't accept me' for a particular subject, and it was Afro-Caribbean pupils who were most likely to think they had been debarred on behavioural grounds: 17 per cent thought this, against 9 per cent of UK/Eire pupils and 4 per cent of Asian pupils.

All the pupils in this study thought they should be doing more examinations, hardly any thought they were doing 'too many' exams.

Table 7.4 *Options thought by pupils to be 'right for ability' by ethnic origin*

	UK/Eire (%)	Asians (%)	Afro-Caribbean (%)	Others (%)	
Yes for ability	68	62	62	63	
More CSEs	2	3	1	2	
More 'O's	8	12	11	7	
Too many exams	0.4	1	0	2	
More 16+	0.8	1	1	0.9	
Don't know which exams entered for yet	20	20	24	22	
					Total
(Numbers)	(766)	(376)	(84)	(307)	(1533)

Table 7.5   *Options thought by pupils to be 'right for ability' by Asians in detail*

	Indian (%)	Pakistani (%)	Bangla-deshi (%)	African/ Asian (%)	Sub continent mixed (%)
Yes for ability	61	63	68	53	79
More CSEs	2	4	5	3	5
More 'O's	13	10	3	21	10
Too many exams	1	1	0	1	0
More 16+ exams	1	1	0	1	0
Don't know which exams entered for yet	22	20	23	19	5
(Numbers)	(44)	(98)	(59)	(58)	(19) Total (376)

The importance of credentials and examination passes, a major message passed over by the schools in their guidance processes, had certainly been accepted. There was a clear accord between teachers and pupils that examinations were important. Ethnic minority pupils were all rather more likely to be examination-oriented than their white peers, and they were rather less likely than UK/Eire pupils to accept the schools' definitions of their abilities, and wanted to take more 'O' levels. Tables 7.4 and 7.5 show that 8 per cent of UK/Eire pupils, 12 per cent of Asians and 11 per cent of Afro-Caribbean pupils thought they should be doing more 'O' levels, and it was most likely that African-Asian pupils thought this. Although about a fifth of all pupils recorded that for some subjects they did not yet know which exam they were entered for, this, as noted previously, varied considerably between schools. There were also considerable differences between schools as to whether pupils thought option placements and exam levels were right for their ability. It was noticeable that in two schools with high numbers of minority pupils, more pupils felt that the school's judgement of their ability and capabilities was faulty.

Option choice as structured inequality

Evidence does seem to be accumulating that normal school processes, not designed to be 'racist' and often operated by liberal and well-intentioned teachers, can have the effect of disadvantaging pupils from particular ethnic groups, in addition to those from lower socio-economic groups and some girls. Curriculum option choice at 13+ is one such process and the process can be regarded as a structural inequality. The disadvantages which are associated with placement in a lower status curriculum, studying a primarily nonacademic, practical curriculum to lower examination levels are becoming increasingly obvious as employment possibilities dwindle and higher level credentials are required for further and higher education and training in new types of manual work. Less obvious is the need for all pupils to be offered some abstract knowledge and critical skills which will allow them to be critical and participatory citizens of a democracy, rather than studying low level courses of supposed immediate 'relevance'. Although ability is supposedly the major criterion for placement in subject and examination levels, ability is an ambiguous concept and school conceptions of ability can be affected by perceptions that pupils are members of particular social or ethnic groups and by the behaviour of individual pupils. Factors related to class, gender, ethnicity, and behaviour *can* be shown to affect the placement of pupils at option time, even those of similar ability. Also, pupils' desires to study certain subjects, or to study to certain examination levels can be deflected, and schools can employ a variety of strategies of persuasion to guide pupils and their parents.

Although teachers involved in option processes can, as most do now, consider their practices, guidance, and advice carefully where ethnic minority pupils are concerned, structural inequalities cannot easily be removed by individual action. It may be that the inequalities and disadvantages inherent in the option choice process will only be removed when the process itself is abandoned. The extension of a core curriculum for all pupils, incorporating academic, technological, and vocational elements; the removal from the curriculum of a number of lower level and 'filler' courses; the development of shorter modular courses, with perhaps credit accumulations, rather than two-year courses, and the implementation of pupil profiles and records of achievement in addition to GCSE exams, are some ways in which the final two years of compulsory schooling could be restructured and educational disadvantages for minority group pupils at option choice time be perhaps correspondingly modified.

Notes

1 This study was funded by the Department of Education and Science and carried out by S. Tomlinson and H. Tomes in 1983–84. The one-year study formed part of a

wider study carried out jointly between the Policy Studies Institute, London and the University of Lancaster, examining 'Factors associated with success in multi-ethnic schools'.

2 The variance components analysis was carried out by T. Hogarth, Policy Studies Institute. The methodology used in the whole study of multi-ethnic schools is described in a publication in preparation by P.S.I.-University of Lancaster.

References

Ball, S. J. (1981) *Beachside Comprehensive – a case study of secondary schooling*. Cambridge: Cambridge University Press.

Barrow, J., Mullard, C., and Verma, G. K. (1986) *The Two Kingdoms: Standards and Concerns, Parents and Schools*. An independent investigation into secondary schools in Brent, 1981–84. London: Borough of Brent Education Department, London.

Byrne, E. M., (1978) *Women and Education*. London: Tavistock.

Department of Education and Science (1975) *Education Survey 21: Curricular Differences for Boys and Girls*. London: HMSO.

—— (1979) *Aspects of Secondary Education*. London: HMSO.

—— (1981) *West Indian Children in Our Schools*. London: HMSO.

—— (1985) *Education For All: The Report of the Committee of Inquiry into the Education of Children from Ethnic Minority Groups*, Cmnd. 9543. London: HMSO.

—— (1985) *Better Schools*. Cmnd. 9469. London: HMSO.

Eggleston, S. J., Dunn, D. K., and Anjali, M. with the assistance of Wright, C. (1985). *The Educational and Vocational Experiences of 15–18 Year Old Young People of Ethnic Minority Groups*. A report to the Department of Education and Science. Warwick: University of Warwick.

Ford, J. (1969) *Social Class and the Comprehensive School*. London: Routledge & Kegan Paul.

Gray, J., McPherson, A. F., and Raffe, D. (1983) *Reconstructions of Secondary Education*. London: Routledge & Kegan Paul.

Hargreaves, D. (1984) *Improving Secondary Schools*. Report of the committee on the curriculum and organization of secondary schools. London: Inner London Education Authority.

Homan, R. (1986) The supplementary school–Development and Implications. In Modgill, S. *et al.* (eds) *Multi-Cultural Education – The Interminable Debate*. Sussex: Falmer Press.

Hurman, A. (1978) *A Charter For Choice*. Slough: N.F.E.R.

Kelly, A. (1979) Why girls don't do science. *Collaborative Research Newsletter* No 4: 61–8.

Middleton, B. (1983) 'Factors affecting the performance of West Indian boys in a secondary school'. Unpublished M. A. dissertation. York: University of York.

Murphy, R. J. L. (1980) Sex differences in GCE examination entry – statistics and success rates. *Educational Studies* 6(2): 169–78.

Pratt, J., Bloomfield, J., and Seale, C. (1984) *Option Choice – a Question of Equal Opportunity*. Slough: N.F.E.R.-Nelson

Reid, M. I., Barnett, R. R., and Rosenbery, H. A. (1974) *A Matter of Choice*. Slough: N.F.E.R.

Ryrie, A. C., Furst, A., and Lauder, M. (1979) *Choices and Chances — a study of pupils' subject choices and future career intentions*. London: Hodder & Stoughton.

Schools Council (1982) *Options For the Fourth — an Exploratory Study in Ten Schools*. London: Schools Council.

Smith, I. and Woodhouse, P. (1984) 'Learning your place'. *E.S.R.C. Newsletter*. 52: 16—19.

Tomlinson, S. and Tomes, H. (1985) *Curriculum Option Choice in Multi-ethnic Schools*. Report to the Department of Education and Science. Lancaster: University of Lancaster.

Wardle, D. (1978) Sixty years on — the progress of women's education 1918—1978. *Trends in Education* Vol. 4: 3—7.

8   Black students –
white teachers

Cecile Wright

The educational attainment of Britain's black population has been the subject of considerable debate in recent years. The prime focus of this debate seems to rest on two issues: the educational attainment of students with different ethnic backgrounds, and the factors which affect their attainment. Firstly, the controversy surrounding the issue of the low educational attainment of black students of Afro-Caribbean origin compared with those of Asian origin or white students, is the concern of inter-ethnic comparison of educational attainment. Writers such as Reeves and Chevannes (1981) and Troyna (1984) have argued that inter-ethnic comparison of attainment is likely to lead to a gross, over-simplified and distorted picture of the nature of the black students', particularly Afro-Caribbean students', educational performance.

The second issue centres on the factors which may influence the educational attainment of black students. The report of the Committee of Inquiry into the education of children from ethnic minority groups (Swann Report 1985) argued that it has long been known that, as far as white students are concerned, poverty and poor housing are linked with underachievement at school and that 'It is now clear, as one would expect, that ethnic minority children suffer in a similar way' (DES 1985: 81–2).

Whilst we acknowledge the existence of socio-economic factors and the influence that these can exert on black students' educational performance, we should not, however, be saying that the school is impotent in this situation. Rather it poses the question of whether there are processes outside the school which generate differences in educational attainment within black groups and between black and white students, and whether there are processes within the school which act to reinforce such differentiation. Putting this a slightly different way, what influence do school practices, procedures, and organization exert on the educational outcome of black students?

To date there is still a lack of critical investigation into school processes to ascertain whether there is in fact a link between these and black students' educational attainment. This is in spite of the dissatisfaction expressed by black parents for many years about the nature of the education their children are receiving. Indeed Stone (1981) and others have informed us that the creation of supplementary schools within the black community, particularly the Afro-Caribbean community, arose out of the concern that the schools seem unable to help their children pass the examinations increasingly needed for employment in Britain. The rise of supplementary schools, therefore, can be seen as a message from the black community which states that the nature of black students' educational attainment lay fundamentally within the structure of the education system, in particular the school. (See also Chevannes and Reeves in this volume).

This chapter presents evidence from my own research which suggests a strong association between school processes and the educational attainment of Afro-Caribbean students. The evidence is taken from an intensive ethnographic and statistical survey of two multiracial comprehensive schools between 1982 and 1984. A cohort of Afro-Caribbean girls and boys from both schools were studied in their fourth and fifth years at school. In addition to extensive classroom observations, assessment data accumulated on each student were analysed, along with an examination of the school's allocation procedures.

The observed classroom relationships between the white teachers and the Afro-Caribbean students is described below. The outcomes of the nature of the social relations between teachers and these students are assessed. Finally, the implications which the evidence presented raises for the conceptualizing of black students' experience of schooling is considered.

Teachers' attitudes, expectations, and classroom interaction

The classroom encounters observed for both schools showed the interaction between the teacher and the individual Afro-Caribbean student to be frequently characterized by confrontation and conflict. Classroom interaction between the teacher and these students often takes the form of the teacher enforcing his or her authority and/or expressing criticism. Moreover, those aspects of classroom life which gave rise to conflict between the teacher and the Afro-Caribbean student were observed to be often incidental to the real business of teaching. For instance, some teachers were observed frequently to intersperse their lectures with remarks or jokes regarding the Afro-Caribbean student's ethnicity and physical characteristics. Such an act on the part of the teacher was observed to cause considerable distress to these students.

Observations suggest that behind the quality of interactions which exist between the teachers and their Afro-Caribbean students were the generally adverse attitudes and expectations which the teachers held regarding these students. Field notes and the dialogue from two of the lessons observed serve to support this claim. Also, later in the chapter we will find in the conversations of the Afro-Caribbean students references to the classroom encounter report for one of the lessons (i.e. Mr Gray's lesson), which demonstrates the degree to which adversities experienced at the hands of certain teachers become firmly fixed in the minds of these students and influence their perception of schooling.

Metal work CSE (Mr Gray)

This metal work class comprised two Asian boys, five Afro-Caribbean boys, and fourteen white boys. The teacher's relationship with most of the students was fairly amicable, but his relationship with most of the Afro-Caribbean boys was observed to be characterized by high degrees of antagonism. ·

Central to the nature of the relationship between the teacher and the Afro-Caribbean boys, was the teacher's classroom management style used for enforcing discipline and learning. In general, the methods used by the teacher were those of taunting, name-calling, and verbal sparring with the students. This management style when applied to the Afro-Caribbean boys (unlike the case for other student categories) was used in such a manner that the students were inevitably forced into highly significant face-winning, face-retaining, and face-losing contests between them and the teacher. Furthermore, the Afro-Caribbean boys considered the teacher's overt lack of respect for their colour as being central to the teacher's treatment of them.

The following exchanges between the teacher and some of the Afro-Caribbean boys serve to illustrate this point.

The teacher was talking to the class. While he wrote on the black-board, a group of four white boys sat talking to each other in an ordinary tone of voice. The teacher, being annoyed by the noise level in the room, threw a piece of chalk at an Afro-Caribbean boy who was not being particularly noisy.

Teacher [*shouting*] Pay attention.

Teacher [*to an Asian boy*] Could you get me that piece of chalk.

Peter (*Afro-Caribbean boy*) Why don't you use black chalk?

Teacher [*turning to the researcher*] Did you hear that? Then I would be accused of being racist. Take this for example. I was down at Lower School; I had a black girl in my class. She did something or another. I said to her, if you're not careful I'll send you back to the chocolate factory. She went home and told her parents. Her dad came up to school, and decided to take the matter to the Commission for Racial Equality. It was only said in good fun, nothing malicious.

Keith (*Afro-Caribbean*) [*aggressively*] How do we know that it's a joke. In my opinion that was a disrespectful thing to say.

Teacher [*raising his voice and pointing his finger at Keith*] If I wanted to say something maliciously racist, I wouldn't have to make a joke about it. I'd say it. I've often had a joke with you, haven't I?

Keith [*angrily*] Those so-called jokes, were no joke, you were being cheeky. I went home and told my mum and she said that if you say it again she would come and sort you out. As for that girl, if it was my father, he wouldn't just take you to the CRE, he would also give you a good thump. My father says that a teacher should set a good example for the children, by respecting each one, whether them black or white. He says that any teacher who makes comments like that in front of a class, shouldn't be in school that's why he said to us if a teacher ever speaks to us like that he would come up to school and sort him out.

Harry [*Afro-Caribbean*] If it was me that you said that to, I wouldn't go home and tell my parents, I would just tell you about your colour.

Keith Teachers shouldn't make racist jokes.

Keith was eventually sent out of the class to see the headmaster for being insolent.

In an informal conversation with the teacher after the lesson, when we talked about the classroom event, it became clear from the teacher's comments, that he recognized that a poor relationship existed between him and most of the Afro-Caribbean boys. The nature of this he attributed largely to the students' low ability and their attitudes. As the teacher states:

'It is very difficult to teach students like Keith Thomas, Steven Hutton, and Calvin Fern, who are really remedials. These students and other black students have this thing about their colour, this chip on their shoulder about being black. They have accused me of being racist. I must admit that I can be racist at times, but I'm not aware of being racist towards them. To an educated person like yourself [referring to the researcher] you don't use the issue of race to explain everything; however, to these black children of no or low ability, they use this as an explanation almost all the time.'

English language CSE (Miss Simms)

This class of middle ability band students was taught English language as a form group. The group comprised three Asian girls, six Asian boys, one Afro-Caribbean boy, six Afro-Caribbean girls, one Chinese boy, three white girls, and eight white boys. There was generally a noisy start to most lessons, and it often took the teacher several attempts to secure silence.

Once silence had been established, however, the students usually settled down to work and appeared to show a degree of involvement in the task they were given. The teacher's relationship with the class and in particular between her and some of the Afro-Caribbean girls was often a strained one.

Teacher I really dislike this group, they are the worst group I have in terms of behaviour and motivation. The problem is, a certain group of students, they make things very difficult. I'm referring to the group of four West Indian girls who sit together. I suppose it's something to do with group dynamics. On their own they are reasonable. This group of girls are always in trouble with other teachers and their parents have constantly to be brought in.

In addition to perceiving the Afro-Caribbean girls as a threat to her classroom management skills, the teacher also held the Afro-Caribbean girls directly responsible for what she considered to be her inability to establish conducive learning conditions. As she states: 'If this group of Afro-Caribbean girls were not in the class, I feel I'd be able to do a much more effective teaching job with the others. . .'

Such a deduction on the part of the teacher, it may be assumed, cannot be conducive to enhancing a good teacher—student relationship. Indeed, observations show the classroom relations between most of the Afro-Caribbean girls in this class and the teacher to be based on frequent open confrontations, which generally took the form illustrated in the following classroom incident:

The teacher was already in the classroom when the students arrived for the lesson. The students arrived five minutes later than normal because they had been to assembly.

Teacher Sit down quietly 4L

[*The teacher stood at her desk waiting for the students to settle down*]

Teacher Will you all settle down quickly, I've waited long enough. On the board is a comprehension question taken from last year's CSE English language paper. I would like you to work through this question, work in your English folder. I will collect your work for marking at the end of the lesson. Now please get on quietly.

The students worked in silence. The turning of pages and a student tapping a pen on a desk are the only sounds. The teacher is sitting at her desk at the front of the room marking a pile of books. The silence continues for ten minutes; then a chair scrapes as an Asian girl leans forward to talk to the white girl sitting in front; four other students begin to talk. There is low level noise in the classroom.

Teacher [*looks up from her marking and barks at the whole class*] Right, quiet please and get on with your work.

The silence resumes, and is then broken by an Asian girl talking aloud to an Afro-Caribbean boy.

Kulwinder (Asian girl) Hey Vincent when will we be having our maths exam?

Other students begin talking amongst themselves. The teacher looks up from her marking as a result of the increasing classroom noise. She looks to the back of the classroom where four Afro-Caribbean girls sit, talking amongst themselves.

Teacher [*in a raised voice*] Will you four girls stop talking and get on with your work.

Barbara (Afro-Caribbean) We are working, we're just talking about the question.

Jean (Afro-Caribbean) It's not only us talking. What about her [*pointing to Kulwinder*] shouting, why do you always pick on us?

Whilst the teacher was talking to the Afro-Caribbean girls, three white boys sat playing with a pocket computer game, which the girls had noticed.

Teacher Whenever I look up you're always talking.

Barbara That's 'cause you only see us, everybody else is talking. Look at them [*pointing to the boys playing with the computer game*] they're not even working. [*Turning to the other Afro-Caribbean girls and talking in a loud whisper*] Damn facety.

The Afro-Caribbeans burst into laughter at Barbara's comment to them.

Teacher [*shrilled*] Barbara and Jean will you leave the room.
The girls leave the room, closing the door loudly behind them.
Teacher [*to the class*] Will the rest of you settle down now, and get on with your work. I'll be gone for just a few minutes.
The teacher leaves the room.

In an interview with the teacher after the lesson, she had this to say about the two Afro-Caribbean girls and the incident which had led her to send them out of the lesson:

'Well I'd say perhaps I have more problems with them than most in the class, perhaps they are the ones whom I'm usually driven to send to Mrs Crane [deputy headmistress for discipline]. I'll put up with so much but they're inclined to become very rude sometimes, which others wouldn't do. They know their limits but those two frequently go over them. It's difficult because I've tried having them sitting separately which doesn't seem to improve things because then they just become very resentful and will try then to kind of communicate across the room, which is almost worse than this business here. As I've said before they're quite good workers, when they get down to it they enjoy the actual work and they usually get good marks. Their work is generally handed in on time and nicely presented. As I've said, I've sent them out quite frequently and I know lots of other teachers have the same problems. I'm not sure what the solution is. I believe things are being done with them'.

Researcher What happened when you sent Barbara and Jean out of the lesson and you followed them out?
Teacher I sent them down to Mrs Crane. I told them to take a note and just wait outside her room. They got into so much trouble last term, she [the deputy headmistress] threatened to bring their parents up. I don't know if it actually got to that. I never know quite what to expect, what sort of mood they will be in, they are either in a bad mood or a good mood. Yes I can't tell really, and I find it difficult because I resent having to jolly them along which I do slightly. Because if I just home in on them straight away at the beginning of the lesson and normally they do start their chattering and things right away. Well I try to put up with so much. They react, they just resent it, if I do tell them off. But then I mean they do accept it. In the past when I've sent them off to Mrs Crane, and after perhaps a blazing row, or having brought her up here [to the classroom], and we have had a big confrontation and I expect them

to be quite cool for weeks afterwards, or really rude. And they haven't been at all. Really I have no reason to believe that they would not come in as charming as anything next lesson, or they'll be troublesome, it just depends on them more than me.

The teacher's conversation, when analysed, provides insight not only into possible factors underlying the incident between her and the Afro-Caribbean girls, but also an indication of the criteria used for judging the girls as 'unteachable'.

Firstly, the teacher considers the Afro-Caribbean girls' behaviour in class to be generally unpredictable, as her own comments suggest; she therefore invariably expected the girls to be 'troublesome' in class, and as a consequence, also expected to be engaged in frequent confrontation with them. Furthermore, this teacher appeared to use the experiences of other teachers with the girls, both to support and explain her expectations and judgement of them. As a result of her expectations any conciliatory act on the part of the girls towards her following a confrontation, she was inclined to treat with a degree of suspicion, as being out of character, and subsequently dismissed.

Secondly, the teacher considers the girls to be academically able and co-operative in their attitude to work, and this was borne out by observations. Yet from her behaviour towards the students it appeared that these features received only secondary consideration from the teacher, compared to the students' alleged 'troublesome' classroom behaviour.

Afro-Caribbean students' views on school and classroom life

Conversations with the Afro-Caribbean girls and boys in both schools, in an attempt to ascertain their perspectives on school and classroom life and their adaptation to their perceived experiences, suggest that these students often wonder whether there is anything more to classroom activity for them than insults, criticisms, and directives.

A discussion with a group of Afro-Caribbean girls in which they talked vividly of their experience of some teachers supports this claim:

Barbara The teachers here, them annoy you, too much.
Researcher In what ways do they annoy you?
Barbara They irate you in the lesson, so you can't get to work.
Group Yeah.
Barbara One day Mr Beresford gave the class a piece of work to do, I type fairly fast and so I finished first. I took the piece of work to Mr Beresford and told him I'd finished the work, he said that I wasn't

the only person in the class and he had to see other children before me. I asked a question on the work and he gave me a funny answer saying 'I should know by using a typist's intuition'. I told him I wouldn't be able to know, if we were told to do straightforward copying, with that he threw the piece of paper at me. I was angry, so I threw it back at him. . .

In the third year, I did sewing with Mrs Lewis, we got on well until one day, she kept telling me off for talking loud, then she accused me of saying 'How now brown cow' and sent me down to Mrs Crane [deputy headmistress for discipline]. She insisted that I did call it Mrs Lewis, even though I kept telling her I didn't know what it meant and that I didn't even know a verse like that existed. I got sent out of the lesson for the rest of that year, which was about four and five months. . .

I was thrown out of sewing by Mrs Lewis, out of French for some reason I can't remember why, out of art, for a misunderstanding with the teacher about wiping glue off some scissors, out of office practice about three times for about a period of two to three weeks each time. . . . I've been in trouble all my school life, I think the girl who I used to hang around with gave the teachers the impression I wasn't worth the bother. I feel some teachers are prejudiced.

Vera Yeah, I agree with her, take the cookery teacher.

Susan For example in cookery, there were some knives and forks gone missing, right, and Mrs Bryan goes 'Where's the knives and forks?' looking at us lot [the Afro-Caribbean pupils in the class].

Vera Yeah, all the blacks.

Sonia Seriously right, in the past most coloured children that has left school they've all said she's prejudiced.

Jean She's told some kids to go back to their own country.

Sonia Seriously right, if you go to another white teacher or somebody, an' tell them that they're being prejudiced against you, they'll make out it's not, that it's another reason.

Jean When Mrs Bryan told Julie to go back to her own country, she went and told Mrs Crane. Mrs Crane said that Mrs Bryan was depressed because her husband was dying.

Sonia So why take it out on the black people. Then she's told black people to do many things, she's even called them monkey.

Sandra As for that Mrs Crane I can't explain my feelings about the woman. Because Mrs Bryan, right she just prejudiced, she comes up to me in the cookery lesson, tell me to clean out the dustbin, and I was so vexed I started to cry, I was so vexed by it. I didn't come to school for two weeks.

Sonia You see the thing is right, they can get away with saying anything to your face, there isn't anything you can do about it.

Jean In geography, this teacher dashed a book at me, and I dashed it back, and I got into trouble for it.

[*Group roared with laughter*]

Vera Most of the things that the teacher says, right, they say things that annoy you they know that you're going to answer them back, so they can get you into trouble. Take Mrs Bryan she'll walk around with a towel, and if you look at someone and smile and she thinks you're talking, she flash water in your face or she'll slap you over the head, but I've just told her that if she boxes me I'll have to hit her back. Because she's got no right to walk round doing that. If you answer her back in any way, then she'll send you down to Mrs Crane then you're in trouble.

Susan Mrs Crane is prejudiced herself because, I mean, she said to Karen that she is only getting bad because she hangs around with too many black people. It's not as if [*shouting in anger*] as she says, black people are going to change you to bad.

Vera Some teachers are all right but others, you can tell that they're prejudiced by the things they do. Every time Mrs Bryan is cooking, even if she's doing say, a boiled egg or something like that, any little simple thing you can think of, coloured people and Asian people have to cook it different. . . . 'Oh, well the coloured people and Asian people always cook their things different. . .'.

Jean [*with disdain*] Is that what she says?

Vera Yeah, she's really facety you know, that's why I don't get on with her, and when I was telling me mum, me mum was going mad because she must think that we're some aliens, or something. . . . If the teachers have no respect for you, there's no way I'm going to respect them.

Mr Newson [new headmaster] all he does now is go straight onto the teacher's side and then the next minute that student is suspended, for doing something really daft. . . . Look at Jane [Afro-Caribbean girl] she got up in the classroom, and she was walking to the door and Mr Webb said to her 'Where are you going?' she said, 'I'm not going nowhere' 'Well', he said to her, 'Well sit down then'. Jane was walking back slow, right, and he just went behind her and pushed her and told her to go and sit down. So Jane turned around and pushed him back. She said, 'Listen you're not my dad so don't push me around' and he goes 'get out and go to Mrs Crane'. Mrs Crane sent her to Miss Roberts [at the time the head of school, who suspended Jane. Vera is claiming that the suspension decision was upheld by the headmistress' successor – the new headmaster]. And Miss Roberts suspended her, Miss Roberts left and just left it at a dead-end like that. They didn't say nothing to Jane's mum, they didn't say nothing to Jane. All they said to Jane was that she can't come back to the school until further notice, and up till now its been eleven weeks, she haven't been back to school. And it was about two weeks ago she had a governor meeting and that's when they told her that she can't come back to school. So you're made to miss out on your education for reasons like that.

Researcher Would you say that the Afro-Caribbean boys have the same experience with the teachers as yourselves?

Vera The boys I know don't get the same treatment because most of the lads are quicker to box the teachers–dem than the girls, you see.

Group Yeah.

Similarly a group of eight Afro-Caribbean boys were asked about their school and classroom experience. They responded as follows:

Mullings The teachers here are too facety, they don't give you a chance.

Michael For example Hill [Anglo-Afro-Caribbean boy] who was expelled.

Paul That just prejudice, he never did nothing wrong.

Michael He never done nothin' much you know. He's half-caste, but he was more to the coloured people dem.

Researcher Why was he expelled?

Michael What it is I think he got suspended three times and he was on report, kept getting bad grade, they just put him in front of the governors. Yet a big skinhead [white boy] right, he go in front of the governors three times already, right, they expelled him. He came back, and dem let him back in a de school yesterday.

Paul Teachers look down on you, Mr Parks, Mr Gordon, Mr Henry, Mr Gray, and some others. I can remember the time I was in metal work, Mr Gray keep saying to me why you've a tan? Why have you got a tan? I say well I've been like this all me life. He say, well you should go back to the chocolate factory, and be remade or something like that [*with anger*] that's not nice at all.

Michael One day I was in there [in the classroom] so I don't know what happened between him and Errol, he came up to me and say, 'Why Paul, Errol, and Delroy is always giving us hassle' and all that. So I said, 'Oh well, you know how Paul and Delroy are, they won't take anything off you lot in'it. If anything, them like to stick up for them rights.' So he said to me, 'You know I like running a joke, Michael.'

119

Keith Mr Gray, right, he says it's a complete joke what he says to black kids, he said one day he was at lower school and he came in [the classroom] and said to this girl, this coloured girl was a bit upset, so he said to her 'What's wrong with you?' and he said, 'I'll have to send you back to Cadbury's to let them wipe the smile on your face' and the girl went home and told her father. And her father took her to the Race Relations Board, and he [Mr Gray] says he's to go to court.

Michael One day I was in there [in the classroom] I don't know what him and Errol had but Errol called him a 'motherfucker', what happened between him and you?

Errol We were messing about right, he said something about black people. So I called him a motherfucker, he looked at me.

Michael He said, him going to dash you out of the school in'it?

Errol He could have but he didn't.

Michael It's like once the man [referring to the teacher] come in the class, and ask me in front of the class, 'Why me coffee coloured?' he say, 'How come Wallace dark, and Kennedy Black, and Kevin a bit browner? How come you that, you a half-breed? Me say, 'No man, me no look like me half-breed.' Me say, 'Just like some a una white like a chalk and another couple a una got blond hair, some have black hair, me no come ask wha that. That's how he is, he just come around, crack him few sarcastic jokes about black kids.'

Paul But they're not nice at all. They're not nice. The jokes aren't nice. The jokes are disrespectful.

Keith They're not jokes man.

Errol You can't call them jokes. When he cracks a joke or whatever he does in front of the class, he just turn round and laugh. You get him and the class laughing at you.

Keith What he is doing is running you down. He's just bringing you down like dirt. Nobody is bring me down [*said with anger*]. Every time I'm chuck out of (*subject*) completely man, because every time in (*subject*) he always keep calling me something about me colour and I answer back.

Errol The teachers are forever picking on the black boys.

Michael Like me now, them no too bother with me because them think, say me a half-breed, you know. Half the teachers in the school think say me a half-breed so they don't too bother me. Just lately they find out, say me black, so they've started bothering me. Like the half-caste kids them they used to left me alone.

Keith They don't give half-caste kids no hassle, no hassle whatsoever. However, if the half-caste kids act black, they pick on them, hassle man.

Errol And the Asians.

Group Yeah.

Researcher Are you all also saying that the Asian students are not treated in the same way by some teachers, as you suggest, the Afro-Caribbean students are treated?

Keith Because with the Asians, right, Asians just keep themselves to themselves like we now, we just want equality with the white people. Asians don't speak their minds, they keep it all in because they are afraid.

Michael They get fling around, they won't say nothing about it.

Keith Because of that Asians are better off than black students that's all I can say.

Paul Yeah, Asians aren't the ones what go around causing trouble with the teachers.

Researcher Are you all saying then, that the Afro-Caribbean or black children, as you put it, go around causing trouble?

Group [*defensively*] No, No.

Keith No, the thing that we want right, we want equality just like the white people, we want equal rights.

Paul I'm not saying that we cause trouble, but I'm just saying the teachers think black boys are always going round causing trouble. That's what they think.

Keith Teachers look down on you.

The Afro-Caribbean boys were asked to explain further how the nature of the relationship which they considered existed between some teachers and themselves affected their behaviour towards these teachers. Using their analysis the students felt that they were forced into a stimulus—response situation; as the dialogues which follow demonstrate:

Paul The school don't respect black students. We are treated badly, we are forever hassled. I can remember the time I was in (subject), Mr X keep saying to me 'Why you've got a tan?' I say, 'Well I was born like this.' He say, 'Well you should go back to the chocolate factory and be remade', or something like that. To me that wasn't a nice thing to say.

Kevin We are treated unfairly, because we are black. They look after their flesh not ours.

Michael They look after fe them white people-dem, you know what I mean, but we get dash at the back all the time.

Researcher You have all said that you feel that you are treated unfairly in the school. How do you feel this makes you behave?

Delroy Bad.

Researcher When you say 'bad' what exactly do you mean by this?

Paul It means that we turn around and make trouble for them.

Delroy Yeah, we try to get our own back on them. We behave ignorantly towards them, and when the teachers talk to us and tell us to do something we don't do it, because we just think about how they treated us.

Paul Like when you walk down the corridor, and a teacher stops you, you just ignore him. When they stop you for no reason you just irated.

Researcher How about you, Errol?

Errol I try to keep out of trouble the best I can. If they cause trouble with me I cause trouble with them it's as simple as that. If you are a troublemaker, right, and you're pretty intelligent, they still keep you down. Look what they've done to Delroy, he's pretty intelligent, yet they keep him down, no wonder he causes trouble. Because I want to get on I try to keep out of trouble.

The Afro-Caribbean girls and boys in their conversations seem to be expressing similar complaints and dissatisfaction regarding their teachers' attitudes and behaviour towards them. Certainly similarities were observed in the way in which they both responded to their teachers' treatment of them. For instance, in the classroom they were both prepared to openly confront and challenge the teacher, using Jamaican patois in their exchanges with the teacher. There was no doubt that in this situation some teachers felt quite threatened by the student use of a dialect they could not understand. The teachers' anxiety served only to accentuate their negative attitudes and behaviour towards those students who used patois. For the Afro-Caribbean students the use of a mode of communication outside the cultural repertoire of the teacher is intended to undermine the teacher's authority. In many instances this strategy was observed to be quite effective.

Another way in which the Afro-Caribbean students, particularly the boys, responded to the poor relationship which existed between them and their teachers was to organize into a large all Afro-Caribbean group which moved around the school at break time baiting the teachers and subjecting them to a barrage of patois. In the words of one student the purpose of their behaviour was to 'get our own back for what they [teachers] do to us.' Moreover, in behaving in this way, these students also entered into a self-fulfilling prophesy, which further appeared to justify the teachers' expectations of them.

The outcome of the Afro-Caribbean
student–teacher relations

As argued so far the relationship between teachers and Afro-Caribbean students within both schools was often antagonistic. There is evidence to suggest that the quality of this student–teacher relationship may precipitate certain sanctions taken by the school against these pupils, the ultimate sanction being the removal of students from the school. Data examined on the suspension and expulsion for the year group studied for both schools reveal a higher proportion of suspension and expulsion amongst Afro-Caribbean students, even though they constituted the smallest ethnic group. In one school, for instance, over half of the students from this year group suspended or expelled were Afro-Caribbean. In addition to this it was found that none of these students expelled from the school in the fourth year were offered alternative education provision, signifying that these students were thus entirely without formal education. Indeed, in the Afro-Caribbean students' conversations above, the issue of suspension and expulsion is emphatically discussed indicating how very real this issue is to their experience of schooling.

Another way in which the Afro-Caribbean students were also found to be denied educational opportunities as a consequence of the adverse relationship between them and their teachers, stemmed from what was found to be their teachers' faulty assessment of their abilities and achievements. Evidence suggests that in their assessment of the Afro-Caribbean students the teachers allowed themselves to be influenced more by behaviour criteria than cognitive ones. That is, the Assessment given would be most likely to reflect the teachers' subjective involvement with the complex behavioural aspects of classroom relations. This in turn led to a situation where Afro-Caribbean students, more so than any other student groups, were likely to be placed in ability bands and examination sets well below their actual academic ability. This indicates that in their assessment of the Afro-Caribbean students' ability the teachers were less able to exercise professional judgement. This claim is clearly demonstrated in Table. 8.1, which shows the allocation of students to examination sets, for one school.

The scores in the table represent the students' third year examination marks. At this school students are allocated to an 'O' Level or CSE couse at the beginning of their fourth year on the basis of their performance in the third year examination. An analysis of the allocation of Afro-Caribbean, Asian, and white students, clearly shows that a higher proportion of Afro-Caribbean students appear to be allocated to examination sets below his or her ability (i.e. Afro-Caribbean student

Table 8.1   *School B: individual students and allocation to exam sets*

Student		Subject marks (out of 100)				Set placement (O=GCE 'O' level)			
		Eng.	Maths	French	Physics	Eng.	Maths	French	Physics
Afro-Carib.	A	73	44	58	–	CSE	CSE	CSE	–
	B	62	63	60	59	CSE	CSE	CSE	CSE
	C	64	45	56	72	CSE	CSE	–	CSE
	D	68	37	82	–	CSE	CSE	CSE	–
Asian	E	51	77	–	55	O	O	–	O
	F	60	56	58	–	O	O	O	–
	G	61	62	55½	–	O	O	O	–
	H	54	55	–	40	O	O	–	O
White	I	61	62	–	62	O	O	–	O
	J	52	57	55	–	O	O	O	O
	K	75	82	77½	72	O	O	O	O
	L	54	75	64	72	O	O	O	O

'D' having attained eighty two per cent in French, is allocated to a CSE set) than is the case for the other two student groups.

The apparent misplacement of the Afro-Caribbean students on the basis of their ability, would strongly suggest that within this school overt discriminatory practices were operating against the Afro-Caribbean students. A suggestion which is perhaps supported by the comment of one of the teachers, who had this to say about the placement of Afro-Caribbean student 'D' in a CSE examination set: 'This student has been on the fringe of trouble all year, her attitude to the teachers is not at all good, she can be a nuisance in class.'

It seems obvious from this teacher's statement and from the allocation figures represented in Table 8.1 that ability is a positive quality in some teachers' eyes, only if it is shown by a white, and possibly an Asian, student.

Certainly, the Afro-Caribbean students in their conversations expressed anger that the teachers had low expectations of their abilities and in some cases prevented them entering for certain public examinations. However they were optimistic that they would be able to undertake the courses at the college of further education, denied them by the school. The following student's comment would appear to suggest this:

'I've been entered for all CSEs: Typing, Maths, English, Social Studies, and Art. I haven't been entered for Office Practice and French. For Office Practice it was my teacher's decision. She said, that I didn't have enough pieces of course work [project] to be recommended, even though a friend [white girl] of mine has less pieces of work and has been entered. I do feel a bit bitter about it but I've decided I will retake it when I go to college.'

An analysis of the overall attainment in the public examinations (that is CSEs and 'O' levels) for all the students in the year group studied for both schools was undertaken. Figures show that the proportion of Afro-Caribbean students entered for, and thus gaining 'O' levels, was dramatically lower than for the Asian and white students. The educational attainment of the Afro-Caribbean students is particularly alarming when it is realized that in one of the schools, the Afro-Caribbean students (for the year group studied) entered the school at eleven plus with an average reading age slightly above the whole intake for the year.

One of the many issues emanating from the research findings presented in this chapter is that of the conceptualization of black students' (particularly those of Afro-Caribbean origin) educational performance in the British school system. It was suggested at the beginning of the chapter that in recent years the educational performance and attainment of Afro-Caribbean students have been conceptualized in terms of 'underachievement'. (e.g. Taylor 1981; DES 1985). The notion of underachievement of Afro-Caribbean students has a number of built-in assumptions. One such assumption is based upon the liberal philosophy of equality of opportunity and the meritocratic ideal, that is, the taken-for-granted idea that schooling serves as an arena for self-realization/actualization, developing abilities to the full, and for maximizing society's talents. Another assumption is that the experiences of different groups of children within the education system are roughly similar. The Afro-Caribbean students' experience of school presented in this chapter clearly casts doubts over these assumptions.

It is evident from the findings in this chapter that within the classroom, in allocation to sets, streams, or bands, and in examination entries, complex processes may be involved which serve to disadvantage black students, particularly those of Afro-Caribbean origins. Moreover, it is clear that assignment of students to groups undertaking a lower standard of work than they are capable of and in turn entering them for lower level examinations or no examinations at all can affect the type of school level qualifications attained. This can exclude them altogether from particular subjects or from their school.

It is also apparent that students subjected to these processes will not attain examination results which reflect their ability. Therefore, inferences derived from comparisons of type or level of attainment in public examinations can raise serious interpretation difficulties, and may even serve to reinforce processes which have given rise to observed differentials.

Fundamentally, it is considered that the nature of the education experience of black students, especially those of Afro-Caribbean origin, may be better understood in terms of 'educational disadvantage' or 'inequality' rather than in terms of 'underachievement.' In advancing this type of analysis, we are drawing attention to the structural and institutional realities within which the situation of the black student within the education system needs to be understood.

Notes

1 The majority of the teaching staff in the two schools studied were white.
2 The names of both the teachers and the students have been altered to preserve anonymity.
3 The English translation of Jamaican patois words frequently used by the Afro-Caribbean students is as follows:

Jamaican	*English*
de	the
dem	them
facety	impertinent/insulting

References

Department of Education and Science (1985) *Education for All: The Report of the Committee of Inquiry into the Education of Children from Ethnic Minority Groups*, Cmnd 9543. London: HMSO.

Eggleston, J., Dunn, D., Anjali, M., and Wright, C. (1986) *Education for Some: The Educational and Vocational Experiences of 15–18-year-old Members of Minority Ethnic Groups*. Staffs: Trentham Books.

Reeves, F. and Chevannes, M. (1981) The under-achievement of Rampton. *Multiracial Education* 10(1): 35–42.

Stone, M. (1981) *The Education of the Black Child in Britain*. London: Fontana.

Taylor, M. (1981) *Caught Between: A Review of Research into the Education of Pupils of West Indian Origin*. London: N.F.E.R.–Nelson.

Troyna, B. (1984) Fact or artefact? The 'educational under-achievement' of black pupils. *British Journal of Sociology of Education* 5(2): 153–66.

9   The unfinished bridge: YTS and black youth

John Wrench

'The bridge between work and school? Looks like the bridge hasn't been finished — we're going to get pushed off the end after this'
(Tyneside YTS engineering trainee. 'A moment to talk' BBC2 1984)

The numerous debates and controversies over 'quality' that have surrounded the Youth Training Scheme (YTS) since its inception in 1983 tend to be sidestepped in the vocalizations of school leavers themselves. Their immediate judgement as to the value of YTS concerns potential for leading them to acceptable employment afterwards. They *want* YTS to be a bridge from school to work. The problem is that, to continue the analogy, it has now been demonstrated that black young people are more likely than white to be 'pushed off the end' of incomplete bridges (the term 'black' is used throughout this chapter to refer to people of Afro-Caribbean and Asian origin). The figures on YTS leavers covering the period April 1985 — January 1986 showed that three months after leaving the scheme 57 per cent of white young people were in full time work compared with only 35 per cent of Afro-Caribbean young people and 34 per cent of Asians (Hansard, Col. 171, 22 July 1986).

The important question to ask is whether such figures reflect endemic racial discrimination within the operation of the YTS. Though critics of the Manpower Services Commission (MSC) point out such statistics as *prima facie* evidence of racial discrimination, there could in theory be a number of alternative explanations unconnected with racism in the processes of YTS. Whilst all the available statistics of entry to and exit from YTS show systematic racial inequality, a defender of YTS might argue that statistics alone are not enough to justify cries of 'racism'.

This chapter reviews the evidence, statistical and otherwise, on the participation of black young people in YTS and comes to the conclusion

127

that, although the figures in themselves could be open to less controversial explanations, when they are taken in the context of the accumulated evidence from numerous academic and labour movement surveys and investigations, as well as the subjective accounts of trainees, managing agents, careers officers, and others, there is only one reasonable conclusion that can be reached: that the established structures of racial inequality which characterize British society are reflected in the operation of YTS, and the ubiquitous racial discrimination so evident in the processes of transition from school to work in pre-YTS days have been continued (if not enhanced) during the time of YTS.

As well as using evidence from previous research this chapter also draws on a number of interviews with careers officers, scheme supervisors, and others concerned with YTS which were carried out by the author between 1983 and 1986 as part of the research programme of the Centre for Research in Ethnic Relations (CRER). In some cases, direct quotations are reproduced from tape-recorded interviews.

Equal opportunity to what?

Before considering equality of opportunity in YTS it is important to raise one or two broader questions about the nature of YTS experience in general. For many commentators the value of YTS experience in itself is questionable, and as Fenton and Burton put it 'to be enthusiastic about having equal access to something one has to be convinced that it is something worth having' (Fenton and Burton 1987: 36). This chapter will not attempt to go over the general criticisms that YTS has attracted (for examples of these see Finn 1986; TURC 1986). It is true that individual schemes can be found which provide good quality training experience and good prospects for future employment (although the two by no means always go together). However, it must also be said there is much that is routinely poor in YTS, reflecting its underfunding, its market led philosophy, and its orientation to the (often short term) needs of employers. On reviewing the evidence from a number of quarters Benn and Fairley conclude that 'not only are there more excellent training and education advances outside the MSC but . . . within it quality appears by chance rather than design, the outcome of commitment by dedicated teachers, trainers, and workers advancing new practices in spite of − rather than because of − MSC directives' (Benn and Fairley 1986: 9).

So is equal access to such a dubious entity an issue for black school leavers? The answer must still be yes. YTS is now a major avenue to work for young people, and cannot be ignored even by those who criticize the quality of its experience. Although some school leavers still do find work straight from school at 16 the number is much diminished since pre-YTS days, and in some parts of the country, notably the areas of higher unemployment in the Midlands and North, the proportion of minimum age leavers who go into jobs is very small indeed. As has already been argued, for most young people the main motivation for participation in YTS is the hope of a job afterwards (see Horton 1986). A West Midlands survey showed that if trainees were confident of finding a job after a year 'they tended to look favourably towards their scheme even though they may have had some reservations about the level of training they were actually being given' (YETRU 1986: 4). Inequality of participation in YTS is inevitably reflected in inequality of access to jobs afterwards. Thus, whether we like YTS or not, we cannot help but be concerned that equal opportunity is observed within it.

Early optimism

When YTS was first announced there was some optimism that it may do something for the circumstances of black young people. Fenton *et al.* (1984: 9) saw that despite the early criticisms of YTS, one aspect of the scheme which received 'considerable praise' was its implied criticism of the educational system for failing to realize the potential of many young people, black youngsters included. In 1983 the equal opportunities requirement was seen to be 'an *integral* part of YTS . . . not something to be tacked on as an afterthought or as a token requirement' (as witnessed by an item received at the April 1983 meeting of the MSC's Youth Training Board: 'Equal opportunities for ethnic minorities'). From the MSC's pronouncements it seemed that equal opportunity was to be a priority, tackled centrally and monitored from the beginning. There were other grounds for optimism to be seen in the shake up of conventional apprenticeships that came with YTS and the concomitant decline of many old practices, such as the age restrictions, the traditional nepotism of craft occupations, catchment areas, and word of mouth recruitment, which had been so effective in excluding young blacks and young women from the better manual jobs (Lee and Wrench, 1987). Furthermore, YTS has now become for many employers part of their routine recruitment procedures, acting as a screening device for potential employees. According to the MSC most employers providing work experience use YTS in this way (Wrench 1986: 15). It might be argued that this could work to the advantage of black youngsters who would be less vulnerable to decisions based on stereotypes at a short interview.

Teachers and lecturers were also persuaded by the MSC's early assurances. It has been argued that one reason why the MSC's educational philosophy implanted itself so quickly in further education is the way that MSC publicity drew on apparently progressive themes (Green 1986: 13). Only later, with the realization that the apparently enlightened stance on equal opportunity by the MSC meant very little in practice did teachers and careers staff become disillusioned.

Evidence of racial inequality

Figures began to emerge even before the end of the first year of YTS, showing the unequal distribution by ethnic group within YTS, with consistent under-representation in those schemes with the greatest potential for leading to employment. In the first year of YTS a small CRE survey found black young people to be under-represented on employer-based and Large Company Unit schemes (CRE 1984a). Over the next years further evidence from the MSC's own statistics and from independent research demonstrated the same pattern. The West Midlands YTS Research Project found that employer-based schemes contained a much lower proportion of black trainees than their percentage in the school-leaving population. At the same time, their representation in private training agencies was in line with their general distribution on YTS (Pollert 1985). The Coventry REITS campaign examined every 1983/84 Mode A scheme in Coventry: only a quarter of private employers offering schemes had a black trainee, with four firms out of fifty-two accounting for half the number of black trainees. They found very few trainees in the personal service or retail sector: in hairdressing, none of the forty-two places were filled by blacks, and there was some indication that black young people top up 'hard to fill' schemes (REITS 1985).

In different parts of the country, similar pattens of inequality were confirmed. In a survey of Sheffield school leavers Clough and Drew (1985) showed that 34 per cent of white ex-trainees found work, compared to 16 per cent of blacks. The MSC's own statistics showed smaller proportions of black young people on Mode A schemes in London and the South East and Merseyside, and so on (Newnham 1986: 20). In short, 'where employment prospects are particularly good . . . the percentage of black trainees on them is vastly lower compared with YTS as a whole' (YETRU 1986: 11).

Given the now undeniable inequality of participation on YTS, the next question to ask is whether this is due to racism at the point of access to the scheme. Before we can adequately answer this question we must consider possible alternative explanations for the statistical imbalance.

'They don't apply'/'They don't make the grade'

In the pre-YTS era employers offering apprenticeships would explain their lack of black recruits with statements such as 'they don't apply' or 'they don't make the grade', using common sense notions of black 'under-achievement' at school. Previous research on apprenticeships showed that neither of these explanations was tenable: young blacks did apply for apprenticeships, and they did so just as realistically as their white peers (Lee and Wrench 1983). Despite being similarly educationally equipped they had much lower success rates, due largely to processes within the recruitment practices of employers. Although the study focused primarily on apprenticeships, the findings illlustrated the more broadly tenable assertion that equality of educational attainment did not lead to equality of opportunity in the labour market.

Under YTS there has been little evidence to suggest that labour market success has now become primarily and directly related to educational achievement. Cross (1987) tested what he called the 'educational level proposition' for inequality on YTS in his study of 1984 Coventry school leavers and concluded, from his data at least, that it was not the educational performance of youngsters which accounted for the differential access to employer based YTS. He found that higher level performance by ethnic minorities tended to lead to places on those Mode A schemes run by training agencies and voluntary organizations, not employer-led schemes. He concluded 'It does not matter what level of educational attainment ethnic minorities achieve, the differential in representation on Mode A1 (employer-based) schemes will not be narrowed. This is because it is factors other than educational performance which affect the chances of being recruited to these schemes' (Cross 1987: 55).

So what are these 'factors other than educational performance' which could account for the low numbers of black trainees on the better schemes? These will be considered next, starting with those that emphasize the *supply* side of the equation, and concluding with evidence for the operation of racial exclusion at the point of entry.

GEOGRAPHICAL FACTORS

There are three main explanations which fall under the heading of 'they don't apply'. The first of these is rooted in *geography*. As one northern careers officer suggested 'I think that there are geographical factors: ethnic minority clients tend to live 'inner city', and because of compounded disadvantage the Mode B provision tends to be inner city, which is only down the road, instead of 3 buses'.

It is true that in the inner city where the majority of the black population is concentrated there have been more Mode B schemes to be found plugging the gap left by the flight of manufacturing industry from such areas over recent years. If there really is a tendency for young people to 'stick local', could the uneven geographical spread of schemes explain the ethnic minority imbalance within YTS? This argument appears to have some plausibility. There could well be a reluctance to travel on the part of young people, particularly as the relatively low status of YTS in the eyes of many of them is not a factor to encourage great effort to travel on their part. Careers officers have long lamented what they see as the 'low horizons' of young people and their reluctance to move far in search of work, and some officers do see this as applying on YTS too. A careers officer based in a special ethnic minorities unit in a northern city reported that in her experience this reluctance of young people to travel any distance for a YTS place was directly related to the factor of cost. For example, in her city, because of the very cheap standard-rate bus fare, young people were willing to travel much further than their counterparts in London, where fares were much higher.

Careers staff are aware that a preference for a local Mode B scheme as opposed to a more distant Mode A is going to lessen the chances of access to future employment. As one told Austen (1987: 61):

> 'I think that most of the Mode B schemes won't lead to jobs. . . . In some cases they'll have a greater amount of time in off the job training, in some cases they'll be doing community work. If they're working in an old people's home they're not really going to have much of a chance of getting a job.'

A preference for local schemes by young people in areas of high unemployment will not reduce their access to *all* Mode A schemes, rather to those which are employer-based. Eggleston *et al.* (1984: 268) quote an unpublished study of YTS provision in three localities which concludes that the higher the unemployment in an area, the more likely it is that Mode A YTS places will have to be provided by organizations such as private training agencies rather than by genuine employers.

To assume that many young people prefer to attend schemes in their local area is quite reasonable: however, to seize upon this as the factor which explains the inequality of black participation on YTS is *not* so reasonable. There are a number of reasons, discussed later in this chapter, which suggest that even if every black school-leaver were as foot-loose as Jack Kerouac this would still make little difference to their access to the better schemes. Furthermore, a CRE report in 1984 draws attention to a study in Southwark which showed that the majority of people on the Mode A schemes studied were white, middle class, and lived outside Southwark. 'It therefore appears that even where there may be Mode A schemes operating locally, black youngsters are losing out to white ones from outside the area' (CRE 1984: 2). This is consistent with the finding by Lee and Wrench (1983) that employers within inner city areas would be willing to recruit apprentices from *outside* the area, whereas employers in the white outer areas of Birmingham were more likely to operate a local catchment area policy.

Sometimes the 'geographical' argument gets refined down even more. One version states that it is not *all* young people who are reluctant to move from their immediate locality, but *black* young people. This particular cultural stereotype has been drawn on before and is still being quoted for YTS. The 1984 Bristol University and CRE research both reported a belief among managing agents that low black representation on schemes reflected their unwillingness to travel. In fact there has never been any evidence that such a phenomenon could account for occupational inequality. Indeed, from a questionnaire adminstered to 125 young people who had left full time education, Eggleston and his colleagues found that the Afro-Caribbean respondents seemed to be the *most* flexible of the unemployed young people they studied, apparently more willing to travel further to work, or contemplate moving to another part of the country to find work (Eggleston *et al.* 1986: 249). Girls of Asian and white ethnic origin were found to be less mobile than boys in the distance they were prepared to travel and in their willingness to move, a difference which was not found amongst the Afro-Caribbean respondents.

THE FACTOR OF CHOICE

There is another version of the 'they don't apply' argument sometimes used by YTS practitioners, an argument which is related to, but slightly different from, the 'geographical' one. This is the argument of voluntary selection — the idea that black young people seek out and prefer those Mode B schemes and others that are less likely to lead to employment, and have actively resisted being placed on employer-based Mode A schemes. Again, up to a point there is some evidence for this. A member of careers staff working in a service where officers were aware of, and attempting to tackle, racial inequality on YTS described regular meetings in her office where schemes with few Asian trainees would be identified, and staff urged to make a positive effort to submit more ethnic minority young people to them. 'But you can only submit them if they *want* to be submitted – it might be an area they are not keen on.' She found particular difficulties with a few protective Asian parents who would only consider a place for their daughter if there were no men on the scheme, or if there were no travelling involved. Such restrictions might preclude access to many Mode A schemes and reduce the choice to those Mode B schemes with no work placement.

It is not only girls who might display a preference for Mode B schemes: some ethnic minority boys also might insist on going to some Mode B workshop schemes because of a desire to be amongst their relatives or friends. Such a phenomenon was not necessarily seen in patronizing terms of a 'cultural gregariousness' but as a clear response to experiences of racism by the young people:

'You've got clients' *choice* as well, and Mode B offers an experience that is attractive to certain types of Black clients. Because, I think, of the disadvantages that they have experienced at school. I think that if you have been put through the mincer in your secondary school and been a prey to discrimination and fairly overt racism then you stick with your mates. That way you can go wholesale to do metal work and go to a Mode B workshop rather than spread out amongst big companies across the county'.

This phenomenon made it difficult for a well-intentioned careers officer to indulge in a little 'positive action' when submitting ethnic minorities.

'The kids let you down when you are trying to do that. You can't wonder – they just don't want to be subbed to all-white, apparently racist employers. You can be as well-intentioned as you want but they think 'Why stick your neck out for a rotten YTS scheme? It might be worth whipping up a bit of bluff and courage if it was going to be a really well-paid permanent job – but a rotten YTS? I will go where I know I will be accepted' (ethnic minority specialist careers officer)

There is, therefore, some evidence in the experiences of careers officers to support this particular 'they don't apply' argument, as there is also for the next one, which emphasizes the preference for black young people to remain in full-time education rather than allow themselves to be put forward to YTS.

THE 'STAYING AT SCHOOL' SYNDROME

The dilemma facing a black fifth former is well known: 'Should ethnic minorities leave school and put their trust in a labour market that discriminates against them, or should they place their trust in education in an attempt to gain the highest qualification possible?' (Eggleston *et al.* 1986: 28).

There is much evidence to show that both Afro-Caribbean and Asian young people show a greater disposition to stay on in education that their white peers. (For a review of this literature see Eggleston *et al.* 1986: 28–33). This might be understood in terms of greater ambition and a determination to gain vocational training and educational qualifications by these young people, but might also reflect a knowledge of the greater difficulties they face in the labour market through racism. One careers officer felt that she was left with a smaller pool of the better qualified ethnic minority youngsters from which to submit to YTS.

'There is a host of reasons why [inequality on YTS] happens: there is discrimination in submission and discrimination in acceptances, let's make no mistake. But another *major* reason is we are not comparing like with like, when you are looking at Mode A and Mode B possibilities. For many years disproportionately high numbers of ethnic minorities have gone on to further education, which leaves a different cohort of work seekers which doesn't compare with the cohort of white work seekers.' (ethnic minority specialist careers officer)

In theory this phenomenon might help to explain the paucity of black trainees on the 'better' YTS. The question of how *much* weight to give this and the preceding explanations will be judged after considering the final possibility: that of racism at the point of entry to schemes.

Racism in YTS

Knowing that racism has been endemic in the labour market for years (Daniel 1968; Smith 1974; Hubbuck and Carter 1980) we have a right to be suspicious about the YTS figures, even if only at first from a 'common sense' point of view. Mackney (1985: 12), noting that the Construction Industry Training Board (CITB) scheme is 99 per cent white in composition, exclaims 'we *know* that it is not due to an innate lack of potential construction skills among black youth'. Such 'common sense' misgivings are reinforced by figures later released by the Birmingham careers service based on the number of standard application letters issued by careers officers in the city in 1985, showing that after being submitted to the CITB scheme white young-sters had a success rate of 60 per cent compared to 4 per cent of Afro-Caribbeans and zero for Asians. Or to put it another way, of seventy black applicants, two were taken on (YETRU 1986: 10). (Although the careers service has been the focus of a number of criticisms over recent years, one of them has *not* been that they routinely submit totally unsuitable applicants to YTS schemes).

The statistics which point to the operation of racism in recruitment are supported by the accumulation of evidence from anecdotes, inter-views, incidents, and prosecutions over the years. In 1984 the CRE and Bristol University reports found 'no small number' of firms feeling free to specify a racial preference for trainees on work place-ments. Later research confirmed this: for private training agency staff trying to place trainees 'the degree of racism in the labour market is a shock, they have said, even to them' (Pollert 1986: 192). Pollert goes on to list a whole catalogue of examples, ranging from the Birmingham FE college lecturers who co-operated with racist prefer-ences expressed by shop proprietors, to the 'Snips Hairdressers' prosecution in Wolverhampton when, of eight girls from a Chamber of Commerce scheme, the six white girls were taken on and the two black girls rejected. Further examples of racism and on-the-job racial harassment were reported by trainees in the West Midlands (YETRU 1986). The problem seems to be greater at the stage of sponsors pro-viding work placements than with managing agents themselves. One careers officer felt that in general the careers service had more in-fluence with managing agents than with employers over recruitment policies as they were relatively dependent on the careers service for trainees. He did concede that the careers service had virtually no control over what happened at the work-placement stage, and that if a managing agent went along with pressure to discriminate from a sponsor, the careers service would be unlikely to hear about it. Other careers officers reported to Austen (1987: 63) that managing agents who had taken on black trainees had problems finding them work-ex-perience placements: 'I know for certain there are some schemes where you "sub" them and you know full well they are going to come trundling back to you because when those schemes try and find them placements they can't because they're black.'

One YTS Mode B supervisor in Birmingham reported to the author:

'We have an office scheme full of black kids because employers still won't put blacks in offices. There is real discrimination for black kids in offices. A black girl has to be very, very good — and we'll still have difficulty placing her.'

The sort of attitude by sponsors which leads to this difficulty for managing agents is revealed in a later interview with the catering manager of a large West Midlands company which was often used by colleges and other YTS training establishments to provide work placements. He explained why he didn't like to take on 'negroes':

I'm not racist really, but blacks are not very good at the job. We had one Asian girl, she was very good at the job and a good worker. It's the negroes — I mean they have a chip on their shoulder and they just don't want to work. They feel that the world owes them a living. We had one once — she came in one day and then rang up the next and said she had tooth ache and we never saw her again.'

Although the transactions between managing agent and sponsor are not open to scrutiny it would be unrealistic to assume that most managing agents saw their role as confronting racism by sponsors. At a public meeting on YTS in Birmingham the manager of a large local authority training scheme announced 'You know it's fine standing on a point of principle — but do I then, because one employer in 20 is refusing — do I then jeopardise the chances for other trainees for whom that training might be beneficial?. . . . If you accept the fact that there are more people than black trainees on YTS and I have a responsibility for them as well.'

Furthermore, under the two years YTS where employers have to *pay* for their use of trainees on work placements, it is likely that such 'pressure to discriminate' cases will increase.

The careers service and racism

Given that racism exists in the practices of sponsors and managers in YTS the final question to ask is whether the careers service itself is also open to accusations of racism or other dubious practices which deflect black young people away from the best YTS. The careers service role as a gatekeeper is far more important under YTS than it was in pre-YTS employment. Before YTS many large employers would not use the service as their major source of access to school leavers, perhaps only turning to it for 'topping up' their numbers. Now, although it is true than managing agents can recruit their trainees direct, the careers service is far and away the most important placer of young people on YTS.

In the past the careers service has come under criticism for a number of alleged sins. Careers staff have been criticised for underrating the abilities and intelligence of Afro-Caribbean pupils (Sillitoe and Meltzer 1985); for exhibiting a lack of awareness or understanding of the realities of racial inequality and the processes of racial discrimination in the labour market (Eggleston *et al.* 1986); for being too ready to make generalized assumptions about the 'special needs' of black young people (Fenton *et al.* 1984); for 'turning a blind eye' to employer racism (Brown 1985) and for protectively channelling black young people away from employers who are seen to discriminate (CRE 1984). It is perhaps not strictly appropriate to refer to *the* careers service as if it were a unitary organization, as there is so much variety in policy and practice between services based in different local education authorities. Nevertheless there is enough evidence to suggest that active confrontation of racism in the YTS labour market cannot routinely be expected from many local careers services. One practice which sidesteps a confrontation with racism is that of 'protective channelling'.

Protective channelling

When in 1984 an employment officer with the CRE blamed the careers service for 'not sending black or Asian youngsters to interviews at firms where they knew they would be turned down' some careers officers protested angrily, arguing that the blame lay with the employers and managing agents who control selection (*YTS Workers Bulletin* 10 April 1985). Other careers officers do not rule out the possibility of this happening. Although Austen's careers-officer respondents felt that it was important to take action against racial discrimination, in the absence of clear guidelines and procedures for dealing with such incidents the temptation was for officers to avoid submitting someone to the offending scheme rather than to make an official complaint. Austen could find no evidence from her study that careers officers acted with racist intentions – they were making judgements and decisions in the context of prevailing conditions in the labour market, and part of their decision was made in the knowledge that black young people would be likely to meet discrimination when attempting to get on some Mode A schemes (Austen 1987). A careers officer told the author

> 'I think where the careers service will fall down – and I *sense* this rather than can demonstrate it – is that people make submissions in a protective sort of way. Rather than think "you're black, you get down to this ropey old workshop" it would be "There's no point sending them to this high-powered up-market, white firm just to have his feelings dashed". I think that probably goes on. It's very difficult to pinpoint' (ethnic minority specialist careers officer)

Critics of the careers service have not generally suggested that careers officers themselves are actively racist — rather that they acquiesce to the racism of employers by 'turning a blind eye'.

Turning a blind eye to racism

Careers staff have been critized for allegedly pretending that incidents of racial discrimination don't exist. As one Midlands community relations officer put it, 'It is the Auschwitz syndrome — people know what's going on but they don't do anything about it. They maintain a wilful ignorance' (Eggleston *et al.* 1986: 188).

Officers from the Commission for Racial Equality will point to the relative rarity of prosecutions under the Race Relations Act which have originated from careers service action. Brown (1985) points to some of the forces at work here. One careers officer told him that although they would try to do something about obvious racial discrimination 'it's such a bureaucratic mess to do anything about it — you tend to lose heart'. Another of his respondents described a dilemma that she perceived:

> 'you've got a scheme which you know will discriminate . . . you've got a youngster who is a white youngster . . . he's ideal for it . . . what do you do? Do you close it down or do you send your white youngster and get him the job? . . . It's a very difficult problem . . . because it always tends to be the ones that are more interesting — that do offer someone a chance — that discriminate.' (careers officer quoted in Brown 1985: 683).

Brown argues that confrontation is made less likely because officers are aware that the majority of discriminatory acts are not made overtly by employers using the service. As one officer put it 'Most employers tend to be a bit more subtle about it . . . but you *sense* there's discrimination.' This reduces the ground upon which a careers officer feels able to force a confrontation (Brown 1985: 683). Acts of racism are not always open and unambiguous: very often a careers officer has little more than suspicions to work on. One officer interviewed by the author expressed a frustration echoed by other respondents:

> 'What happens is a host of very grey foggy problems which emerge, where things don't 'smell' right but you can't actually nail them down. . . . So an employer comes up with a vacancy: you might feel, for whatever reason, that there is something "Iffy" about it, nothing to go on . . . there is nothing tangible, and you think "Perhaps the best we can do is to watch this one, we will keep an eye on it and if it happens again. . . ." But then you might not get another vacancy for six years. So it's terribly difficult to do anything about it'.

Even when careers officers are relatively aware of issues of equal opportunity and sensitive to incidents of employer racism, further action is not always forthcoming. Careers officers often do find themselves in a difficult position because of the very nature of the role of the careers service. As one officer put it 'It has such a problem deciding where its client group is, and deciding whether it backs employers or whether it backs kids'. At a time of high unemployment when vacancies are scarce pressure increases to back the former and in this context racial discrimination causes extra problems for careers staff. One member of careers staff described how difficult it was for her when an employer was being 'bolshie' because of the pressure that she felt was on her not to lose the vacancy. 'In training days, that's what I've picked up generally – "Try not to lose the vacancy – try to be as tactful as possible" '. She added 'I suppose some of us would rather lose it if he is being like that anyway'.

A careers officer conceded:

'I think all of us – with the best will in the world – would rather it all went away, really. Not that people want to cover up discrimination, or don't care about it – I don't think any of my colleagues feel that – but I think they aren't certain how to handle it.'

The difficulties of the situation meant that careers staff might err on the side of caution. One careers officer lamented

'It's a minefield of an area, it is very frustrating, it is just so difficult to tie anything down . . . you have to guard against the surge of anger, of emotion, you feel when you think that something is not right. Because there is a world of difference between feeling that something is not right and being able to do something about it. It comes with having a very weak law and the careers service serving two sectors: having the young person as a client and also having the employer as a way of earning its living. To totally alienate all employers would shut us down.'

In recent years a number of individual local careers services have initiated a more positive stance in raising their equal opportunity awareness and in confronting racism. In one such service an officer reported that since the recent start of training on identifying and tackling racial discrimination three or four cases of discrimination had been challenged and followed through to some conclusion.

'I can't believe that it is mere coincidence. I think it is down to people actually noticing something and feeling now that we can do something about it rather than choosing to ignore it, which is sometimes the easier option.'

Similarly an employment officer with the Commission for Racial Equality related how for years the CRE had not heard of any cases of racial discrimination from a local careers service until the CRE got involved in a local exposé and prosecution of racial discrimination on YTS, whereupon they had six cases reported to them in nine months.

'Unless you believe the employers have suddenly gone bananas and started coming up with racist remarks to careers officers then you've got to believe that it has really been going on all the time and that the careers officers haven't known how to handle it, or have been really scared of actually reporting it to the Commission'.

Observations such as these suggest that there must be many incidents of racial discrimination within the youth labour market which remain invisible to those outside the careers service.

Conclusion

The fallacy within some of the more simplistic analyses of inequality of YTS is the implicit image of young black school leavers as passive and inert objects on a conveyor belt from school to the labour market, having things done *to* them by a range of gatekeepers to future opportunity. The actions and choices of young people themselves must be acknowledged in any analysis of the processes of inequality in the labour market. We should not be surprised that many able black young people do prefer to stay at school rather than put themselves forward to YTS; we should not be surprised that a young person may express a preference for a Mode B workshop environment, and that some young people do give priority to local rather than more distant schemes. What we *should* find surprising is the suggestion that this way lies the real explanation for the unequal distribution of black young people on YTS. Explanations which emphasize the *supply* side of the picture, in this case those related to the characteristics, behaviour, aspirations, and culture of the black young people themselves, are seized upon too readily by those who find explanations in terms of the operation of racism unpalatable or inconvenient. It may well be that many able black young people do not put themselves forward to YTS. This does not alter the fact that, in general, black young people are often particularly keen to get good jobs with training, skill, and prospects, and that when they do put themselves forward to those YTS schemes which are most likely to satisfy their aspirations they are deflected and rejected by processes which can only be called racist. (Moreover, it could well be that it is the perception of racism on YTS

141

which deters some black young people from putting themselves forward in the first place). To date, these processes of racial discrimination have not been seriously tackled by anything like an effective equal opportunity policy on the part of the MSC; nor is it being successfully challenged in practice by the routine operations of many careers services.

There are other relevant areas that this chapter has not had room to address. One is a critique of the equal opportunity policy and practice of the MSC which has been shown to lack any understanding of the type of policies that would be needed if there was indeed a genuine desire to challenge the historical and structural causes of racial inequality in the labour market (for such a critique see Pollert 1986; Mackney 1985). Neither has there been room for a critique of the corresponding ethos of the careers service, an organization with immense regional variation in the provisions it makes for ethnic minority clients, ranging from the enlightened to the backward, but one where even careers officers who are actively committed to anti-racism can be frustrated by the structures within which they are working (for a fuller critique see Cross, Wrench, and Barnett, in press).

In the days before YTS a survey into ethnic minority participation on YOP was critical of the predominant attitude that it found among MSC staff:

'We have been appalled to see just how many times black and Asian youngsters are bracketed with the handicapped and afflicted. How on earth can groups of normal young people – with all the range of human talents and diversities – develop their potential when they are continually referred to as having "special needs" analogous to the physically and mentally handicapped, the educationally disadvantaged, and the ex-offenders' (Cross *et al.* 1983: 32).

Yet in August 1986 the President of the Institute of Careers Officers wrote in *Youth Training News* that one aspect of careers service work in YTS was 'ensuring that the needs of ethnic minority groups, low achievers, and the disabled are catered for'. The persistence of this tendency to juxtapose the 'needs' of ethnic minority young people alongside those of low achievers and the disabled, in this case by a careers officers' representative in an MSC publication, is a cause for some despair, particularly as it says nothing about the main 'need' that black people do have: 'for the colour of their skin not to influence their access to training and labour market opportunities'. (Fenton *et al.* 1984: 5)

The continuation of racial inequality in YTS is blamed by many on the MSC in its weak practical commitment to equal opportunity.

Fenton and Burton argue that 'This failure to accept the centrality of equal opportunities and to recognize that it is entirely consistent with other goals in YTS constitutes the major stumbling block to significant improvements in the prospects of black youth today' (Fenton and Burton 1987: 43).

It is certainly true that inequality in YTS is a major problem for black young people. A more contentious point, however, is in fact whether equal opportunity is 'entirely consistent with other goals in YTS'. It might just as well be argued that the problem is a failure to realize that equal opportunity is largely *inconsistent* with other goals in YTS as it is currently organized.

There had long been a problem of racism in the labour market before YTS, when many employers were able to run rampant with the whole gamut of their prejudices in recruitment. In the case of selecting candidates for manual and routine clerical jobs they were free to operate highly subjective criteria of what Jenkins (1986) has called 'acceptability', (for example, appearance, manner, attitude), rather than more objective, functionally specific selection criteria such as trade or educational qualifications. Only very occasionally would clear racial discrimination come to light, perhaps via controlled investigation (e.g. Hubbuck and Carter 1980). For years it was a situation which produced relatively little pressure for change: no one really expected rogue employers to take note of the views of outraged liberals over their in-house recruitment procedures.

One unintended consequence of the centralized manipulation of the labour market that comes with YTS has been a more public outrage over the injustices within the scheme. Race and gender inequalities have become more noticeably a public issue; this is in part because some of the same rogue employers are now in receipt of public money as part of a scheme in which equal opportunity is supposed to be central. The vociferous lobbying of assorted pressure groups which have been mobilized on the issue of race inequality since YTS began has apparently caused the MSC at least a degree of embarrassment. The MSC has responded in line with some of the suggestions made by its critics: for example following the start of the new two year YTS in 1986 it declared an intention to insist on positive proposals for equal opportunity from providers before awarding Approved Training Organization status to employers. The MSC has also implemented a scheme to monitor the numbers of young blacks on employer-based schemes with set targets for improvement in each area, starting in Spring 1987. The question remains as to whether the new procedures will have an effect on equality in practice, or whether we will see ritualistic acknowledgements of equal opportunity alongside new developments in tokenism and ingenious new ways of complying with the letter rather than the spirit of MSC directives by employers in order to satisfy MSC criteria and gain ATO status.

The fundamental problem will remain: quite simply, effective equal opportunity action is something which runs counter to the underlying philosophy of the whole scheme. The MSC's YTS intervention has been called 'a national policy which enshrines employers' needs above all others, and thus also enshrines employers' prejudices and backward practices' (Benn and Fairley 1986: 5). The clear message which has been given out with the destruction of the old training boards and the introduction of YTS is that 'training is something which should be left to employers: they know best'. It therefore goes somewhat against the grain to want to claw back freedoms which have just been handed out so decisively.

Is it possible to have genuine and effective equal opportunity policies in an employer-led system? In a *Guardian* feature in September 1986 it was reported that the intention of the MSC to improve *quality* on schemes was having the consequence of alienating many of the individuals and commercial organizations operating in YTS, one problem being the increased bureaucracy entailed in monitoring trainers and employers (Lee *et al.* 1986). It is interesting to note that if the word 'quality' is replaced by 'equality', much of the analysis within the article still holds true, including the conclusion that 'Quite simply, the drive to impose standards has clashed with the free market organization and philosophy which were basic to the schemes'.

This contradiction at the heart of YTS helps to explain why certain analyses of racial inequality within the scheme are more popular than others amongst those directly involved in YTS provision. If equal opportunity is seen to be only a question of the allocation of 'special needs' provision to ethnic minority young people, this can be quite easily accommodated within the current organization and philosophy of YTS. All that is needed is the occasional addition of extra resources for what were some of the old Mode B schemes, or more currently, for 'premium places'. And if the reason for the obvious and ubiquitous racial inequality on schemes is seen to lie not with employer racism in the context of a malfunctioning and tokenistic MSC equal opportunity policy, but within all those factors of 'supply' which are ultimately rooted in the behaviour of black young people themselves, then there is no corresponding implication that something needs changing within the scheme. The contradictions do not become exposed. And that is precisely why evidence for all of those 'They don't make the grade/They don't apply' arguments, rather than racism, are seized upon with such enthusiasm in order to explain the inequality suffered by black young people in YTS.

I would like to acknowledge the assistance in some of this work of Christel Burns, research assistant at CRER during 1984/5.

References

Austen, R. (1987) YTS, Black girls and the Careers Service. In Cross, M. and Smith, D. I. (eds) *Black Youth Futures*. Leicester: National Youth Bureau.

Benn, C. and Fairley, J. (eds) (1986) *Challenging the MSC on Jobs, Education, and Training*. London: Pluto Press.

Brown, K. M. (1985) 'Turning a blind eye': racial oppression and the unintended consequences of white 'non-racism'. *Sociological Review*, 33(4): 670–90.

Clough, E. and Drew, D. (1985) *Futures in Black and White*. Sheffield: Pavic Publications.

Commission for Racial Equality (1984a) *Racial Equality and the Youth Training Scheme*. London: CRE.

—— (1984b) *Equal Opportunities and YTS*. Unpublished.

Cross, M. (1987) Who goes where?: placement of Black youth on YTS. In Cross, M. and Smith, D. I. (eds) *Black Youth Futures*. Leicester: National Youth Bureau.

Cross, M., Edmonds, J., and Sargeant, R. (1983) *Ethnic Minorities: Their Experience on YOP*. Sheffield: MSC Occasional Paper No. 5.

Daniel, W. W. (1968) *Racial Discrimination in England*. Harmondsworth: Penguin.

Eggleston, J., Dunn, D., Anjali, M., and Wright, C. (1986) *Education for Some: The Educational and Vocational Experiences of 15–18 Year Old Members of Minority Ethnic Groups*. Stoke: Trentham Books.

Fenton, S., Davies, T., Means, R., and Burton, P. (1984) *Ethnic Minorities and the Youth Training Scheme*. Sheffield: MSC Research and Development Series No. 20.

Fenton, S. and Burton, P. (1987) YTS and equal opportunity policy. In Cross, M. and Smith, D. I. (eds) *Black Youth Futures*. Leicester: National Youth Bureau.

Finn, D. (1986) YTS: the jewel in the MSC's crown. In Benn, C. and Fairley, J. (eds) *Challenging the MSC on Jobs, Education, and Training*. London: Pluto Press.

Green, A. (1986) The MSC and the three-tier structure of further education. In Benn, C. and Fairley, J. (eds) *Challenging the MSC on Jobs, Education and Training*. London: Pluto Press.

Horton, C. (1986) *Nothing Like a Job: A Survey of Unemployed School Leavers Who Could Have Gone on the Youth Training Scheme But Did Not*. London: Youthaid.

Hubbuck, J. and Carter, S. (1980) *Half A Chance? A Report on Job Discrimination Against Young Blacks in Nottingham*. London: CRE.

Jenkins, R. (1986) *Racism and Recruitment: Managers, Organisations, and Equal Opportunities in the Labour Market*. Cambridge: Cambridge University Press.

Lee, D., Marsden, D., Hardy, M., and Rickman, P. (1986) How YTS tied itself in knots. *Guardian* 16 September.

Lee, G. and Wrench, J. (1983) *Skill Seekers: Black Youth, Apprenticeships, and Disadvantage*. Leicester: National Youth Bureau.

Lee, G. and Wrench, J. (1987) Race and gender dimensions of the youth labour market: from apprenticeship to YTS. In Lee, R. L. and Loveridge, R. (eds) *The Manufacture of Disadvantage: Stigma and Social Closure*. Milton Keynes: Open University Press.

Mackney, P. (1985) Mobilizing against the racism in YTS. *NATFHE Journal* December: 12–19.

Newnham, A. (1986) *Employment, Unemployment, and Black People*. London: The Runnymede Trust.

Pollert, A. (1985) *Unequal Opportunities: Racial Discrimination and the Youth Training Scheme*. Birmingham: Trade Union Resource Centre.

—— (1986) The MSC and ethnic minorities. In Benn, C. and Fairley, J. (eds) *Challenging the MSC on Jobs, Education, and Training*. London: Pluto Press.

REITS (1985) *YTS or White TS? Racial Discrimination and Coventry's Youth Training Schemes*. Coventry: REITS.

Sillitoe, K. and Meltzer, H. (1985) *The West Indian School Leaver*. London: Office of Population and Census Surveys.

Smith, D. J. (1974) *Racial Disadvantage in Employment*. London: PEP.

Trade Union Resource Centre (1986) *The Great Training Robbery Continues*. Birmingham: TURC.

Wrench, J. (1986) *YTS, Racial Equality and the Trade Unions, Policy Paper in Ethnic Relations No. 6*, CRER, University of Warwick; also in M. Cross and D. I. Smith (eds) *Black Youth Futures*. Leicester: National Youth Bureau, 1987.

Youth Employment and Training Resource Unit (1986) *'They Must Think We're Stupid': The Experiences of Young People on the Youth Training Scheme*. Birmingham: TURC.

10 The black voluntary school movement: definition, context, and prospects

Mel Chevannes and Frank Reeves

The effort being made by various Afro-Caribbean groups to provide, outside mainstream schools, a form of education that better satisfies what they believe to be the needs of black children is most inadequately described as 'supplementary' education. The term 'supplementary' seems to suggest that the classes organized by black people since the late 1960s are merely a means of supporting the aims of the local authority schools — little more than a quantitative extension of the school day. It is not, of course, possible to 'supplement' what does not exist in the mainstream. The schools cannot properly be termed 'alternative' either, because given their present status and level of resourcing they can make no pretence at providing an adequate or entire alternative to the nine to four, five days a week statutory system. Neither can the provision be called 'complementary': Afro-Caribbean groups' views on the inadequacy of local authority education is such that they would be unlikely to consider making a contribution to its 'completion' in its present form. Better to refer to these schools for Afro-Caribbean children as part-time, voluntary schools for blacks in recognition of the purpose of their foundation.

The black voluntary school is a practical gesture, however rough and ready, in support of a broader black political and educational ideal which has directly arisen from an assessment by Afro-Caribbeans of their social position in Britain and of the part that the existing white-dominated education system plays in its perpetuation. It is essential to recognize in any discussion of black voluntary schools that their origin lies in the self-conscious organization and practical mobilization of the Afro-Caribbean population in Britain. According to John la Rose, active in the black education movement since 1969 and founder member of a black publishing business, the black education movement began as a result of the concern of parents that their children were not achieving as they should in British schools (in Collymore 1980d: 2). This growing realization by parents resulted in a significant development in Afro-Caribbean political consciousness and organizational forms.

Discussion of the so-called 'black supplementary' school movement has usually concentrated on the formally stated objectives and more obvious organizational and curricular aspects of the schools themselves. As a consequence, the political context in which the schools have been set up has been de-emphasized and certain of their aspects overlooked. This is a pity because, as when confronted with other British institutions such as the police, this peculiarly Afro-Caribbean response has stripped away much of the ideological camouflage which hides the conflicts of interest and distribution of power in the British education system as a whole. By comparing a number of the initiatives taken by Afro-Caribbeans in London and the West Midlands in setting up black voluntary schools, it is possible to draw up a list of their common features, thus defining and identifying the phenomenon under discussion here and helping to distinguish it from other educational projects with which, in the past, superficial comparisons have sometimes been drawn.

Provision primarily for black pupils

A primary feature is that the schools have been set up for the benefit of children of Afro-Caribbean descent: they are indeed black schools in aim and composition. The fact that there may be no deliberate colour bar (a white or Asian child may be allowed to enrol or a white volunteer invited to help) has little bearing on the organizers' view that the schools have been set up to provide in a predominantly black environment for the needs of black children. Black children attend because they are deliberately recruited from families where the parents believe in the need for their children to undertake extra study with children from the same racial group and to obtain support from teachers who understand what it is to be black in a white society. Teachers and helpers, as well, involve themselves in the school in the knowledge that they are being of service to the black community.

Under the heading 'the separate schools debate' the Swann Report (DES 1985: 498–517) is critical of 'the moves by certain ethnic minority communities motivated primarily by religious concerns, to establish their own "separate" schools as an alternative to the existing mainstream system'. But in regard to the Afro-Caribbean dimension of the debate, the report only considers the possibility of full-time black schools and cites the private, fee-paying Seventh Day Adventist

School which was established in north London in 1979, and where pupils and teachers are almost exclusively black. It is unfortunate that alternative forms of provision – such as the allocation of a day or half-day to students to attend voluntary schools of their choice – go unmentioned. The reason for needing to mention the 'half-way' solution to the demand for exclusive ethnic, racial, or religious education is that it more closely reflects the feeling manifest in those groups which support black educational projects. The black voluntary school movement is admittedly predicated on the need for some part of a black child's education to be conducted in a black-dominated environment, but not on a requirement that the child be entirely separated from the educational mainstream – a demand supported at present by only a small minority of Afro-Caribbeans.

Collectivism

A second important characteristic of the black voluntary schools is their 'collectivism'. They provide for any black child who chooses to attend, irrespective of educational attainment or ability to pay. The intention of such schools, whatever the outcome, is to contribute to the social standing and cultural level of the black community as a whole rather than to the advantage of a handful of privileged black pupils at the expense of the rest of the black community. In a society where educational attainment is measured on individual perform-ance, this characteristic may be difficult to recognize in practice, but it serves to distinguish the voluntary school from private coaching.

While admittedly some black parents might see voluntary schools as a conveniently cheap form of private education for their children, these schools were never set up either to bestow on any child the privi-lege of individual advancement at the expense of other children, or to supplement teachers' meagre wages. In general, while forced to make minimal charges for books, equipment, refreshments, and so on, voluntary schools are seldom financed from fees alone and are based on the principle of free education according to need, never on the ability to pay. All they might share in common with private coaching is the element of parental choice, the desire of parents to contribute to the improvement of their children's educational performance, and hours additional to the mainstream school day. While there may be a tradition of private coaching among some social classes in the Carib-bean (see Stone 1981: 171), the black voluntary school is not a mere transposition of this parental disposition to a new context, but a specific assessment of, and response to, the education available to black children in Britain.

Writing in the American context about black people's campaign to control their local schools, Wilcox (1971) draws attention to the difference in the demands of 'middle class' and 'poor' blacks. While the former seek 'quality, integrated education outside the ghetto', the latter attempt 'to build a constituency among parents and community leaders' in order to establish a black community-centred and controlled school in the recognition that their destiny is tied to the plight of the poor black community as a whole (Wilcox 1971: 128). A similar choice of individual or collective strategy is available to blacks in the British context. The black voluntary school movement, however, appears to be firmly based on the principle of joint collective action.

Community basis

Organizations which operate outside of the statutory framework, which are not usually in receipt of public funds, and which are seen by most professionals as peripheral to full-time provision, must rely for their support on their clientele. The black voluntary school, when set up by community activists, must depend on community and family networks in the local black population for its staffing, students, and material resources. The organizers of the school must be capable of recognizing the views of black parents and of satisfying their requirements: not an easy task to fulfil when confronted with the political and tactical disagreements which are to be found in any racial or ethnic group. Nevertheless, part of the success of the voluntary school rests on the organizers' ability to establish close relationships with parents and children, to recognize and demonstrate an empathy with their aspirations and anxieties, and to reassure them, through the care and attention given to individuals and through the curriculum on offer, that the educational exercise has a relevance to their economic and social aspirations.

One of the differences between the local authority day school and the black voluntary school is that whereas the former might find community support desirable in achieving its educational aims, for the latter it is essential to its survival. The voluntary school is sustained by community support and, in turn, sustains community networks through its negotiation of objectives, regular contact with parents, group meetings, fund raising, home visiting, and related social activities.

Community participation

As a consequence of their roots in the black community and need to maintain continuing support if they are to prosper, the voluntary

schools are generally participatory in form, encouraging the involvement of concerned black professionals and parents in decision making
and activities. Whatever the formal structure of the school, whether it
is run by an association of parents or by a single-minded headteacher,
at an informal level opinions will be sought, common goals arrived at,
and attempts made to satisfy the needs of black professionals,
volunteers, parents, and pupils.

With limited resources and an organization consisting mostly of
volunteers, it is only by arriving at a unity of purpose and by accepting
a self-imposed discipline that the project can be successfully maintained. This situation has strengths and weaknesses. The strengths lie
in the organization's lack of coercive measures and complete reliance
on good will (except possibly in the case of those schools where
teachers' salaries are funded externally), the weaknesses, in the inability of such organizations to withstand any major disagreement or
to impose uniform standards of performance on staff. If, for example,
volunteer staff do not turn up regularly or on time, with subsequent
disruption to established routines, very little remedial action can be
taken apart from issuing general exhortations.

Solidaristic ethos

The success of the voluntary black school lies in its ability to generate
a strong group solidarity based on common experiences of being black
in a white society – perceived by teachers, parents, and students alike
as hostile and unfriendly. The school constitutes a black environment, insulating, protecting, and supporting the individual against
the unpredictability of white behaviour and the constant difficulty of
interpreting outcomes in a context of widespread white prejudice and
discrimination.

Black students can share their experiences of white-run educational
institutions with black teachers, in the knowledge that they will
receive a sympathetic hearing and sound practical advice. In
addition, teachers, parents, and children are likely to share a
common cultural tradition, and to understand each other's interests
and concerns. Family, religion, friendship, and neighbourhood networks will support the educational endeavour and the school will
become an expressive forum where friends meet to exchange
information and make common arrangements. For example, when
floods devastated Jamaica in 1983, an opportunity was provided to
inform pupils about the geography of the island and to involve them
and parents in fund-raising exercises. Or in deference to the local

Pentecostal church, teachers will ensure that the date of the school summer project does not clash with the church's national convention.

Often ex-pupils will come back to the school to talk to teachers or friends and to help with fund-raising activities, and the school may involuntarily assume the role of a community centre or youth club. The successful voluntary school will certainly generate the feeling that this is 'our place'.

The curriculum

The curriculum of the black voluntary school is invariably conceived of in terms of the school's primary purpose, which is to raise the social standing of the black community as a whole by improving black children's educational level and by inference, their future job opportunities. It is in regard to the means and order of achieving this aim that emphasis will differ. Should pupils first be encouraged to develop an understanding of their position, both past and present, as black people in a white-dominated society, and the group solidarity and common sense of purpose and of ambition which will be needed in the struggle to overcome this disadvantage? Or should they first be given extra help in the basic school subjects, such as mathematics and English, in order that they might compete immediately and more effectively in the education stakes as determined by the education system and job market?

Sam Morris, Deputy Chief Officer at the Community Relations Commission, described the success of the black studies course being taught at the Tulse Hill School in Brixton: 'Some black fifth formers had become completely uninterested in their lessons. Subjects like history, geography, and English literature had little appeal for them. Then black studies as a subject was introduced. The students immediately became interested and as a result their interest was aroused in the other subjects which they had hitherto neglected' (Morris 1973: 245). An anecdote from the Black Arrow School, however, indicated that the 'ideological' approach is not without difficulties. After a series of lessons on Mary Seacole, Cudjoe, Marcus Garvey, etc., the students of one class asked when they were going to study something that would be useful to them in getting a job: computer science. They found black studies of some interest but were more concerned about their immediate employment prospects. The ideological and practical objectives are not, of course, mutually exclusive and, as a result of the participatory nature of the voluntary schools, an expression of pride in being black will emerge in the classroom even where a teacher is apparently entirely committed to a no-nonsense basic skills curriculum.

Voluntary schools, however, can usually be placed on a basic skills/Afro-Caribbean consciousness-raising continuum, most managing to combine a course in basic literacy and numeracy with a black studies orientation involving some mention of Afro-Caribbean culture, struggle, and the achievements of black people. The balance of the resulting curriculum will depend on the ideological orientation of the organization as set against the educational instrumentalism of parents and children.

The collectivist, solidaristic, and curricular features of black voluntary education clearly distinguish it from other arrangements with which it has superficially been compared: for example, the efforts by some parents to extend the social skills of their children by arranging private music, dancing, or horse-riding lessons. Although there is no reason why music, dance, and sport of various kinds should not form part of the black school curriculum, its essence lies not in developing those skills *per se*, but in collectively fortifying the black child's psyche with the confidence and will to succeed in the basic academic subjects: if this requires additional aesthetic, kinaesthetic, and social skills (for example, African dance) and a knowledge of the unique Afro-Caribbean historical experience, then so be it, but it shares little in common with the basic amateur ballet lesson, however comforting such a though might be. Nevertheless, it is possible, for example, that a karate lesson for black young people might fulfil the black educationalists' aim, if the purpose is collectively to discipline the mind and body in a manner which inspires self-confidence.

Parallels have also been drawn between the voluntary schools and the classes arranged by and for Asian groups in the various Asian languages. Language is seen as an integral part of any culture, and both Asians and Afro-Caribbeans as racial minorities in Britain have emphasized the importance of preserving and developing their distinctive cultural features in full knowledge of the ignorance and insult with which such cultures are frequently met. Linguistic and other cultural traditions play an important role in sustaining the solidarity of minority groups, but the black education movement cannot be viewed solely as a means of sustaining language or culture in this way. It has a structural rather than cultural imperative, being based primarily on an economic and political analysis of the position of the black population relative to the white, and only secondarily on the defence of ethnic social institutions against the pressure of British ethnocentric attitudes and practices.

Nevertheless, the language question is frequently and hotly debated in the black voluntary education movement. There has been a growing awareness of the part that Caribbean creoles/black British English have played in sustaining the solidarity of Afro-Caribbean young people in Britain and of providing them with a symbolic linguistic marker, capable of identifying them as members of an in-group, and of excluding from their circle authority figures, such as teachers.

Dalphinis believes that 'the positive backing of creoles through their inclusion in mainstream educational systems would have beneficial educational effects upon both the educators and educated, although it would be unlikely to put an end to "the resistance of black youth" ' (Dalphinis 1985: 272). Such a view, however, is not universally shared by Afro-Caribbean parents, of whom many still associate 'patois' with the low social class status of the uneducated Caribbean rural poor and believe that Afro-Caribbeans' existing low status in Britain is due in part to their inability to speak or write standard English or, alternatively, to young people's overt resistance (expressed linguistically in their persistent use of patois) to the white-dominated school: a self-indulgent resistance that they must be taught to curb if they are to benefit from British education and society.

The resulting acrimonious debate between hardline black 'culturalists', who seek unapologetically to institute Caribbean creole or 'nation language' as a medium of instruction, and 'pragmatists', who regard this as a form of black self-damnation, has at times divided the black voluntry school movement, although it is unlikely that many of the schools in practice have ever made wide use of creole except in the field of the creative arts: drama, poetry ('Jamaica labrish'), folk stories ('Anancy') and the like.

While Asian groups have found little difficulty in accepting local authority organization of mother-tongue classes after day school hours, and in arguing for mother-tongue to be incorporated as part of the primary school curriculum in areas of Asian settlement, it is unlikely that Afro-Caribbean educational aims and aspirations could be met in this way because far more than tuition in culture and language is being postulated and asked for, and even if language alone were being considered, the debate over the status and effects of teaching creole would result in major political controversy.

Although the black voluntary schools may be accommodated by, or actively supported by the black-led churches, it is important to recognize that they are not simply extensions of the churches' Sunday school programmes. They might have come into being as a result of church support but they are always much more than a prayer meeting or bible lesson and are not denominational in a religious sense.

The comparison sometimes drawn between the black voluntary and the Muslim school movements can be misleading as it plays down the importance of the politics of colour and class implicit in the former and the supremacy of the religious way of life of the latter.

On the same grounds, the black voluntary school should be distinguished from the private Christian religious foundation. For example, on being asked whether the John Loughborough Seventh Day Adventist School with fees of £600 was a 'West Indian' school, Orville Woolford, the black head teacher, said that he hoped it would be an integrated school for children of all races, but pointed out that as the Adventist church in London was predominantly black West Indian, the school was likely to reflect that composition. Although it was natural, therefore, that the school community and staff should be predominantly black, the major factor in the selection of staff was that they should be Adventists. In her article on the school, Yvonne Collymore commented that 'children who are not Seventh Day Adventists are also welcome, but looking at one of the rules, "a clean tidy haircut of reasonable length is an essential part of the uniform", I wondered how many Rastafarian children would take advantage of this offer' (Collymore 1980b: 4). It is nevertheless understandable that schools where black pupils are in the majority should be compared.

Ideological orientations

While the black voluntary school movement can be regarded as emerging from a general desire on the part of the black population for their children to succeed educationally and economically, it is also sustained by well-established and sophisticated political philosophies that have, over the last hundred years, helped black people to order and explain their social experiences, to channel their anger of rejection, and to seek political solutions.

Henry (1979), former teacher and Handsworth community development worker, mentions American Black Power, African socialism, and Jamaican Rastafarianism as three of the political traditions from which blacks have constructed their political understanding. Garveyism, which had considerable influence on both the development of Black Power and Rastafarianism might also be usefully mentioned, all four of these providing an intellectual context for the continuing development of a black ideology and its application to new circumstances in Britain.

In different ways writers and activists such as Claudia Jones in the 1950s and Obi Egbuna, Gus John, Darcus Howe, Bernard Coard, and Farrukh Dhondy in the 1960s and early 1970s contributed to the flowering of black alternative thought which was disseminated to a wider audience through meetings and campaigns and in papers and journals such as the *West Indian Gazette, West Indian World*, and *Race Today*. Visits from United States Black Power leaders Malcolm X in 1965 and Stokely Carmichael in 1967, inspired and sustained a somewhat eclectic movement and assisted in the process of 'black conscientization'.

In a series of informative articles in the *West Indian World* on black education, Yvonne Collymore stressed the importance of early campaigning by the West Indian community in relation to educational provision: the North London West Indian Association's action against banding in Haringey, the Caribbean Educational and Community Workers' Association's opposition to the placing of West Indian children in ESN schools, and the setting up of Bogle L'Ouverture publications, all in 1969. 'The first two initiatives', she claims, 'alerted parents to the dangers facing their children if education authorities were allowed through harmful policies and practices to deny West Indian children equal opportunity for learning. The third initiative was one of the earliest and most adventurous efforts in self help' (Collymore 1979).

It is difficult to lay bare the complex ideological strands which give support to the black voluntary school movement but some or all of the following ideas or practices deriving from Garveyism, Pan Africanism, Black Power, Rastafarianism, and contemporary black British thought are identifiable in the rhetoric and actions of the project organizers:

CONDEMNATION OF WHITE SOCIETY AND ITS MATERIALISM
The Rastafarians in particular reject the worldliness of 'Babylon', the term chosen to describe an evil, godless, white world and its multifarious agents: politicians, police, probation officers, social workers and, not least, teachers. As a broad generalization, the movement is distrustful of white intentions and critical of white teachers' motives and values and the effects on black children of the white-dominated day school.

WHITE RACISM AND DOMINATION
According to Carmichael and Hamilton (1967), white teachers, no matter how liberal, are unable to escape the overpowering influence of their whiteness on themselves and on black people. Among some black organizations there is a marked reluctance to make maximum use of white volunteers, a position usually justified in terms of the need to provide black pupils with suitable black 'role models'.

DANGERS OF WHITE PATERNALISM

For the Race Today Collective, liberal institutions (of which the white school might be offered as a paradigm) laying claim to philanthropic motives, and invariably presenting blacks as victims, have to be exposed as insidious forms of social control (Howe 1973: 3). The lesson is that offers from the State to assist in voluntary education projects have to be examined carefully for signs of manipulation and domination.

BLACK SOLIDARITY

Black Power calls on black people 'to unite, to recognize their heritage, to build a sense of community' (Carmichael and Hamilton, 1967: 44). The community base of the voluntary school is of utmost importance.

RACIAL PRIDE AND BLACK NATIONALISM

Marcus Garvey sought deliverance for black people in a new world in which they would no longer be slaves or serfs, but creators of a new black civilization. Black skin would become a glorious symbol of national greatness in an independent negro nation in Africa. The voluntary schools frequently seek to inculcate pride in being black.

AFRICAN LIBERATION AND ANTI-COLONIALISM

Pan-Africanism is primarily an anti-colonial political movement seeking the liberation of Africa from European material, cultural, and ideological domination and stressing the importance of integrating and uplifting the African people to equip them for life in a modern, industrial state. In the context of black voluntary education, Pan-Africanism may be interpreted as a warning against the uncritical acceptance of white values, or against the dangers of allowing white academics to colonize the minds of black children. The voluntary school becomes a base from which to fight a guerilla war against the domination of exploitative white concepts.

IMPORTANCE OF ASSERTING BLACK PEOPLE'S CONTROL
OVER BLACK CHILDREN'S EDUCATION

Garvey wanted 'complete control of our social institutions without interference by any alien race or races' (Garvey 1967: 140). The message of Black Power was that the liberation of blacks was unlikely to come from reliance on the institutions of white society. As Carmichael and Hamilton put it, 'given the illegitimacy of the system we cannot then proceed to transform that system with existing structures'

(Carmichael and Hamilton 1967: 42). Black Power, they continued was 'a call to Black people to define their own goals, to lead their own organizations and to support those organizations'. The ghetto school had to be rescued from the white-dominated school board and transformed into a base that served the interests of the black community. If whites refused to take notice parallel community institutions would have to be set up. Once more the importance of black political control is stressed.

SELF-HELP
Locally the practical expression of the need for decolonization and anti-imperialism might be seen in the insistence that black groups retain their political and economic autonomy – the black community school serving as a prime example.

COMMUNITY INTUITIVISM: THE BLACK COMMUNITY KNOWS BEST
Distrustful of white definitions of education, Garvey stressed its naturalistic dimension: education was not something fed into the individual, but a God-given gift 'let out' by an act of self-realization. The development of this inner knowledge meant that a person could become educated 'without even entering the classroom' (Garvey 1967: 16). The black community would intuitively recognize the education needed for its survival and prosperity: the voluntary school would listen to its parents and pupils.

CULTURAL ASSERTIVENESS AND BLACK VISIBILITY
Rastafarianism provides young people with an example of how to assert themselves in a hostile white world. It makes available the external symbols and style, the dreadlocks, tams, and headwraps, the wearing of the colours, dietary taboos, with which to parade their cultural and political identity in front of those who refuse to acknowledge them as equals. Farrukh Dhondy (1974) wrote of the 'infectious resistance' of blacks in the education system; they were a force which revealed the day school's social control function and exposed the false ideology of liberalism. From this it might be inferred that the voluntary school's task is to encourage students' spontaneous self-confidence and assertiveness in opposition to the prevailing view that they can do no right.

BLACK STUDIES
The traditional school curriculum took no account of black people, usually omitting all mention of their contribution to world and national history: black studies would form an essential part of the new black-controlled curriculum.

Context

The existence of the black voluntary school is predicated on the black population's unsatisfactory experience and appraisal of British education — an experience composed of all the classical ingredients of social alienation: powerlessness, meaninglessness, social isolation, and self-estrangement.

POWERLESSNESS

With regard to powerlessness, undoubtedly the most salient demand of the black school movement is to obtain some influence over the process of educating black children. Parents as a whole have traditionally had little say in a state education system originally part instituted to fulfil the middle-class mission of civilizing the working classes. If white British workers were considered unfit to make decisions about their children's education and to participate in the government of schools, it is scarcely surprising that black colonial immigrants should have experienced similar exclusion. The black population has been deprived of control over its children's education both in a real sense (the 'community' of black parents has little say in an education system dominated by professional teachers, examination boards, and universities) and in a nominal sense — there are proportionately very few blacks serving on education committees, governing bodies, or as teachers.

Black parents know they have little chance of obtaining redress from teachers who treat their children unfairly. The school, they believe, is unlikely to respond sympathetically to any form of personal or community intervention. Most teachers are white and considered by black students to be insensitive to the ever-present racial dimension of the class or school yard. *Talking Chalk*, containing accounts of black pupils', parents', and teachers' experiences of education, provides numerous examples of their inability to control the white-dominated environment of the day school, whether at the level of the governing body, the staff meeting, or the classroom (Jamdaigni *et al.* 1982). Black parents feel themselves unable to influence school management decisions, the way their children are treated on a day-to-day basis, the conduct of the classroom, or the content of the school curriculum. Meanwhile, black pupils struggle to gain greater mastery of their immediate situation by developing collective strategies which often run counter to the educational aims of the school and are possibly injurious to their own career prospects.

It is for these reasons that the black voluntary school is set up in the first place. It is an admission that the white day school is for the moment irreclaimable foreign territory, and that black control is at present only possible in a separate institution which is collectivist, community-based, participatory in form, and solidaristic in ethos: the elements absent in the black experience of mainstream schooling. The inescapable conclusion is that the black voluntary school is the only available means by which black individuals and communities can achieve the power and autonomy necessary to make decisions about their own children's future.

MEANINGLESSNESS
At a general level, the meaninglessness of education for the black population arises primarily from a realistic assessment that the schools' claims to provide equality of opportunity or parity of esteem are illusory. Far from providing each individual with the same life chances, the schools confirm the class destiny and status of working-class children 'by virtue of the starved education which they provide' (Miliband 1969: 241). In the course of their educational career, children are differentiated, examined, graded, and certificated, the results having a direct bearing on their future career and life chances. Given the stereotypical white assessment of black intellectual ability, the economic and social-class background of black parents from the Caribbean, the paucity of educational facilities made available in the Caribbean to previous generations, and the continuing racial discrimination in education and employment in Britain, it can come as no surprise that many blacks have little faith in the school's claim to be educating children to their 'full potential' (Reeves and Chevannes 1981).

Most older black pupils are instrumental in their approach to education, being primarily motivated by a wish to improve their prospects in the labour market. Those who find school work difficult, who cannot see why it should be of interest to them, or suspect that it is unlikely to improve their chances of employment, are inclined to reject the formal curriculum in favour of more immediately expressive activities. Education will be meaningless if pupils are unable to see a relationship between their school work in total or part, and their future roles as citizens or workers. This perhaps helps to explain the emphasis placed by the black voluntary school on the development of basic enabling skills, the raising of social expectations, and the attempts to establish a realistic link in the pupils' minds between their study and their intended occupation. It is always difficult for middle-class educationalists to understand the urgent instrumentalism of those whose lives are circumscribed by economic considerations.

Midwinter, referring to the needs of the majority 'who will live forever in the deprived area' of the cities, argues strongly for 'the social-environmentally based curriculum' which 'begins with the child's experience and works purposefully outwards' (Midwinter 1972: 18–19). Black children, subject to racial discrimination, but supported by family resources arduously forged in centuries of struggle for survival, are likely to wait in vain for a curriculum that reflects their personal experiences. In this respect, again, black children are unable to create a relationship between their everyday life and the school curriculum, with resulting lack of purpose and involvement. It is not without reason that the black voluntary school movement seeks to provide black studies as part of its curriculum – not as an academic historical study of Africa and the Caribbean but as a celebration of continuing black struggle and achievement in the face of adversity.

ISOLATION

A black minority living among an unfriendly white population is bound at times to feel lonely, vulnerable, and isolated. Depending on residential concentration of racial groups, local schools will vary in their racial composition and in the number and proportion of Afro-Caribbean children in attendance. While on occasion Afro-Caribbean students might form a majority, in most schools they will be in a minority among whites and Asians. Governors, influential parents, the head, and most of the teachers will be white.

Black teachers may have to face the ostracism of white colleagues. One black teacher has described how when she first started teaching she went into the staff room to be greeted with 'Good Lord, we've got them outside, do we have to have them in here as well?' (Jamdaigni *et al.* 1982: 56).

Lacking knowledge of the British education system, intimidated by the hierarchy of the school and the 'professionalism' of the teachers, black parents may decide to forego the privilege of attending parent-teacher meetings, open days, or careers conventions, with adverse effects on communication between the school and the black population.

In a context in which there is evidence to show that teachers and other students have low expectations of Afro-Caribbeans, black pupils may sense they are constantly under examination and may experience the stress that invariably accompanies such critical exposure. The feeling of social isolation in the school, and of being on the defensive, and unable to relax, will generate a number of responses: of withdrawal, of seeking out and mixing only with those of a similar colour, of ignoring or denying one's colour, of pretending against all the odds to be white, of proudly and aggressively parading one's differences in the face of white disapproval or of openly rebelling against all manifestations of school discipline, and so on.

One response, of course, has been to attend the black voluntary school where among the black majority a black skin takes on a new and positive role: a membership badge for the fraternity of colour. The black voluntary school, 'solidaristic in ethos', is a place where blacks feel at ease, are supportive of one another, and are more ready to admit their educational weaknesses and to seek help in redressing them. Paradoxically, the cost of attempting to relieve social isolation is one of creating a separate black institution which might be interpreted as increasing the social distance and reducing still further the contact between whites and blacks.

SELF-ESTRANGEMENT

The fourth dimension of social alienation, self-estrangement, is always more difficult to delineate. In the context of the black experience in Britain, it might easily be related to the social psychological studies of identity, ably summarized in Milner (1983). The conventional theory is that self-rejection among blacks arises as a result of their living in a culture and society dominated by whites and in which they are always depicted and treated as inferior. Blacks are then presented with the choice of whether to deny their true identity by identifying with whites (the effort of identity-maintenance in the face of the reality subjecting the individual to high levels of stress) or to identify with blacks and to accept the values of a white society that projects them as inferior. A picture is presented of a vulnerable individual struggling alone against these possibilities, a reality perhaps for the solitary black child in an all-white environment. But for many black people there is another solution – a collective strategy of changing the values assigned to the attributes of the group.

Milner's studies of the white orientation of black British children show a substantial decline in 'misidentification' over a five year period. Milner believes that 'black consciousness has grown, black social and political organizations have flourished, and black culture has evolved a specifically British variant, all of which has given black children and youth an alternative, acceptable image of their group with which to identify' (Milner 1983: 161).

The inspiration for the black voluntary school movement owes much to the realization of the need to develop a collective strategy for raising the consciousness of the black population in the face of the limited stereotypical images of black people available in white popular culture. In particular, Bernard Coard's widely-read *How the West Indian Child is made educationally sub-normal in the British school system* (1971) helped to focus the attention of the Afro-Caribbean population on the inferior quality of the British education their children were receiving and of the dangers the white school posed to the black child's identity. Coard graphically describes his own experience of the reluctance of his class to draw black children as *black* and gives an account of the Clarks' black and white doll experiment, before making a series of recommendations which include the need to recruit as many black teachers as possible, to make black history and culture part of the curriculum of all schools, and for black people to open nursery and supplementary schools in the areas in which they live (Coard 1971: 38–9).

Teachers in the Black Arrow School were determined to suppress another instance of what they interpreted as damaging self-denigration: the practice of some black pupils of referring insultingly to the darkness of skin and other negroid features of their fellow black pupils.

The self-image of the black child has remained a prime concern of the black voluntary school with emphasis being placed on the importance for black children of black professional role models operating in a black educational environment with a curriculum of black studies. At a political level, the campaign to expurgate children's books and curricular material of all negative references to black people has been pursued with vigour.

Prospects

The criticisms of state education implicit in black voluntary education fall into two categories: those levelled at the racial attitudes and discriminatory practices of the school and its teachers (racialism) but also those directed at educational institutions generally. Many of the educational principles elicited by the black voluntary school movement's critique are echoed by advocates of alternative and community education and deschooling.

For example, Poster (1971) lists curriculum relevance, social service to the community, democratic control of the school, democracy in the school, assistance from the community, and cultural provision for the community, as some of the aims of community schooling. Pointing out that it is not in the public interest to accept a system of education which destroys rather than develops human potentiality and blames its human resources while inadvertently perpetuating the injustices which limit its efficiency, Clark (1971: 122–3) advocates alternative forms of public education as competitors to the present state monopoly.

As a consequence of these resonances, the black voluntary education movement is capable not only of generating political support among the Afro-Caribbean population and those concerned for racial justice, but also of finding right-wing and left-wing allies in the more general field of social policy. Where reservations exist, they are more likely to be found among professional white educators, conscious of the movement's outspoken criticism of existing white education institutions and its attempts to 'interfere' in what have traditionally been regarded as professional matters.

Right-wingers are struck by the possibilities of encouraging self-reliance, of breaking up the state educational monopoly by transferring control to individual consumers. The idea of promoting racial minority independent education as an *alternative policy* for dealing with the problems of educational failure, under-resourcing and the inadequacy of the existing education services may also undermine more direct political demands for greater equality, racial justice, and an end to racial discrimination.

Conscious of the enduring class inequalities in education opportunity and outcome, left-wingers will regard the black community's efforts as a laudable egalitarian project, an extension of traditional working-class demands for free universal education, to be directly compared to the socialist Sunday school movement, and as a possible way of overcoming known obstacles to black equality of treatment. Left-wingers will also subscribe to the values of community participation in and control of state schools, yet will hold grave reservation about the possibility of independent black private schools. These will be seen as socially divisive on ethnic, racial or religious grounds, just as other forms of private education are seen as divisive on grounds of social class. Clearly considerable significance must attach to the distinction between separate full-time schools for blacks, whether private or state-run, and black voluntary ('supplementary') education.

The future of the black voluntary school movement will depend both on its perceived usefulness to the black community and on its relationship with the mainstream education system and policy makers. In as far as it is possible for us to pretend to be objective in our assessment of the education on offer (there are no generally agreed criteria of assessment, and the educational provision varies enormously depending on school, teacher, and subject area) it is likely that the benefits of the voluntary school are more indirect than direct, the school's unrecognized 'latent' functions being of far greater importance than those overtly stated or 'manifest'.

A consideration in any assessment must be the very small proportion of Afro-Caribbean children between the ages of 5–16 who attend the voluntary schools at all, or on a regular basis. Numbers are often exaggerated for the benefit of sponsoring bodies and other official agencies, but to take as an example the town of Wolverhampton, with a comparatively well-developed voluntary school sector and a population of just over 3000 Afro-Caribbean children between the ages of five and fifteen years, even the highest estimate would give an enrolment figure in 1984 of only 3 per cent, with the likelihood of perhaps 2 per cent attending on a regular weekly basis. In addition, no more than 10 per cent of black children in any year would attend a holiday project run by a black-led organization. On the grounds of participation alone the effect of the direct voluntary educational input on the black school population must be small.

The number of hours spent in the schools – three hours on a Saturday morning or two evenings per week – and the length of the interval between successive meetings might also be thought to lessen the schools' impact. Lack of consistency in the content and methods of the day and the voluntary school, the intermittent attendance of volunteer helpers, inclement weather, long travelling distances, lack of school equipment, and shortage of storage space in buildings that are hired on a temporary basis, are other factors which might detract from the value of the voluntary school experience.

But all this should be set against the positive help offered to children, often on a one to one or small group basis, in the academic school subjects, particularly English and mathematics, in their social relationships, in the developments of their cultural identity through the study of African and Caribbean history and creative arts, and in understanding the political struggle of black people in Britain and elsewhere. Also to be noted are improvements in children's orientation to study and an increase in the racial and political consciousness of children and parents.

Indeed, many of those involved in the black voluntary school movement would claim that its most important contribution is to the political development of the black community. It strengthens community support networks and communication channels and helps to disseminate knowledge about the structure and functions of local government services. The school can also help in the mobilization of the black community around issues which concern it, particularly in the field of education. As a self-help institution under the control of black people, the school has an important symbolic role: it serves as an example of independent black achievement.

The voluntary school supports the black population in a number of other ways, less frequently mentioned. It frequently provides help and advice to parents in their dealings with the day schools, particularly

165

at times when parents need to assert their rights, when children are in trouble or are being pressurized to make career choices. Teachers in the voluntary schools can become close friends of pupils and their families, giving them advice on vocational matters, providing them with emotional support over a sustained period, and assisting them with contacts in professional circles.

More often than not the voluntary school will have direct links with the day schools and other social services in the area in which it operates. As an organization, it will act as a pressure group seeking to improve educational and other facilities for the black community. Where relationships with day schools are friendly and supportive, black teachers and parents may be invited to help in organizing activities on the day schools' premises.

Although there might be a danger of staff at the day school attempting to relieve themselves of children whom they regard as 'discipline problems', referrals are occasionally made by the day school to the voluntary school. Day school teachers have been known to volunteer for work in the voluntary school in order to gain knowledge and experience of work with Afro-Caribbean people and the trust and confidence of the black children in their classes. Black teachers and helpers are also able to develop their professional and organizational skills by working in the voluntary school. One particularly painful lesson is that black teachers do not have privileged access to the souls of black children and must earn their respect by demonstrating genuine commitment and competence.

The future of the black voluntary school movement will depend on four related factors: the availablility of resources, the issue of political control, black political unity, and changes in British social institutions. If more resources were made available, the black voluntary sector could be strengthened and extended. At present, for example, most voluntary schools confine themselves to work at the primary and secondary levels, with greater emphasis at the primary because of the difficulty of providing teachers and equipment at more specialist advanced levels. Initiatives in further, adult, and higher education are unusual despite the black population's need for vocational education, adult literacy classes, and access links with higher education courses. A strong case can be made for making money available to black voluntary schools in order that teachers may be paid and equipment purchased.

Questions of independence and autonomy, however, are raised for self-help organizations which come to depend on external funding: white agencies, the local authorities, the Department of Education and Science, the Home Office, the Manpower Service Commission, or the Commission for Racial Equality would be the only feasible sources of income on the scale required and they, quite understandably, would want to ensure that they obtained value for money. In turn, the black voluntary education movement would be centrally concerned with its autonomy in respect of its right to make decisions on the suitability of the education on offer to black children.

Forced to be separatist in practice as a result of the failings of the white education system, the black voluntary education movement is divided over the extent to which it should maintain its separatism as a principle or as a tactic as new circumstances arise. Those organizations outspokenly critical of the ubiquitous racism of white institutions are unlikely to win, or to wish to win, the support of white funding agencies. The knowledge of the availability of money and of the attached strings may lead to a modification of a position of principle but often not before acrimonious debate has weakened the unity of the group. Of course, changes which assist black people in gaining access to, or winning greater control of British institutions – nurseries, schools, youth clubs, training agencies, and so on, may lessen their demand for exclusive places of their own: in effect they may be able to control to a limited degree facilities financed directly by the local authority.

In conclusion, in order to point the way forward, it is worth mentioning one recent West Midland development in the field of black education. A consortium of four black community organizations joined forces and approached a local community college for help in providing teachers for the consortium's educational endeavours. A black education consortium prospectus of vocational and academic courses was published and widely distributed among the black population. The black organizations provided the premises for the classes, helped to find and to enrol students and assisted in recruiting suitably qualified staff to teach the courses on a college outreach basis. The college employed and paid the part-time teachers and encouraged them, if they were not already professionally trained, to take appropriate teaching qualifications in their spare time. In a subsequent year more black organizations joined the consortium and the scheme was enlarged to include the local adult education and youth service and the polytechnic.

Black students have been enrolled in ever larger numbers while the community college has managed to recruit more black full-time and part-time staff in accordance with its official equal opportunities policy. There is no reason why such collaborative ventures should not be extended to the primary and secondary sectors. In the meantime, universities and polytechnics might make use of their links with black voluntary education to increase their intake of black students on courses for teachers, thus eventually establishing 'access loops' between the schools, further and higher education, and back to the schools.

© *1987 Mel Chevannes and Frank Reeves*

References

Blauner, R. (1963) *Alienation and Freedom: The Manual Worker in Industry*. Chicago: University of Chicago.

Carmichael, S. and Hamilton, C. V. (1967) *Black Power, The Politics of Liberation in America*. New York: Vintage.

Cashmore, E. (1979) *Rastaman: The Rastafarian Movement in England*. London: Allen and Unwin.

Clark, K. (1971) Alternative public school systems. In Gross, B. and Gross, R. (eds) *Radical School Reform*. London: Victor Gollancz.

Coard, B. (1971) *How the West Indian Child is Made Educationally Subnormal in the British School System*. London: New Beacon Books.

Collymore, Y. (1979) Ten years of protest and struggle for education. *West Indian World* (12.10–18.10): 5.

—— (1980a) Caribbean Teachers' Association launches new teaching and counselling project. *West Indian World* (22.2–28.2): 6.

—— (1980b) Moves to set up a supplementary school association. *West Indian World* (28.3–3.4): 5.

—— (1980c) New Seventh Day Adventist School: blacks lead the way. *West Indian World* (2.5–8.5): 4.

—— (1980d) Development of Black Parents' Movement. *West Indian World* (2.11–8.11): 2, 9.

Dalphinis, M. (1985) *Caribbean and African Languages*. London: Karia Press.

Department of Education and Science (1985) *Education for All: The Report of the Committee of Inquiry into the Education of Children from Ethnic Minority Groups*, Cmnd 9543. London: HMSO.

Dhondy, F. (1974) The black explosion in schools. *Race Today* 6(2): 44–7.

—— (1978) Teaching young Blacks. *Race Today* 10(4): 80–6.

Dubois, W. E. B. (1947) *The World and Africa*. New York; Viking Press.

Foner, N. (1975) The meaning of education to Jamaicans at home and in London. *New Community* 4, (Summer): 195–202.

Garvey, A. J. (compiler) (1967) *Philosophy and Opinions of Marcus Garvey*. London: Frank Cass.

Giles, R. (1977) *The West Indian Experience in British Schools*. London: Heinemann.

Gross, B. and Gross, R. (eds) (1971) *Radical School Reform*. London: Victor Gollancz.

Henry, I. (1979) White schools, black children. *The Social Science Teacher* 8(4): 134–5.

Howe, D. (1973) From victim to protagonist, the changing social reality. *Race Today* 5(1): 3.

Jamdaigni, L., Phillips-Bell, M., and Ward, J. (1982) *Talking Chalk: Black Pupils, Parents, and Teachers Speak about Education*. Birmingham: AFFOR.

John, G. (1972) Commentary. In Humphry, D. and John, G. *Police Power and Black People*. London: Granada, Panther.

Johnson, B. (1985) *'I think of my mother': Notes on the Life and Times of Claudia Jones*. London: Karia Press.

Midwinter, E. (1972) *Priority Education. An Account of the Liverpool Project*. Harmondsworth: Penguin.

Miliband, R. (1969) *The State in Capitalist Society*. London: Weidenfeld & Nicholson.

Milner, D. (1983) *Children and Race, Ten Years On*. London: Ward Lock.

Morris, S. (1973) Black studies in Britain. *New Community*, 11(3): 245–8.

Moyo, B. (1984) Night school develops day-time curriculum. *Express and Star* 17 January: 9.

Nagra, J. S. (1980) 'Asian supplementary schools and the attitudes of Asian children and parents towards the teaching of the mother tongue'. M. Ed. Dissertation, University of Birmingham.

Padmore, G. (1956) *Pan Africanism or Communism?* London: Dennis Dobson.

Phillips, M. (1982) Separatism or black control? In Ohri, A., Manning, B., and Curno, P. (eds) *Community Work and Racism*. London: Routledge & Kegan Paul.

Poster, C. D. (1971) *The School and the Community*. London: Macmillan.

Reeves, F. & Chevannes, M. (1981) The underachievement of Rampton. *Multiracial Education* 10(1): 35–42.

—— (1983) *Notes on the development of a black supplementary school, Wolverhampton*. Afro Caribbean Education Trust.

—— (1984) The political education of young blacks in Britain. In *Educational Review*, 36(2): 175–85.

Sharron, H. (1984) Night school. *The Times Educational Supplement* 6th January: 15.

Smith, M. G., Augier, R., and Nettleford, R. (1969) *The Rastafari Movement in Kingston, Jamaica*. Kingston: Institute of Social and Economic Research.

Stone, M. (1981) *The Education of the Black Child in Britain. The Myth of Multiracial Education*. London: Fontana.

The Times News Team (1968) *The Black Man in Search of Power*. London: Nelson.

Tomlinson, S. (1984) *Home and School in Multicultural Britain*. London: Batsford Academic.

Wilcox, P. R. (1971) The community-centred school. In Gross, B. and Gross, R. (eds) *Radical School Reform*. London: Victor Gollancz.

11 Attacking racism in education

Bob Carter and Jenny Williams

Current conceptions of racism in practice

It is a commonplace that academics are overconcerned with definitions and terminology, whereas in the 'real world' it is actions that count. Like many commonplaces this contains some truth. But it also relies upon a false assumption about the relationship between ideas and action, between theory and political practice. According to this assumption, theorizing can be disregarded if it does not result in practical policies or is not of immediate and direct relevance to particular groups of activists. This divorce of theory from practice is not only false but dangerous. In antiracist politics, the failure to grasp the ways in which theory and practice inform each other has already had highly divisive consequences. When new policy developments are controversial, when there is an increase in resources and effort devoted to new forms of action, then it is particularly important that the theoretical assumptions behind political and professional practices are made explicit. There is a growing acceptance on the part of teachers, academics, and politicians that racism in education should be the focus of analysis and reforming policies. This presumes that the meaning of 'racism in education' is clear and unambiguous. In this chapter we propose to examine some of the ways in which the term racism is used in education. We wish to pay particular attention to the role of notions of culture and ethnicity in underpinning interpretations of racism. Finally, we want to suggest an alternative understanding of racism and draw out some of its implications for antiracist reform.

THE SWANN REPORT
Any commentary on the Swann Report (1985) must begin by acknowledging its many differing emphases and contradictions, some of which can be and are being used by radical teachers, administrators, and others as part of their own campaigns. We wish to focus our

170

attention upon the first two chapters, since these set out the ideological framework within which the Committee's concerns are shaped and developed.

Chapter Two, 'Racism: theory and practice', in contrast with most official reports, attempts to spell out the meaning and importance of racism. This takes twenty-eight pages and includes lengthy discussions of prejudice, stereotyping, the media as a source of stereotypes, the roots of racism in the different receptions given to refugees and migrants and their expectations about life in this country, teacher attitudes and behaviour towards ethnic minority pupils, inter-ethnic prejudices, institutional racism, a wider, general climate of racism, racist attacks, and 'racial' tensions in schools. It is difficult to distil one representative definition of racism from this miscellany, but the following comes closest:

> 'In view of the elements of prejudice which we have identified, it is perhaps inevitable that ethnic minority groups, who are relative newcomers to this country, should find themselves subject to possibly the most insidious and pernicious form of negative prejudice in our society – racism.'   (1985: 14)

This interpretation of racism rests on the analysis which precedes it in Chapter One, 'The nature of society'. Here the notions of nation, culture, ethnicity, and 'race' are linked in a particular way.

At the beginning of the Report ethnicity is chosen as a central explanatory concept. Though the Report does not provide a single definition, it suggests that ethnicity plays a crucial role in determining an individual's place in society. Ethnicity can be characterized by skin colour or by 'shared cultural attributes'. Apparently it is both an objective, unalterable category, and a subjective, alterable description dependent on the 'eye of the beholder'.

This subjective, cultural aspect of ethnicity allows Swann to make a series of seemingly obvious, common sense assertions concerning racism and the problems arising from it. According to Swann, individuals are members of many different groups (age, gender, class, profession, and so on) but they are also part of a wider national society by virtue of common *shared* characteristics (e.g. common language, common political and legal system), which taken together give that society a degree of unity and its members a form of corporate identity. Thus Swann is able to claim the existence of a common identity as the basis of ethnicity:

> 'In Britain today there are members of many diverse and numerically smaller ethnic minority groups living alongside a majority group which, though far from homogeneous in its actual composition,

history, and origins, is nevertheless regarded as, and tends to regard itself as, sharing a common ethnic identity.' (1985: 4)

Viewing ethnicity in this way provides Swann with its central motif: racism as a threat to the balance of a genuine pluralism. The task facing the pluralist society is to seek 'to achieve a balance between, on the one hand, the maintenance and active support of the *essential* elements of the cultures and life styles within it, and, on the other, the acceptance by all groups of a set of shared values distinctive of the society as a whole.' (Emphasis added. 1985: 6.)

As with all balances, this one involves obligations for both partners (for a comparitive account of the pluralist dilemma, see Bullivant 1981). All ethnic groups must abide by the law, and seek to change it only through 'peaceful and democratic means' (no more rioting please). In return, the government has to ensure equal treatment and protection by the law, equal access to education and employment, equal opportunity to participate fully in social and political life, equal freedom of conscience and cultural expression.

Swann's understanding of nation and ethnicity, with its repeated emphasis on stability, cohesion, and common identity, is one that ignores structural divisions and conflicts of interest betwen different groups. This means that racism is primarily presented as individual prejudice, based on negative cultural stereotypes. This view of British society as 'relatively homogeneous' before the arrival of a culturally diverse immigrant population means first, that the relationship between racism, colour, culture, and class need not be explored and, second, that discriminatory behaviour is seen to be merely a conse-quence of practices and procedures designed to 'meet the needs and expectations' of a culturally homogeneous 'white' society. Colour in-equalities are explained by cultural intolerance and misunderstand-ing. The facts of discrimination and the nature of its operation can be put aside in favour of a general understanding by all of the unfortu-nate effects of racism.

Significantly, it is in the paragraph 'Relationship with the police' that this view is put with the greatest candour:

'Here again, the essential element seems to us to be not so much the actual facts of the situation, although there is considerable evidence in some cases to justify communities' concerns, but equally the wide gulf in trust and understanding which exists between ethnic minority communities and "established figures" which in itself is symptomatic of the overall climate of racism which we believe exists.' (1985: 33)

Where, one might ask, does this 'wide gulf' come from if it is not rooted in the 'actual facts of the situation'? It is not police brutality which is the issue for Swann, but a cultural gulf that makes the ideology of common interests difficult to sustain.

This analysis of racism, within the context of cultural pluralism, leads directly to the major recommendations of the Report. 'Education for all' means, at the curriculum level, correcting cultural misunderstandings, and at an institutional level, making 'ethnic' concessions towards a common cultural unity. Chapter Six, for example, recommends the ending of compulsory worship and the removal of the privileged status of Christianity in schools. In return the demands for separate schools and mother tongue are rejected. The only cultural divisions that are worthy of discussion are those which relate to ethnicity and religion. Therefore the myth of a previous 'cultural unity' is implicit and at times explicit. The history of social conflicts around schooling in this country reveals a continuing struggle to impose particular cultural definitions of merit and worth. A notion of 'cultural unity' is therefore difficult to sustain, as is the assumption, present in Swann, that the only divisions within schools meriting attention are those based on ethnicity.

This failure to set individual prejudice and racism within any model of structural inequality and conflict means that the relationship between curriculum reform and wider structures of power and inequality is ignored. Thus the basis for reform can only be individual good will and the pursuit of social harmony (see Troyna 1986: 178 for a fuller account of Swann's 'conception of the State which is neutral, which will be responsive to the call for antiracism and which is waiting to be provided with the technical means by which it may operationalise this orthodoxy').

THE POLITICS OF RACISM AWARENESS
The popularity of Racism Awareness Training (RAT) courses has been a key feature of antiracist initiatives over the last few years. We are concerned here only with those practitioners who have based their work on the writings of Judith Katz (1978): for example, Ruddell and Simpson (1982), Satow (1982) and the Racism Awareness Programme Unit (RAPU) founded in 1978. These have been subject to critical analysis elsewhere (see particularly Sivanandan 1985 and Gurnah 1984). Our interest is limited to their analysis of racism.

In contrast to Swann, RAT appears to avoid references to ethnicity in favour of a resolute focus on institutional racism. Central to its approach is the formula: racism = power + prejudice. According to this, as a consequence of history and numerical preponderance, power in British society is in the hands of white people. Two consequences are held to follow from this. First, only white people in Britain can be racist. Second, even though particular white individuals may not consciously adopt racist attitudes, they will still be racist because, as white people, they will unavoidably be implicated in the institutional practices and procedures which white people have developed for white advantage. The concept of racism on which this argument rests can be said to consist of the following propositions:

1 Power is personal: all white people, individually, have, by virtue of their whiteness, power over black people. Power is thus severed from its connections with economic relations.
2 All white people are racist, not because of the coincidence of whiteness and class privilege in the UK but because they are white. This in turn implies that:
3 There is an 'essence' of racism that history has deposited white psyche, part of white peoples' collective unconscious. As Sivanandan puts it: 'There is no escaping it [racism] and because the system is loaded in their favour, all that whites can be, even when they fight racism, is antiracist racists: if they don't they are just plain, common or garden racists' (Sivanandan 1985: 18).
4 Separatism is the consequence of this view of racism, since racial oppression is a product of whiteness, of biological skin colour, and is therefore unalterable. If oppression is derived from biology, what is the point of struggling against it? A similar argument has been developed about radical feminism by Murphy and Livingstone (1985) and we have drawn heavily on their discussion.

In short, the racism = power + prejudice formula rests on a personalized view of power and an understanding of racism which sets it aside from economic relations. White power and white attitudes within particular institutions become the focus of policies. The political implications of this are far reaching. Though deliberately eschewing a notion of ethnicity, RAT analyses take for granted a relationship between colour and culture. It is implied that colour constitutes a basis for community. It is only on this basis that it can meaningfully be argued that the *purpose* of racism is to benefit all white people. A community of interests is constructed on the basis of colour: *the* black or white community, white schools, and so on. Within this paradigm racism can only be fought by changing the personal exercise of power, by persuading whites who have power to exercise it in the interests of blacks because colour is the most significant division between them. Why should white people do this? Again, as with Swann, because it is morally the correct thing to do or because colour divisions and inequalities pose a threat to the psychological well being of whites and to the continuing exercise of power in its current form.

RACISM AND EDUCATIONAL INEQUALITIES

Missing from both the RAT and Swann perspectives is any rigorous exploration of the relationship between racism, colour discrimination, and other inequalities. Even more radical approaches, operating with a concept of institutional racism, share a similar failing. There is an assumption that racism is directly, unambiguously, and solely responsible for 'racial' inequalities and that this can be inferred from statistical comparisons. There is a readiness to regard colour differences as the elemental form of social division. The Commission for Racial Equality (CRE) formal investigation into Birmingham LEA referral and suspension of pupils (CRE 1985) epitomizes both the strengths and weaknesses of this approach. In a thorough investigation of the patterns of school suspensions in Birmingham between 1974 and 1980 the CRE concluded that pupils of Caribbean and African origin were proportionately four times more likely to be suspended from secondary schools than white pupils. According to the report neither residence in the inner city nor single parent families accounted for this over-representation. Instead it is assumed that the statistical comparison demonstrates the existence of racism and discrimination.

What form does this take? Unfortunately political and professional concerns within Birmingham LEA have resulted in much important data being omitted from the report, so obscuring the answer to this question. Hints are given that some 'middle ring' schools are over-reacting to newly arrived black pupils and that some teachers are intolerant of Rastafarianism or incapable of assessing cultural variations in the manifestation of insolence. These hints, which relate directly to the behaviour of teachers in particular schools, are in contrast to the claim that:

> 'evidence pointed to institutional, rather than direct or intentional, discrimination as the main reason for the differential pattern of treatment. The term "institutional discrimination" is taken to include all those practices and procedures employed by a school or local authority which, intentionally or otherwise, have the effect of placing members of one or other racial or ethnic group at a disadvantage that cannot be justified.'　　　　(CRE 1985: 2)

There is clearly some muddle in this discussion as to where the 'intentional' aspect of these practices is located. More importantly the practices and procedures are not spelled out. We need to know in some detail what these are and how they operate. Then the nature of the reforms needed to combat 'racial' inequalities can be pinpointed. Instead, Birmingham LEA, as a result of the CRE investigation, has instituted new procedures which centralize decision making about suspensions. The assumption appears to be that the reasons for the earlier patterns can be found in teacher prejudice, stereotyping, ignorance, incompetence, or racism; that administrators and local politicians will not make such mistakes; and that equality of outcome (i.e. a 'fair' representation of suspensions in statistical terms) would represent 'racial' justice. None of these assumptions is necessarily correct. A quite different but equally oversimplified scenario would examine the interconnections between the very high unemployment of black youth and the willingness of such youth to tolerate the boredom of school in return for qualifications or references which have little material reward. In other words, to see direct material inequalities as the crucial context within which teacher pupil relationships are played out.

What we are suggesting is that although research such as this is extremely valuable in indicating inequalities of outcome, such statistical statements can be interpreted in a variety of ways. The role of racism and discrimination and the forms they take in the production and reproduction of outcomes must be demonstrated clearly and concretely. An example of what we mean is the detailed ethnographic study undertaken by Cecile Wright (1985) in two Midlands schools in which she studied school records, interviewed teachers, and observed classroom interaction. Such detail allows individual prejudice, discriminatory acts, and institutional procedures to be scrutinized in ways that can provide a basis for effective policy initiatives. (See also Chapter 8 in this volume).

Reconceptualizing antiracism in education

The consequences of the above analysis for antiracist initiatives now need to be spelt out. Before discussing alternative policies we need to make plain our definition of racism. The core of racism is the assignment of characteristics in a deterministic way to a group, or groups, of persons. These characteristics are usually articulated around some cultural or biological feature such as skin colour or religion; they are regarded as inherent and unalterable precisely because they are seen as derived from one's 'race'. 'Race-ism' then employs these 'race-ial' characteristics to explain behaviour, feelings, attitudes, and ways of life.

It is important to recognize that 'race-ism' does not rest on the objective fact of 'race'. 'Races' cannot be said to exist in any valid biological sense; they are socially constructed. Groups of people become racialized, defined as a 'race'. They are held to possess certain unchangeable characteristics which are constitutive of their 'race'. 'Race' is therefore constructed through a process of ascription. An attribute (skin colour, religion, country of origin, language) becomes the basis of an individual's identity. It is thus considered to be an unalterable feature of those human beings so defined: for example, greed comes to be regarded as an aspect of 'Jewish-ness'; criminality comes to be regarded as an aspect of 'West Indian-ness'.

Racism is therefore more than the sum of individual prejudice; it becomes an organizing principle of popular consciousness. The manner in which particular individuals interact with racism, the way in which it shapes their beliefs, ideas, and attitudes is not our prime concern here; rather it is with the ways in which power and racism intersect.

People in positions of power can, and do, organize the distribution of resources such as income, housing, and employment in racialized terms. One effect of this is to reinforce racialized perceptions and 'race-ism'. In the UK low income, poor housing, and low status jobs are seen to be associated with colour, are seen to be a consequence of blackness. This means that the processes by which poverty is created are rendered invisible by making poverty appear to be a result of colour.

The significance of regarding racism in this way becomes obvious when considering notions of ethnicity and culture. Anderson (1983) has argued that nations are 'imagined communities' which, at certain historical moments and for some social groups, provide an organized and lived sense of reality, a way of selecting, organizing, and interpreting individual and collective existence. This concept of 'imagined community' can also be applied to social groups constructed around cultural and ethnic bases; the notion of 'the Jew', 'the Muslim', 'the West Indian' are social constructions.

This is not to deny the existence of varied and distinctive cultures. Nor is it to deny that these are important to individuals. We are insisting though that cultures have to be understood historically, as creative responses to social circumstances and material conditions. They do not impart unchangeable features of identity to individuals and they do not unalterably determine their behaviour through some mysterious 'way of life'. To use the concept of culture in this way is to strengthen the language of racism.

A major feature of racialization in the UK has been the State's leading role in the construction of ethnic and cultural communities. This has been particularly evident in education. For example, in much discussion of alleged 'black underachievement', 'Asian' and 'West Indian' cultures are polarized and contrasted as though each group were homogeneous, as though cultures were permanent, fixed,

177

and unchanging and as though racism were experienced equally and with the same consequences by every black person. One effect of this association of underachievement with 'blackness' has been to render opaque the processes of competition and credentialling that are integral to schooling in the United Kingdom.

Education research and policy that is based on oversimplified 'ethnic' divisions between 'Asians/Afro-Caribbeans/whites' should be rejected. Class, gender, age, and even spatial and geographical divisions within each group must be part of any discussion of educational needs, inequalities, and rights. This entails a consideration of the relationship between 'racial' inequalities and class inequalities within education.

The early optimism surrounding the struggles to mitigate class inequalities through educational reform has largely evaporated. Recent emphases on selection, vocationalism, and competitiveness have been accompanied by savage cuts in educational provision and expenditure. It is in this situation of retrenchment and diminishing resources that antiracist policies have to operate. If their aim is merely to alter the composition of winners and losers, to redistribute scarce rewards, then they are unlikely to appeal to the vast majority who will continue to fare badly in an inequitable system.

Antiracist struggles need to demonstrate their importance to wider movements of social and political reform and to efforts to challenge credentialling, competitive schooling if they are to receive popular support. The establishment of antiracist policies as part of equal opportunity policies, as for example in Manchester and ILEA, is one way that campaigns have been developed. Though concerned directly with altering the distribution of resources, rewards, and employment within a local authority, they may also contribute to a general attack on monetarism and the shift of resources away from the poor.

This would require an LEA to look closely at its own policies, its own distribution of resources and recruitment procedures. Those antiracist policies which do little more than blame teachers and schools for racism and exhort them to alter their practices will simply arouse cynicism and provoke disenchantment. LEAs need to examine their own decision-making processes, allocation of resources, designation of catchment areas, school closures, suspension procedures, and creation of special units. These are decisions where racism and class issues interlock.

Power within institutions, and the power of institutions, need not originate from nor only express itself through individuals. Power is not just personal. This means that policies must distinguish between the structures that result from the specific histories of buildings, recruitment patterns, the training and certification of teachers, the allocation of resources, ideological definitions of knowledge, and ability through the examination system, and the roles of particular individuals who occupy particular positions because of their professional and political suitability. Whilst there are opportunities for individuals to initiate changes, these are invariably constrained by political and institutional forces which shape options, the understandings of options and the context within which reforms have to be implemented.

An example may make this clear. In an edition of its journal *Issues in Race and Education* the London NAME group considers the problem of assessment in schools, stating in the first paragraph that 'testing procedures are often potent mechanisms for institutionalized racism.' (London Name 1984: 1.) Yet there is little demonstration of how this is supposed to operate. Two case studies of referrals for special education are given, where it is assumed that because the children are black there is sufficient evidence of differential treatment. Insensitive, arbitrary decision making is not necessarily institutionalized racism. The London branch of NAME takes for granted that difficulties of assessment where English is not the community language are the result of teacher racism. However, assessment is a fundamental part of competitive schooling in the UK. It is designed to discriminate between one child and another. It is worth noting in this context that the combination of intellectual and behavioural judgements made by teachers about black students, so graphically described by Cecile Wright in her chapter in this volume, closely resemble judgements made about certain types of working-class pupils (see, for example, the work of Willis 1977, Hargreaves 1967, and Lacey 1970). The 'racial' aspects of the selection process are not peripheral adjuncts that can be lopped off without altering the nature of the process itself.

So long as education is concerned to allocate individuals within an already determined structure, teachers will be gate keepers distributing scarce rewards. It is obviously a key antiracist task to remove a colour element from this distributive, hierarchical system, but this will not alter 'standard' inequalities. It will not alter the life chances of the majority of pupils. Providing policies on the assemption that it will, is to raise a false optimism among parents and children and to connive with the established myth that better-educated pupils will abolish unemployment and economic decline.

A variety of policies have been developed by LEAs to modify institutional structures. Many of these are prescriptive: ordering head-teachers to designate a staff member responsible for multicultural-ism/antiracism, to set out formal procedures to deal with racist abuse, to translate school communications into community languages, to allocate specific resources for multicultural/antiracist work. Instructions may also be proscriptive: the establishment of certain rules about staff behaviour, such as a code of conduct which makes racist offences a disciplinary matter, or the removal of traditional decision making from headteachers to local authorities. Other mechanisms include formal contacts with outside bodies, often representatives of black groups, who are incorporated into decision-making structures with little real power, such as appointment panels for Section 11 posts or consultative committees for curriculum reform. Sometimes teachers move beyond this token commitment and do develop whole school policies which involve a majority of staff. It is rare, though, for pupils and parents to play a significant part in such initiatives.

All these means of fostering institutional reform provide ways of modifying power structures, by giving greater power to specific individuals or groups, by altering conditions of service or by changing the nature of accountability. Two contrasting strategies seem to be emerging. The first relies on removing from the school a variety of decisions and increasing the power of LEA officials and politicians, on the questionable assumption that they are less likely to make decisions which perpetuate 'racial' inequalities. The second tries to open up the power structure within the school and between the school and local groups, to foster some form of democratic structure and community participation and to produce whole school policies to which staff and others are committed.

It is necessary to subject these innovations to analysis, to measure their efficacy in achieving antiracist goals. This means that the goals must be specified in detail and with clarity. As Dummett suggests, we need a 'series of practical steps, moving towards clearly defined aims each time and taken after careful thought and observation' (Dummett 1985: 11).

We have argued earlier and elsewhere (Carter and Williams 1985; Williams 1985) that to label racism, discriminatory behaviour, and material inequalities as institutional racism does not help in the formulation of policy. However, it is crucial that policies are developed to remove colour inequalities in education and to prohibit discriminatory behaviour by teachers. Vague exhortations to abolish institutional racism are not enough, nor are policies which assume that no change can occur until the attitudes of the majority of teachers have been altered. A more practical way forward is to focus upon discriminatory behaviour. The distinction drawn by Dorn (1985) between individual and institutional discrimination is valuable here. German summarizes the distinction thus:

'The Act [1976 Race Relations Act] defines direct and indirect discrimination and, while the former is generally capable of recognition by reasonable people, the latter concerns a web of customary procedures and practices which militate against the interests of ethnic minority groups in particular and about which there is little awareness of their ill effects. . . . The latter has also been termed unwitting, unintentional, or institutional discrimination.

(German 1983: 8)

Individual discriminatory acts should be the object of policies and individuals should be disciplined. The imputation of racist intent in institutional discrimination is frequently difficult and sometimes inappropriate; it may even be irrelevant. For instance, the over-representation of particular groups of students in lower streams in schools may be the result of colour discrimination by teachers. It may also result from the teacher's inability to motivate groups of pupils to take school work seriously; it may be the result of a misallocation of resources earlier in the pupil's school life; it may be a self-chosen response to racism inside and outside the school, leading to a rejection of school about which the individual teacher can do very little. Policies must be as clear as possible in their depiction of these processes.

In ALTARF (1985) there is a helpful article outlining the different decisions and judgements which can be made on the basis of the evidence for black over-representation in ILEA support units. This evidence demonstrates that the social class composition of such units has been discussed since 1979. The article then sets out a detailed series of questions which need to be posed, concerning the nature, purpose, and organization of support units. This is what we mean by being specific. It is far more practical an aid to reform than labelling all practices as institutional racism.

Conclusion

Attacking racism in education requires an analysis of racism and of the place of education in reproducing inequalities. We have argued that many interpretations of racism fail to deal with the fundamentally political processes by means of which groups of people come to be defined as 'races'. The resulting emphasis on cultural or colour differences derogates other sources of inequality and confers on education an exaggerated significance in the amelioration of racism and discrimination.

181

Education does not create structural inequalities. It is unreasonable to suppose therefore that such inequalities will be significantly modified through educational reforms. This is especially pertinent when the current crisis in education leaves little room for innovation or maneouvre. Ideologies of equality of opportunity, of human capital, are being reworked in ways that involve restratifying examinations and increasing competition. 'Racial' inequalities need to be understood and challenged in this context. Strategies that unite a wide range of groups, providing the bases for alliances and linking educational reform to wider struggles, may succeed in doing this.

Some of the ways in which these alliances may be formed, and the sorts of struggles around which they may be effective, are outlined in other chapters in this book. Central to our argument, though, is the belief that schools by themselves cannot eradicate racism. It may be possible for teachers and others involved in education to modify discriminatory practices at both the individual and institutional levels and such efforts must be fully supported, but this is not the abolition of racism. The struggle against discrimination in education must be seen as part of the wider political struggle against racism; indeed the former will only be successful insofar as this is recognized.

© *1987 Bob Carter and*
Jenny Williams

References

Anderson, B. (1983) *Imagined Communities*. London: Verso Books.

All London Teachers Against Racism and Fascism (ALTARF) (1985) *The NUT, Racism and Support Units* Newsletter No. 16, June/July: 10–13.

Barnett, P. (1984) Some notes on institutional racism. *Education Journal* April: 11–13.

Berkshire LEA (1983) *Education for Racial Equality*. Policy Paper 1: General Policy. Policy Paper 2: Implications. Policy Paper 3: Support. Summary Leaflet.

Brown, C. (1984) *Black and White Britain: The Third PSI Study*. London: Heinemann Books.

Bullivant, B. (1981) *The Pluralist Dilemma in Education*. Sydney: Allen & Unwin.

Carter, B. and Williams, J. (1985) Institutional racism: new orthodoxies, old ideas. *Multiracial Education*. 13(1): 3–8.

Cochrane, R. and Billig, M. (1984) 'I'm not National Front myself, but . . . . *New Society* 17.5: 255–8.

Commission For Racial Equality (CRE) (1985) *Formal Investigation into Birmingham LEA Referral and Suspension of Pupils*. London: CRE.

Committee of Inquiry into the Education of Children from Ethnic Minority Groups (Swann Committee) (1985) *Education For All.* Cmnd. 9453 London: HMSO.

Dorn, A. (1985) Education and the Race Relations Act. In M. Arnot (ed), *Race and Gender: Equal Opportunity Policies in Education.* Oxford: Pergamon Press.

Dummett, A. (1985) *In the Shadows of Understanding: Institutional Racism.* Links 21 London Third World First: 7–13.

German, R. A. (1983) Some thoughts on institutional racism. *Education Journal* November: 5–6.

Greater London Council (1982) Race equality and ethnic minorities. *Future Strategy Report 1983–85.*

Gurnah, A. (1984) The politics of racism awareness training. *Critical Social Policy* Winter: 6–20.

Hargreaves, D. (1967) *Social Relations in a Secondary School.* London: Routledge & Kegan Paul.

Hatcher, R. (1985) On education for racial equality. *Multiracial Education* 13(1): 30–46.

Husbands, C. (1983) *Racial Exclusionism and the City: The Urban Support for the National Front.* London: Allen & Unwin.

Katz, J. (1978) *White Awareness: A Handbook for Anti-Racism Training.* Oklahoma: University of Oklahoma Press.

Lacey, C. (1970) *Hightown Grammar.* Manchester: Manchester University Press.

London NAME (1984) *Issues in Race and Education.* 42: 1–15.

Murphy, L. and Livingstone, J. (1985) Racism and the limits of radical feminism. *Race and Class* XXVI(4): 61–70.

Racism Awareness Programme Unit (RAPU) Lambeth Institute, Elm Park, London.

Ruddell, D. and Simpson, M. (1982) *Recognising Racism.* Birmingham: Education Department.

Satow, A. (1982) Racism awareness training: training to make a difference. In Ohri, A. *et al* (eds) *Community Work and Racism.* London: Routledge & Kegan Paul.

Sivanandan, A. (1985) RAT and the degradation of the black struggle. *Race and Class,* XXVI(4): 1–33.

Troyna, B. (1986) 'Swann's song': the origins, ideology, and implications of *Education for All. Journal of Education Policy* 1(2): 171–81.

Williams, J. (1985) 'Redefining institutional racism'. *Ethnic and Racial Studies* 8 (July): 323–48.

Willis, P. (1977), *Learning to Labour.* Farnborough: Saxon House.

—— (1983) Cultural production and theories of reproduction. In Barton, L. and Walker, S. (eds) *Race, Class, and Education.* London: Croom Helm.

Wright, C. (1985) School processes: an ethnographic study. In Eggleston, S. J., *et al. Educational and Vocational Experiences of 15–18 Year-Old Young People of Ethnic Minority Groups.* A Report to the Department of Education and Science. Warwick: University of Warwick.

12 'Race' and education: two perspectives for change

Richard Hatcher

The central debate within multicultural education is between two currents. One, which I will call left antiracism, proposes a perspective for antiracist education based on a structural theory of racism and a class analysis of education. The other, the dominant current in the field, has responded to the left critique of cultural pluralism, and the increasing pressure from the black communities, by reworking multiculturalism to incorporate a notion of institutional racism and draw on the reforms achieved in the last few years. I will call it the new multiculturalism.

They offer competing perspectives for the way forward. I want to briefly outline them, and to argue that the new multiculturalism, though it offers many positive proposals, is based on concepts of racism and of educational change which are incapable of achieving them.

Of course, within the new multiculturalism there are variations of perspective and differences of policy. What justifies it being regarded as a distinct and coherent current is the common analytic and strategic framework within which these variations are posed. The new multiculturalism is now in the process of becoming institutionalized in a significant minority of local authorities, and to a much greater extent at an academic level in departments and colleges of education. The new multiculturalist case has perhaps been most theoretically developed by James Lynch and James Banks, most recently in *Multicultural Education* (Lynch 1986a) and *Multicultural Education in Western Societies* (Banks and Lynch 1986).

The new multiculturalism

Because strategy flows from theoretical and conjunctional analyses, it is useful to begin by looking at the governing ideas of the new multiculturalism.

A LIBERAL DISCOURSE

We can begin by making a distinction between liberal and socialist approaches to social analysis (CCCS 1981: 139). What broadly characterizes socialist perspectives is their location of social problems, including racism, in the capitalist organization of society. Liberal analyses, however radical, differ from this in insisting on the progressive character of modern societies and locating the source of problems elsewhere, typically in dysfunctional social elements persisting from the past. The concept of class, if it features at all, becomes simply an index of disadvantage.

The new multiculturalism, including its more radical versions, with its characteristic emphasis on multicultural education as the necessary modernizing reform for a liberal democracy, and its disavowal of class, falls within this liberal paradigm. Its proponents explicitly dissociate themselves from left antiracism. While there is recognition that ' "Anti-racism" has alerted the movement to the harsher realities of cultural pluralism, and has played a valuable role in that' (Craft 1986: 93), they reject the left's 'strident and confrontational approach' (Lynch 1986a: ix) and echo Tory attacks on the left's 'so-called antiracist education' as 'propaganda' (Parekh 1986: 30).

These characteristic disclaimers may serve a necessary tactical function in aiding the institutional acceptance of the new multiculturalism by establishing its moderate credentials, but they flow from a fundamental difference of analysis of racism itself.

A CULTURALIST CONCEPT OF RACISM

The new multiculturalism rejects structural explanations of racism, and doesn't engage with current debates on the political and economic contexts of present-day racism. Although institutional as well as individual racism is recognized, it is analysed in terms of cultural processes. The key concept is ethnicity, drawn from the 'ethnic relations' school of the sociology of 'race'. Perhaps the most elaborated account within the multicultural debate of the cultural basis of racism comes from James Banks, who defines the problem as one of whites and blacks being trapped in 'ethnic psychological captivity'. 'Inevitably conflict in society is thereby accentuated'. The task of multicultural education is 'to assist the individual . . . to reach out to and achieve a higher stage of ethnic and cultural existence . . . so that there exists sufficient cultural and social overlap for society to function' (Lynch 1986a: 13–14).

A COMMON INTEREST IN SOCIAL COHESION

The dominant theme that runs through the new multiculturalism is of cultural diversity as a threat to social cohesion. (The same theme is echoed in the opening chapter of the Swann report.) The absence of class, and therefore of conflicting class interests, renders the notion of social cohesion unproblematic and unexamined it is simply in everyone's interest.

CHANGE THROUGH RATIONAL DISCOURSE

The way to achieve this new 'national covenant' is not through 'strident rhetoric and useless confrontation' but through rational discourse (Lynch 1986b: 192). 'It is . . . in the very existence and generation of dilemmas that democratic societies find their momentum to peaceful and creative change and reform, through processes of persuasion and discourse' (Lynch 1986a: 183).

MULTICULTURALISM IN EDUCATION

The key concept of multicultural education is 'acculturation', 'a process of mutual and pluralist acculturation for children and teachers' (Lynch 1986b: 178) aimed at 'releasing our education system from its monocultural prison and opening it up to the liberating influences of other cultural perspectives' (Parekh 1986: 26). In practice in the classroom racism in the curriculum is seen as being mainly due to 'a process of omitting any significant knowledge about Black people . . . from the normal curriculum' (Davis 1986: 16).

In other words, multiculturalism is not counterposed to antiracist education; 'antiracism is implicit in multiculturalism' (Grinter 1985: 9).

THE AUTONOMY OF SCHOOL

How are these changes to be implemented? In spite of racism in the wider society and the 'sad catalogue of inactivity by government', schools have sufficient autonomy to achieve 'the eradication of the ideology of racism from the structures and procedures of education' particularly because of the decentralized nature of the British school system (Davis 1986).

'Race' and class

The left alternative to the new multiculturalism offers a different strategy for educational change, based on a different analysis of racism and therefore of antiracism. Underlying the left perspective is the question of the relationship of 'race' to class.

It is necessary first to dispose of two erroneous and opposite interpretations. One is to assert that there is no necessary connection between racial oppression and class oppression, that they have entirely independent dynamics, and that to link them together handicaps the antiracist struggle. The other is to reduce racial oppression to an economistic notion of class oppression, and deny its relatively autonomous effectivity.

Against these it is necessary to reaffirm a perspective which sees that 'class struggle in a racist social formation is inextricably linked with the antiracist struggle: the battle to affirm one's humanity and to abolish racist culture, racist political institutions, and racist exploitation in the productive processes is a manifestation of class struggle' (Marable 1985: 6). Racism entails the power to discriminate. 'In a capitalist state, that power is associated with the power of the capitalist class − and racial oppression cannot be disassociated from class exploitation. And it is that symbiosis between race and class that marks the difference between the racial oppression of the capitalist and pre-capitalist periods' (Sivanandan 1985: 28; see also Hall 1980).

This concept of racism as working in the interests of capital, against the interests of the working class as a whole, is the crucial basis for the antiracist struggle. It enables us to explain why whites should be opposed to racism, by establishing the material class basis for white working class antiracism.

Can we point to a tradition in the white working class that translates this potential for antiracist unity into actual alliances with black struggles? The historical record shows the working-class movement of the advanced capitalist countries to be deeply infected with racism and national chauvinism. But there is another, albeit minority, tradition of class-wide solidarity that needs to be stressed. Historically there has always been a current of opposition to racism in the white working class, from the fight to abolish slavery through to the present.

In West Germany, Castles identifies within the labour movement today, 'a growing consciousness of the need to fight racism' (Castles 1984: 225). In France, the rise of racism against North African immigrants under Mitterand is being challenged by a mass movement of labour and youth, called *SOS-Racisme* (Robin 1985). In the USA, Manning Marable describes the long tradition of white participation in black struggles, through to the 1983 civil rights march on Washington of 300,000, one third of them white, including a substantial trade union presence (Marable 1985). In Britain, the Anti-Nazi League and Rock Against Racism represented a massive popular movement against racism in the late 1970s, and the 1985 miners' strike demonstrated the mutual solidarity of the black communities and the bastions of the traditional white working class, symbolized by the

NUM's support at the 1985 Labour Party conference for the right of black people to organize within the Labour Party.

In other words, the white working class contains two contradictory responses to 'race'. For specific historial reasons the antiracist response has been a minority one, but nevertheless it represents a real current within working class politics and culture, including that of its youth. Its existence today is of crucial importance for antiracist education, for two reasons. First, because it provides the potential basis for alliances with wider forces outside education to press for antiracist reforms within education. Secondly, because it provides the potential basis within the culture of white youth in schools for antiracist teaching.

Culture

Though culture is the central concept around which the new multiculturalism is constructed, the concept itself is given only a taken-for-granted, common sense meaning, impoverished both theoretically and in terms of concrete lived experience.

It is a concept of culture innocent of class. So, for example, Banks postulates that personal identity arises out of the interaction of three spheres of identification — ethnic, national, and global — with no mention of class location or consciousness (or gender) as sources of personal identity (Lynch 1986a: 91). Class is crucial to the understanding of culture, because cultures do not exist in simple relations of overlapping circles representing degrees of cross-fertilization, but in relations of domination and subordination which shape and structure the values, beliefs, and patterns of behaviour of dominant and subordinate cultures. Dominant cultures, the cultures of ruling classes, express their hegemonic aspirations. Subordinate cultures are shot through with the experience of domination and resistance to domination. School is one of the sites where these dialectical but asymmetrical cultural relations reproduce and contest each other (Giroux 1983: 66, 100). Yet the new multiculturalism's concept of culture is not informed by close concrete analyses of the reproduction and production of the cultural relations of 'race' either in school or outside.

Of the ethnographic studies of school that have been undertaken few have focused on racism. Further studies are needed to provide the basis for antiracist teaching, because it can only succeed if it engages with the real, lived experiences and consciousness of pupils, composed of varying combinations of elements which oppose the dominant culture, which reinforce it, or which coexist with it as alternative forms, neither

reproductive nor oppositional. In the case of black pupils, oppositional and alternative forms combine in a 'culture of resistance'. But
what basis is there for antiracism in the culture of white pupils?

An important study of racism among white, mainly working class,
youth was carried out recently by Cochrane and Billig (1984). They
found that racist views were held by a large proportion of white fourth
form and fifth form pupils. Their interviews give insights into the
political determinants of racist youth culture.

> ' "You'd think at our ages we wouldn't be colour prejudiced because
> we've been to school with them. We're not really, but things have
> happened." Above all, what has happened is the growth of un-
> employment: "I mean, we're leaving school soon, and half the jobs
> have gone. You try and get into a factory, it's just all Indians. And
> when I leave to get a job, I bet I won't be able to get one."
>
> "It's just getting worse and worse," one of the girls said, emphasiz-
> ing again the feeling that the world was slipping beyond their con-
> trol, and the only perceived "solution" required the hardening of
> personal feelings: "I've got friends who would like to stay in this
> country, but it it was either get them all out or keep them all in, I'd
> rather get 'em all out." When challenged, this hardened attitude was
> readily justified by a familiar litany about Black violence, Asian
> cooking smells, and so on." '   (Cochrane and Billig 1984: 257)

The comments of these white youths reveal the interaction of politics
and culture in the shaping of individual subjectivities by racism.

However, there is also, as we have noted, an antiracist tradition
within the working class. The most graphic illustration in recent years of
the powerful and creative popular energies that opposition to racism
can tap and stimulate is the experience of Rock Against Racism and the
Anti-Nazi League in the late seventies. *New Society* wrote:

> 'The three great carnivals, Victoria Park, Brockwell Park, and
> Belle Vue, Manchester, were extraordinary moments of popular
> protest. And while the Anti-Nazi league organization in the trade
> unions was ideologically effective as counter-propaganda, the
> people mobilized on the demonstrations and the pickets were the
> younger people coming to antiracism and antifascism through the
> "moral" perspectives offered by Rock Against Racism and the
> popular music culture . . . by members of a generation deeply
> influenced by sexual politics and by working-class people in the
> inner city areas, who found in multiracialism and cosmopolitanism
> a culture to be defended rather than eradicated.'
>
> (Widgery 1986: 94)

This is a dramatic example of the creation of opposition to racism out of a specific conjunction of politics and culture. White working class youth cultures today are sites where these contradictory responses to 'race' clash. The problem for antiracist teaching is to find ways in the classroom of engaging with and building on those antiracist elements within the cultures that young people bring to school, and relating to popular antiracist culture outside.

Antiracist teaching

The focus of the new multiculturalism in terms of classroom practice is on 'other cultures'. The argument against it was definitively put in the Institute of Race Relations submission to the Rampton Committee:

'While multicultural studies may, in explaining differences in customs and culture, help to modify attitudes, such studies are primarily an extension of existing educational techniques and methods, and, as such, allow racism within society, and within the educational system, to pass unchallenged. . . .

Ethnic minorities do not suffer disabilities because of ethnic differences, but because such differences are given differential weightage in a system of racial hierarchy.

Hence, our concern was not centrally with multicultural, multi-ethnic education but with antiracist education (which by its very nature would include the study of other cultures). Just to learn about other people's cultures is not to learn about the racism of one's own. To learn about the racism of one's own culture, on the other hand, is to approach other cultures objectively.'

(Institute of Race Relations 1982: iv)

At the core of antiracist education is learning about the racism of British culture. Part of that is the study of the history of black-white relations. But that history has also to be connected to the lived experiences of young people today. We need much more study of the processes of development of antiracist consciousness and the role that teachers can play. Giroux suggests three levels at which such processes work. Firstly, the level of unconscious mental structures:

'If we are to take human agency seriously, we must acknowledge the degree to which historical and objective societal forces leave their ideological imprint upon the psyche itself. To do so is to lay the groundwork for a critical encounter between oneself and the dominant society, to acknowledge what this society has made of us and decide whether that is what we truly want to be.'   (Giroux 1983: 149)

Secondly, the level of common sense as contradictory consciousness arising out of practical activity: 'the Gramscian view of common sense points to a mode of subjectivity characterized by forms of discursive consciousness imbued with insights into the social reality as well as with distorting beliefs that mystify and legitimate it' (Giroux 1983: 151).

Thirdly, the level of critical consciousness which is able to, in Gramsci's words, 'make coherent the practical problems raised by the masses in their practical activity'. (Giroux 1983: 153). In education this entails making problematic pupils' experiences and critically interrogating their common sense understandings, including those of school itself, as 'the basis for exploring the interface between their own lives and the constraints and possibilities of the wider society'.

Giroux's work, drawing on Gramsci, offers a theoretical basis for a radical pedagogy which is particularly fruitful for antiracist teaching.

We need to be looking at approaches which explore the contexts of racism in British society which deconstruct and build on the direct personal experiences and concerns of pupils, which involve off-site investigations of real life situations, which bring community campaigns against racism into the classroom, which locate racism and ethnic cultures in the matrix of social processes in which they are embedded, including their international and historical contexts, which can begin in the primary school, which entail democratic forms of pupil-teacher relations, and which pose the questions of power to change. (Blackwell *et al.* 1985). Then perhaps schools can help young people like those who spoke to Cochrane and Billig (1984) come up with better solutions than those offered by racism. But of course we are now on the terrain of political education, not multiculturalism.

'Race' and Tory education policy

What future is there for multicultural or antiracist teaching in the new Tory education?

Tory discourse on 'race' and education occupies the same rhetorical terrain as the new multiculturalism, situated between the terms of the 'pluralist dilemma', social cohesion and cultural diversity. It articulates them in a different way: not social cohesion through cultural pluralism but social cohesion in spite of cultural pluralism. This assimilationist goal does not entail a simple *exclusion* of ethnic cultures (that would be counter-productive), but their deradicalization and *incorporation*, insofar as they do not undermine the overriding thrust of policy towards social cohesion, as subordinate and peripheral elements into the hegemonic ideology that the Tories are reconstructing. The only extended policy statement to have come out of the Tory party on multicultural education, the Monday Club policy paper *Education and the multiracial society*, reflects government thinking:

> 'Britain has a great and inspiring heritage. Our children need to be fed on it, to be encouraged to make its values their own. Such an approach to education will unify, not divide; nurture shared pride and common loyalties, not cynicism and racial hatred. There should be a commitment, not to an out of date and dogmatic education, but to one that takes its stand on what are, for want of a better word, traditional values. This concept has room for multiculturalist insights. It should take account of different traditions and teach respect for them.'
>
> (Pearce 1985: 7)

We can see this complex process of incorporation in practice. Section 11 money continues to fund multicultural support services, DES courses promulgate multiculturalism, ESG projects are set up to improve 'race relations', and Tory LEAs endorse multicultural education. But these concessions need to be placed in the context of the real priorities of Tory education policy, as expressed in recent policy documents from the DES, designed to establish a new framework for the curriculum. Multicultural education typically features, if at all, in general statements of aim, but is absent when it comes to the more specific and operationable curriculum objectives.

In the White Paper *Better Schools*, which is an overview of government policy, the section on general school objectives includes the need 'to help pupils to develop . . . tolerance for other races, religions, and ways of life' (DES 1985: 14). But in the more detailed subsequent sections on primary and secondary schooling, there is no mention of multicultural objectives. In fact, the emphasis is quite the opposite: to inculcate 'the nature and values of British society' (primary) (DES 1985: 20), and 'consolidating pupils' understanding of the values and foundations of British society' (secondary) (DES 1985: 22). Chapter 8, 'The education of ethnic minority pupils', states that 'all pupils need to understand, and acquire a positive attitude towards, the variety of ethnic groups within British society. These objectives will be embodied in the statements of curriculum objectives . . .' (DES 1985: 61). But an analysis of the DES curriculum documents does not bear out this claim.

For example, the paper *The organization and content of the 5–16 curriculum* (DES 1984), when it comes to 'Important elements of the curriculum (which) are not subjects', speaks of the need, *not* to include a multicultural dimension, but on the contrary to 'become familiar with the broadly shared values of our society' (DES 1984: 3). And the only mention of bilingualism in it is with reference to Welsh.

The Swann Report is written within the new multiculturalist framework. Sir Keith Joseph reasserted that 'schools should preserve and transmit our national values in a way which accepts British ethnic diversity and promotes tolerance and racial harmony' and moved swiftly to reject some of its key recommendations on the day of its publication, simply for questioning the requirement for a daily act of collective worship, the dual system of county and voluntary schools, and the Section 11 regulations (see *The Times Educational Supplement* 22 March 1985).

At a local level, those Tory LEAs who, under pressure from the 'riots' and a large black electorate, supported more radical bipartisan policies on education for racial equality, are now retreating into the more Thatcherite policy framework for the inner cities that is being constructed.

It is evident that there is no significant place within the new Tory education for antiracist education, including many of the more radical demands of the multiculturalists themselves. Government policy is based on strengthening the dominant culture, on increasing inequality, on cutting spending, and on tying education more closely to the economy, which, being itself permeated by racism, will tend to make education in its own image, as is already the case with discriminatory YTS provision. The racist consequences of government education policies are reinforced by its economic policies (mass black unemployment; the crisis of the inner cities), and its policies specifically on 'race', including discriminatory immigration legislation and the criminalization of black youth.

Strategies for change

The hostility of the government to the new multiculturalists' case means that the 'agendas for change' that they devise have no means of being translated into practice. Hence the strategic reliance on 'teacher autonomy'. Of course, there is space for oppositional activity by teachers in schools, but to believe that it is sufficiently large to accommodate the new multiculturalism, let alone antiracist education, without either government sponsorship or the mobilization of broad popular support, is to misunderstand the relationship between school and 'society', and the project of the present government. Schools are more determined than determining, and this government is steadily and successfully eroding that limited autonomy further through a battery of measures to increase centralized control: of the curriculum, of INSET, of examinations, of funding (including the role of the MSC and the attack on local government), and of the teaching force itself (the issue underlying the 1985–1986 pay campaign), in order to ensure that they will 'deliver' the new Tory education (Simon 1984, 1986).

Furthermore, the government can rely on popular support, or at least hostility to antiracist measures, from a substantial section of the public and teachers themselves, a problem which the multiculturalists evade in three ways. First, by conceiving of the school-public relationship only in professional-client terms, emphasizing the need for schools to establish more responsive consultation with black parents, but excluding the notion of the mobilization of collective pressure on schools from sections of the public, for or against antiracist reforms. Yet a reactionary appeal to popular educational sentiments is precisely one of the government's main strategies, coupled with increasing centralized control, to force the schools to change direction. Recently the popular press has waged a systematic campaign to marshall public opinion not just against the 'antiracist extremists' of ILEA and Brent but against the multiculturalism of Swann, and in defence of Honeyford.

Secondly, by conceiving of teachers as undifferentiated, malleable, unproblematic; there is little analysis of the range of teachers' personal and professional ideologies, and how they are a major factor in educational continuity and change on the issue of 'race', though Whitty has shown, in the case of attempted innovations in political education, how effectively they can be blocked by teachers' traditional values and practices (Whitty 1985).

Thirdly, the multiculturalists argue that whereas left antiracism will have 'an alienating impact on what is a largely conservative profession', the new multiculturalism undertakes, in Banks' words, 'to reform the school within the context of the basic assumptions about schooling that are held by most teachers' (Grinter 1985: 8, 10), a recipe for all the capitulations of gradualism in the face of those 'traditional values' the Tories invoke.

The alternative is to recognize that the implementation of antiracist reforms in education, including many of the more radical policies of the multiculturalists, requires political struggle. This is the strategy that the new multiculturalists explicitly reject.

For Bhikhu Parekh, the school 'cannot spearhead a political movement, and if it ever tried to do so, it would lose its educational character and become an arena of struggle between large social and political forces over which it can exercise no control' (Parekh 1986: 31. See also Grinter 1985).

Isn't it evident that opposition to racism cannot but be political? Hasn't the school always been an area of struggle between large social and political forces? Doesn't history show that every meaningful reform, in education or on 'race', has been won through struggle? It is surely the lesson of the educational reformism of the 1960s that it was the failure to mobilize popular forces in their support that led to the progressive movement being so easily displaced by the reactionary offensive of the last decade. The ironic fact is that without the antiracist struggles in education and outside over the last decades, there would be no new multiculturalism today. It required militant tactics including demonstrations and boycotts to get rid of Honeyford. If they had relied on 'rational persuasion', he would still be the headteacher of Drummond Middle School. How much more pressure then will be required to reorientate the whole school system towards antiracism?

The project of the new multiculturalists

We can now summarize the project of the new multiculturalists. The context is British capitalism in crisis, its hegemony threatened by, among other things, black resistance, now driven to rebellion on the streets. The failure of the new multiculturalism to analyse that context, its deliberate nonengagement with the political debates around 'race', and those on education, its apparently innocent evolutionism, and its hostility to political struggle, all flow from the nature of the project that the new multiculturalism sets itself. That project is not to see what part schools can play in strengthening black resistance by opposing racism, but to act as the State's policy adviser on how to recompose the hegemonic ideology by incorporating within it a selectively expanded cultural repertoire.

The ideological terrain of nation, culture and social cohesion on which it works is also that occupied by the 'new racism' (Duffield 1984). The new racism starts from the premise that it is human nature to form groups based on similarity of culture, and that the nation is defined in terms of a common culture. The presence of ethnic minority cultures threatens its cohesion. The point of difference with the new multiculturalists is that they believe that a new definition of the nation, incorporating a plurality of cultures, can restore social cohesion. But the acceptance of the same culturalist terrain of debate as the new racism is disastrous for the liberal position, because of course the right are *correct* in saying that the social cohesion of British capitalism is threatened by ethnic minority cultures which generate vigorous resistance to racial oppression. The right recognizes that a real conflict of interests exists which can't be reconciled by multiculturalism. That

195

is why the present Conservative Government doesn't accept the new multiculturalist solution. Concessions under pressure may be necessary, but they risk feeding the appetite they are intended to appease. This Government will not grant any of the more radical, multiculturalist demands: it rejects the whole liberal consensual approach to 'race'. Since the new multiculturalism rejects any strategy of mobilizing a popular political struggle for its demands, because that would destroy its credentials as a policy adviser, it has no strategy except, unrequited, to make a virtue out of necessity and exaggerate the autonomy of teachers from the outside world. The real natural sponsors of the new multiculturalism are of course not the Tories but a Kinnockite Labour government, but ironically its commitment, largely rhetorical though useful in creating more space for radical antiracist teachers, will be undermined by the racism that its policies fuel, as the Callaghan and Mitterrand governments have proved.

The struggle against racism in education

First, what do we mean by political struggle? Its principal strategy has to be the construction of a broad popular movement for antiracist education. At its core is the self-organization of black people, as parents, teachers, pupils, and the wider communities.

Their most immediate allies are white teachers actively involved in antiracist education. There are organizations that bring together teachers and non-teachers on a long-term basis, such as NAME, ALTARF, CARE in Avon, CARS in East London. Some are purely local groupings. NAME is of course a national organization, the largest and potentially the most effective in many respects. It is at present in transition from multiculturalism to antiracism. There is certainly a need for a national organization, locally rooted, vigorously campaigning against racism in education. How effectively NAME can play that role depends not only on how radical are the antiracist policies that it adopts, but also how successful it is in translating them into campaigns of action, with all that entails in terms of political orientation and democratic functioning.

But to achieve radical reforms in state education more powerful forces must be mobilized. What potential allies do the organizations of the labour movement represent: the unions, particularly the teachers unions, and the Labour Party?

THE NATIONAL UNION OF TEACHERS
The NUT is the largest teachers' union and has taken the most progressive stance. The 1986 Conference marked a step forward: it

adopted an explicitly antiracist stance; it began to take positions on issues beyond the classroom (e.g. on racist laws); and it recognized the need to increase black representation on Union bodies. These positions are not sufficient, but they do increase the opportunities for practical action, and reflect the growing influence of the antiracist movement within the Union. At a local level, Birmingham NUT almost unanimously passed a motion of solidarity with the Handsworth Defence Campaign after the 'riots'. Inner London Teachers Association has responded to the continuing police harassment of black youth by calling for police to be excluded from schools. Perhaps the largest mobilization of teachers against racism since the 2,500 strong rally that launched ALTARF in 1978 was the recent demonstration by East London teachers in support of the campaign by CARS (Campaign Against Racism in Schools, a local alliance of black and trade union bodies) against racism at Daneford School. (Lawrence 1986). After police arrested eleven people picketing the ILEA Divisional Office, over seventy schools took unofficial strike action and over two thousand teachers took part in a demonstration. *The Times Education Supplement* reported (10 January 1986) that: 'As a response to the pressure and the school's problems, the ILEA has drafted in a team of inspectors, released extra resources, and put together a £180,000 package to help Tower Hamlets schools tackle problems of racism'. These examples illustrate the potential of the NUT to be a major force for antiracist education, in alliance with black organizations.

THE LABOUR PARTY

The antiracist movement cannot avoid the question of political parties, government, and State. It is only at those levels that solutions ᴛᴏ the fundamental issues of racism can be found; otherwise grassroots activity remains merely casework. What attitude should it take to the Labour Party? Clearly not one of uncritical reliance, given its dismal record on 'race' and on educational reform. But it would be wrong to dismiss it as just the same as the other parties. The crucial difference is Labour's social composition and base, which lies in a class which has no objective interest in being divided by racism. The contradictory consciousness within the working class on 'race' also runs through the Labour Party, and provides the basis for a struggle within the party, often against the leadership, for antiracist policies. That struggle is led today by the Black Sections campaign, which is perhaps the largest black political movement in Britain.

The antiracist struggle in the Labour Party influences millions of people. At stake are the policies on 'race' of the next Labour government, and the policies today of the Labour-controlled majority of city councils, where battles are going on over policies on 'race' and education To take the best known example, ILEA's antiracist policy, for all its limitations, was very much the product of a left Labour GLC influenced by black campaigning organizations (Hatcher 1987).

Alliances for change

The practical experiences we have, some of which I have referred to, are limited, but they demonstrate that effective antiracist alliances can be built among teachers, the black communities, and the labour movement, without the antiracist struggle being compromised. I do not minimize the difficulties of overcoming histories of complicity in racism and perceived conflicts of interest today. Unity has to be built and rebuilt in the struggle for common objectives. The problem now facing the antiracist movement in education is how to articulate politics with culture. How to construct a growing web of connections, at school, local, and national levels, between the antiracist struggle in the classroom, which is still a largely unexplored terrain of cultural politics, to the antiracist struggle outside. How to go beyond reactive, single-issue campaigns, to proactive campaigns which can harness broad popular movements to a planned programme for antiracist education in schools.

But local councils, however committed, are limited in what they can achieve, because of economic and ideological factors outside their control and because of the increasing curtailment of their powers by government. The question therefore of *government* is a decisive one for the antiracist movement, with a particular significance for white areas where schools are not subject to direct pressure either from the black communities or from radical local authorities. To put it bluntly, there is no possibility of a generalized antiracist education in British schools in the foreseeable future, especially outside the inner cities, except under a Labour government committed to antiracist policies. That means that the struggle for antiracist education is inextricably linked to the struggle for a Labour Party and a Labour government of a different kind from those which have capitulated to, and so reinforced, racism in the post-war period. This is the real antiracist struggle that is taking place in Brent, in Bradford, in Birmingham today.

If the terms of the antiracist struggle are becoming clearer, so also are the social forces with which the developing antiracist movement can ally: left currents within the Labour Party and the unions, the women's movement, the anti-imperialist, and peace movements. These are the principal elements of a new alliance that has been gradually taking shape since the late 1960s, and that is being painfully built and rebuilt in and by every major social struggle in Britain under the Thatcher government.

The task now facing the movement for antiracist education is to continue to construct a growing web of connections at school, local, and national levels, between what happens in classrooms and the wider political struggles outside, in the form not only of campaigns to implement or defend specific reforms, but also of a comprehensive programme for antiracist education in schools, around which unity can be built among the social forces capable of installing it.

© *1987 Richard Hatcher*

References

Blackwell, B., Catterall, B., Mendelsohn, R., Westaway, J., Whitty, G., and Young, A. (1985) *Urban Studies: Making Sense of Cities*. London: CUES.

Banks, J. and Lynch, J. (eds) (1986) *Multicultural Education in Western Societies*. London: Holt, Rinehart & Winston.

Castles, S. (1984) *Here for good*. London: Pluto.

CCCS (Centre for Contemporary Cultural Studies) (1981) *Unpopular Education*. London: Hutchinson.

Cochrane, R. and Billig, M. (1984) 'I'm not National Front myself, but . . .' *New Society* 17 May: 256–9.

Craft, M. (1986) Multicultural education in the United Kingdom. In Banks, J. and Lynch, J. (eds) *Multicultural Education in Western Societies*. London: Holt, Rinehart & Winston.

Davis, G. (1986) Strategies for change. In Arora, R. and Duncan, C. (eds) *Multicultural Education*. London: Routledge & Kegan Paul.

DES (1984) *The Organization and Content of the 5–16 Curriculum*. London: HMSO.

—— (1985) *Better Schools*. London: HMSO.

Duffield, M. (1984) New racism . . . new realism: two sides of the same coin. *Radical Philosophy* (37): 29–34.

Giroux, H. (1983) *Theory and resistance in education*. London: Heinemann.

Grinter, R. (1985) Bridging the gulf: the need for antiracist multicultural education. *Multicultural Teaching* 3(2): 7–10.

Hall, S. (1980) Race, articulation, and societies structured in dominance. In UNESCO *Sociological theories: race and colonialism*. London: UNESCO.

Hatcher, R. (1987) Education for Racial Equality Under Attack. *Multicultural Teaching* 5/3, Summer.

Institute of Race Relations (1982). *Roots of Racism*. London: IRR.

Lawrence, D. (1986) Paper Policies. *Socialist Teacher* (31): 7–8.

Lynch, J. (1986a) *Multicultural Education*. London: Routledge & Kegan Paul.

Lynch, J. (1986b) Multicultural education: agenda for change. In Banks, J. and Lynch, J. (eds) *Multicultural Education in Western Societies*. London: Holt, Rinehart & Winston.

Marable, M. (1985) *Black American Politics* London: Verso.

Parekh, B. (1986) The concept of multicultural education. In Modgil, S., Verma, G., Mallick, K., and Modgil, C. (eds) *Multicultural Education: The Interminable Debate*. London: Falmer Press.

Pearce, S. (1985) *Education and the Multi-racial Society*. London: Monday Club.

Robin, G. (1985) Hands off my mate. *International Viewpoint*. 17 June.

Simon, B. (1984) Breaking school rules. *Marxism Today*. September: 19–25.

—— (1986) The battle of the blackboard. *Marxism Today*. June: 20–6.

Sivanandan, A. (1985) RAT and the degradation of black struggle. *Race and Class* XXVI(4): 1–33.

Socialist Teacher (1986) December (34).

Widgery, D. (1986) *Beating Time*. London: Chatto & Windus.

Whitty, G. (1985) *Sociology and School Knowledge*. London: Methuen.

Name index

201

Subject index